Fawcett Crest Books
by Barbara Howar:

LAUGHING ALL THE WAY

MAKING ENDS MEET

# MAKING ENDS MEET

Barbara Howar

A FAWCETT CREST BOOK

Fawcett Publications, Inc., Greenwich, Connecticut

*MAKING ENDS MEET*

THIS BOOK CONTAINS THE COMPLETE TEXT OF
THE ORIGINAL HARDCOVER EDITION.

A Fawcett Crest Book reprinted by arrangement with Random House, Inc.

ISBN 0-449-23084-8

Alternate Selection of the Literary Guild, Summer 1976
Selection of Contempo Book Club, August 1976
Feature Alternate of the Doubleday Bargain Book Club,
December 1976

Printed in the United States of America

10   9   8   7   6   5   4   3   2   1

For my father

# MAKING
# ENDS
# MEET

# 1

LESS and less could she hold back the memory. She hardly bothered to try anymore. She had come to enjoy the punishment. By letting go only a little, it would be 1943 again and she would be lying on the davenport of Leyla Tuttle's porch that encircled the big white clapboard house situated on what everyone knew to be the last good dune left on the Myrtle Beach oceanfront. With no effort, Lilly could see her own youthfully scrawny leg, its sandy bare foot pushing against the screening to keep the glider moving just slightly; she could still feel that familiar soothing motion as she lay there with the faded Sleepy Doll under her chin, the doll's eyes permanently closed in sleep, its body limp without its zippered back stuffed with pajamas.

It was always a little after six. Lilly could tell the hour by the number of planes that swooped down, one by one, to buzz the roof of the house, the signal that the second lieutenants had finished another day practicing war and were taking their planes back to the base. This was how the women in the front room knew it was time to start dressing for the evening.

Generally her mother remembered to get her out of the way, but sometimes Lilly got to lie unnoticed on the porch to watch for the pilots as they came up the steps, two at a time, whistling, tossing brimmed soft hats into the air, and peeling off leather flight jackets more suited to their dashing image than to the hot South Carolina summer. The young men had only first names. Sparks, Mac, Smiley, Jerry. Each talked of towns in Pennsylvania or New Jersey, places far away. Their heads were neatly crew-cut, their jaws smooth and arrogantly square, and although Lilly had no way of knowing for sure, she was somehow certain that these second "louies" who called each night and all day Saturday and Sunday were younger than her mother or her mother's friends.

The pilots brought PX whiskey and cartons of Luckies and Camels; for Lilly there were boxes of Hershey bars without almonds or an occasional sack of Walnettos or Double Bubble Gum which she would squirrel away in the zippered innards of the Sleepy Doll. Looking back, Lilly guessed that she was deeply in love with each of them, believing them to be flawless the way only a nine-year-old girl can do. When the uniformed men were around, her face would remain strictly passive, but her heart would tighten each time presents were extended by tanned arms wearing wristwatches on expansion bracelets. She would accept her bribes and disappear; she had to, of course, for her own room was next to the one for the colored maid who became surly and policed Lilly closely if the drugstore deliveryman had not come to call by eight. On those nights she would go obediently to her room and lie on top of the bedspread with a couple of the Hersheys tucked beneath the small of her back to soften them. Waiting, one thin bare leg dangling from the bent knee of the other, she would swing her foot in time to the music coming up from downstairs and dream that the wonderful summer would go on forever. When the candy bars were mushy, she would dab at them, sucking at the chocolate and her dirty fingers until she fell asleep.

On better nights Lilly might creep back out on the porch, sometimes just to listen, sometimes to stare brazenly through the windows. Late in the evening the dancing would get slower and closer, the conversations more muffled. Sparks or Smiley would pair off with her mother's friends, those equally sleek and restless ladies who had left husbands at home to endure the city heat and had come to Myrtle Beach to share the house that summer. They would settle on the far end of the darkened porch, their long silences broken only by piercing giggles or hoarse whispers while the night would fill with soft songs about foolish hearts and how people were not supposed to sit under apple trees with anyone else. Still later, the Victrola would give out raucous choruses about airplanes diving off into the wild blue yonder, music that would bring Smiley or Sparks or Jerry, rumpled and lipsticked, back into the front room to grab each other around the neck and to sing loud promises that nothing indeed could stop the Army Air Corps.

When Sparks or Jerry made "first louie," there would be special Sunday celebrations where a black houseman would carry in steaming platters of barbecued chickens cooked outside in smoldering pits in the sand. There might be as many as twenty pilots crowded around the dining-room table, all of them drinking pink wine from iced-tea glasses and toasting the beautifully dressed women; the men always bowed and included Lilly in each speech. Her mother would often make a production of scraping the hot fresh corn from the cob, explaining that "my Lilly's front teeth are taking so long to come back because they are growing themselves extra pretty, aren't they, baby?" Lilly would grin and then gum her way through hot biscuits with strawberry preserves, careful always to save room for the fried peach pies and the homemade ice cream. After lunch the ladies would retire to the porch, and Lilly would be sent away to take her afternoon rest.

Later, in the evening, the ladies would hang crepe-paper strips over the long front room and Lilly would color-crayon a big sign that said WELCOME FIRST LOUIES. The group on those nights would be larger and gayer, the singing more determined, even defiant. Somehow it seemed to Lilly that happy parties were all a part of war and that nothing could ever be so glorious as to leave Myrtle Beach to "finally get into the fight." Sparks or Jerry would go away after that, and for a while they would send back little V-mail letters that were read aloud—funny bragging accounts of places Lilly had never heard of before. Eventually the messages would stop coming, and whoever left never came back. Her mother's pretty friends —Leyla, Grace or Mary Nell—might be pale and drawn for a while and would sit sadly under the beach umbrella wearing silver pilot's wings pinned to their Lastex bathing suits, crying a little and drinking straight out of ugly brown beer bottles. And then it would all begin again.

That summer was Lilly's earliest awareness of her mother; she thought of her as Clara and called her by that name because everyone else did. In those days Clara seemed always to be surrounded by sunshine and friendly faces, and there had been so much laughter, so much to do, as if those moments were to be the only ones that mattered.

"We ought all of us to sing and dance and be merry because tomorrow we just might all be dead." Clara was always saying that, doing that, and it had seemed the right, almost courageous way to live. Lilly loved that about her mother, her adventure and daring, and had adored Clara's spontaneous bursts of enthusiasm and affection. Once the two of them had walked down the empty beach together just as the sun was setting; their bare backs were still warmed as they strolled along, arm and arm, pausing only to collect shells or to throw into the dunes the sticks of wood washed up by the tide. Clara had

11

spun Lilly about that day, taking her by both hands in a playful game of ring-around-a-rosy.

"Just look," Clara had said, lifting her arms to include the blue sky, the sparkling whitecaps. "It is all so beautiful it makes me want to cry. Beautiful and clean. The way you are, darling girl." Clara had dropped onto the dry sand and then pulled Lilly into her lap, brushing back her wild curls that the breeze kept dislodging.

"Clara has never been so happy. Do you know that?" She had looked lovingly at Lilly as she spoke. "Part of being happy comes from having you as my little friend. You and me. Free as ponies."

Clara had lifted Lilly to her feet and raced ahead of her, leaping over the patches of tall sea grass and running zigzag in and out of the flat waves that slid up on the shore. Lilly had followed along behind trying to keep up with Clara's long strides, skipping in her wake and watching with a thumping heart the beautiful young creature who, by some wonderful miracle, was her very own mother. Her chest had hurt with joy. She loved Clara so much that it caused a funny kind of pain and there was nothing she wanted more than to bounce along after her lovely mother forever. Lilly thought that if she could have only one true wish, she would choose to have Clara for herself always.

Mac was the pilot who came around the most that summer, a solid, boxlike man with a lot of brown hair too curly to be cut so short. He was there every day and would hang his dog tags around Lilly's neck and talk to her while he polished his shoes, those strange boots that came almost to the ankle and fastened with leather straps. He worked over them while Lilly sat silently, never once giving away that, next to her mother, he was by far the most pleasant part of her day. He would talk as he worked, telling her about New York City, the Statue of Liberty, the Rockettes—"all ladies worth fighting a war for, huh?" He once played a small role in *Brother Rat,* and since the first of June he had recounted the plot to her almost daily. Even when it was well into August, she did not let on that she could recite the story perhaps even better than he. Often he told her of a kid sister just her age back home and the reminder could fill Lilly with a rage that made her want to sulk and pout. Mostly, though, he just buffed his boots, making snapping sounds with the polishing cloth and whistling a funny little tune through his teeth.

"Now then, Lilly," he would say, holding up his shoes for

inspection, "can you see your pretty face in these clear enough for me to put them on and dance your Ma around?" Lilly would pretend an indifference she did not feel, as if any display of her pleasure would cause it to disappear. Watching as he buckled the straps, she waited rigidly, knowing that he was about to grab her up in a mock embrace to swing her high over the painted porch floor and then to bend her backwards into an exaggerated dip.

"Ginger Rogers'll never sleep another wink when she hears about you, kid."

It would be all Lilly could manage not to throw herself around his legs.

The night Mac got his captain's bars, he pinned them to her mother's blouse, telling her gently that it was nothing to be so serious about. "Every louie knows captains don't get downed, honey. That's the main rule of war."

Later Lilly had heard them talking on the porch. She was crouched on the outer side of the railing in the tall sandy grass putting spit on her mosquito bites to keep from scratching. She could not understand everything being said, only enough to fill her with a sudden sense of exclusion.

"Clara, honey," Mac had said, "please don't cry. It can all work out if you wish it hard enough. Everything will be just the way we want. All you have to do is take Lilly home and get her settled in school. Then you come to San Francisco.

"Lilly's a great kid and I love her just as much as you do. But there is no place for her now. She'll be better off this way. You know he'll come around after a while; he'll give you a divorce, you'll see. When the war's over, honey, why, Lilly can even spend summers with us. He'll get over it. Ole Mac is never wrong about these things."

Hugging her legs to her chest, occasionally licking her kneecaps and smelling them, Lilly had rocked back and forth in the dark. It had been almost daylight when she had finally got into her bed and fallen asleep with her clothes still on. That same afternoon, on a lined tablet she carefully wrote a letter to her father, took the silver dollar he had given her at the beginning of the summer, and barefoot, dodged the hot tar road to the drugstore and mailed it at the counter in back that served as the post office. When the envelope slid out of sight, the hard fury inside Lilly had dissolved, causing shivers so hard she had to wrap her skinny arms around her haltered chest to stop the shaking.

With the rest of the money, she had bought two Pronto-

Pups and two frozen root beers; the change was spent riding the Tilt-A-Whirl at the amusement center. She vomited that entire night and the next day had run a fever. On Thursday the doctor came to see her and promised to call again on Saturday but never did. On Friday her father had arrived in his big maroon Chrysler. He covered her in a scratchy wool blanket and put her on the back seat of the car. Lilly's face had remained pressed against the gray velour upholstery throughout the long ride home. In all her nine years it was the only automobile trip she could remember taking with both her parents. Even as accustomed as she was to the silence between them, she sensed that day a new and permanent heaviness in their quiet.

# 2

LILLY shook her head to clear it, then slumped lower into the lounge chair in the empty screening room, patting her folded tortoise-rimmed glasses against the palm of her left hand, counting nervously with each tap the number of years since that memory of Myrtle Beach had been reality. Thirty-one years. Thirty-one long, goddamn years.

Irritably she altered her posture to burrow more deeply into the womblike seat so that her head was resting against the back of the chair. She reminded herself that she was grown now, forty years old; it was high time to stop fishing from the past to torture herself. She was doing so much of that lately. And for what? What earthly purpose did it serve to rehash things best left forgotten? She shifted positions once more, impatiently fidgeting with her notebook, opening and closing her glasses with loud clicking noises. Surely after thirty-one years the things of childhood lack the hard core of fact. Everything was edited, wasn't it? Even movies?

She sat deliberately straight now and waved her hand over her head for the projectionist to start the film. The agent from Warner Brothers was late as usual and she was tired of waiting for him. Time on her hands was dangerous these days. A person could go crazy sitting around by herself in an empty theater, if she wasn't already crazy to begin with.

The picture came up on the screen immediately: it was *Mame*. Unconsciously she started to hum the overture and her foot was bouncing to the tune as the studio agent slipped into the seat beside her. He seemed pleased that she was so involved with the orchestration and he moved his little Gucci-shoed foot in time with hers. Lilly threw him a tense smile and nodded, already bored; she had endured the story of Mame in all its versions—the movie reproduction of the hit Broadway comedy based on the hit comic novel—and now, inevitably,

15

it had to be set to music. Well, there would be no mention of the word "hit" in her review today, that much she knew already. She leaned over to speak to the agent.

"Christ, couldn't you people just give Lucille Ball a gold watch and a testimonial dinner instead of putting us through this?"

"Come on, Lilly. Give it a chance, will ya?"

She looked at the little man next to her, even squinted to recall him. Studio representatives looked so much alike. Small, nervous, anxious for approval. She wanted to pat his carefully lacquered head and tell him it was all right, that it was, after all, only a movie. Only a movie! Hell, her literature, her religion, her whole goddamned conscience, for Christ's sake. Who was she to comfort him? She of all people? Looking at the small man, Lilly could not help but think of Peter; he despised most agents—said CMA threw them back when they were over five feet tall. That was the first remark he'd made when she showed him some snapshots of the children; he'd said that, at ten, Teddy was already too big to be an agent and that she should thank God for that.

She smiled in spite of herself and spoke aloud without realizing it. "Thank God for vitamins too. There's something to be said for the pharmaceutical industry after all."

"What? Oh. Yeah, honey. That's right." The little man beside her was not listening. "Now catch this sight gag. It's terrific."

Whatever his name is, Lilly thought, they're all the same; they agreed with everything she said. Right up to the time when she tore apart whichever film they were flacking.

There certainly had been a day when the gentlemen in Hollywood had not concerned themselves with her opinions. And not so very long ago, either. She had had to buy a ticket at a local theater to see a movie, then grab a cab and make some fast notes on the ride to the TV studio, where, exhausted, she would fall into her chair on the set with just enough time to steady her breathing before taping her review for the evening news. Now that her face and acerbic views appeared three or four times a week on a hundred and eighty-one stations, the studio executives arranged these private screenings at her convenience, even sent down to Washington a Rick or a Sam or a Chuck in a four-hundred-dollar Cardin suit to hold her hand and kiss her fanny for approximately ninety minutes every other day. Where they had once ignored her, they now hated her. Being hated made for better treatment.

16

It had been George Sabberstein, a Pulitzer Prize-winning busybody, as Lilly often called him, who had gotten her that first job on local television. And then, a year or so later, he had again reorganized her life by asking how much longer she could possibly be content reviewing movies for only a single Washington station. The question had surprised Lilly; she felt just fine about things as they were.

"You know," he had said, "you never have told me what you make per shot." George was very blunt.

"About the same as your average streetwalker."

"Then why don't you do a couple of tapes for us? We could air you on UPI's outlets in the hinterlands. They go to movies out there, too, you know. If our subscribers are as hot for your snot-nosed attitude as I am, they just might pick you up. Who knows, babe, you could become the Judith Crist of Podunk."

As toward all change, Lilly had been indifferent. "George, the unwashed public is not ready to look to Washington for movie appreciation."

"Honey," he had responded sadly, "nothing that comes out of this fucking town surprises anybody anymore. Why not movies? Even the way you make fun of them, it isn't any more ridiculous than politics. If UPI will take a chance on it, why not you?"

That had been five years ago and her caustically honest commentaries on both the films and the film-making process had indeed caught on. George had persuaded UPI to videotape a couple of syndicated newspaper columnists to be sold over the wire service too; the whole package had earned him a substantial raise and she was, as promised, on her way to becoming the queen of film critics for Middle America. Even the trade journals took her seriously; she fell, they said, somewhere between the intellectual Pauline Kael and the outrageousness of Rex Reed. Some said it was her lack of reverence. Others credited the down-home accent, saying it lent a credible folksiness to her presentation. *Variety* compared her to Johnny Cash selling Amoco gas; it was her least favorite analogy. But whatever the reason, it appeared she did have the common touch. When she told them in Toledo that an overlong, highly touted extravaganza was not worth three hours and three dollars, she was believable. Well, it was hardly the kind of power one dreamed of exercising in the Nation's Capital, but it did, as Lilly told the *Hollywood Reporter*, keep her out of the pool hall.

Toward the end of *Mame* she began to make notes: Paul

17

Dindel calls this a screenplay? Patrick Dennis never grows an inch between 1928 and 1948! Bea Arthur should be Mame . . . !

Reading her scribblings in the semi-dark, the Warner's agent began to argue. "Lilly, for God's sake. The studio has a fortune in this one. We need the little towns to put it over. Give us a break."

She slumped even lower in her seat, making her eyes level with the agent, but she said nothing.

"Listen, Lilly, the Lucy fans will hate you for knocking this. They don't know Canby from Gilliatt out there but they'll give it a chance if you go easy." Lilly was embarrassed that he was pleading with her. She wished she could remember his name.

"Look"—she turned to him calmly—"I've spent so much of my life in darkened picture shows, I should be a mushroom. I bought it all for years, and in some crazy, convoluted way, the movie industry created me—their very own monster."

His stricken face made her relent.

"Come on"—she smiled—"we both know that nothing I say or do will really make one goddamned bit of difference to the success or failure of this or any other film. Except in the smallest way at the box office."

The man cringed at the monetary reference.

"Throw up, if you will," Lilly continued, "but I really believe movies are the best art form we've come up with yet and when I see good writers and good actors go without work so that some dim-witted studio head can cram a recycled script down our throats, I'm not going to tell you or anybody else that it's anything akin to entertainment, much less culture.

"Look, give me a decently scripted idea, something well directed and acted, and I'll give you the best bloody review ever. I may be a cynic but I'm no whore." Lilly swallowed at her words. For months now she had been trying to capsulize herself and she had just stumbled inadvertently into partial enlightenment with a tiny man whose name she did not know. The irony of the situation was not amusing; instead, there was only that vague sense of depression she had come to recognize so easily of late. Fleetingly Lilly wondered if, at forty, she was a cynic but still not a whore, then what was she? What was available between the two?

When the film ended, Lilly gathered her things. Preoccupied, she walked up the slight incline of the theater's narrow aisles and went out the unattended door onto the street. She had forgotten the young man behind her until he opened the door of the cab. It was sleeting and the long hair of her fox coat was damp; she began absently brushing off the beads of moisture, much as if she were brushing away uncomfortable thoughts.

The agent leaned into the rear of the taxi. "Lilly, you're helping destroy the film industry. You know that, don't you?"

This time the irony made her smile. She looked at him tiredly, speaking more to herself than to him. "The motion picture business is about the only thing in my life that is falling apart without any help from me." Then, with enormous physical effort, she leaned forward and gave the driver her destination.

At the television station Lilly went straight into the taping studio, avoiding her own small office, the one partitioned off in a corner of the newsroom. She had a cluttered desk there and an almost identical one downtown at the UPI bureau— two places to belong and neither of them very important to her anymore. Sandy, the girl who helped her part time at the station, would be waiting in the office with a list of Lilly's calls. There would not be one from Peter; she sensed this already but she did not care to have her disappointment confirmed—not yet, anyhow. No, it would be better to wait and check with Sandy when she finished taping her review. But it would be the same old story. She'd steel herself, Sandy would bubble over, chatting and repeating station gossip until Lilly interrupted to ask about her messages.

"Sandy, are there any calls besides these?" Lilly would shuffle through the pink slips, waiting, her heart standing still.

"No. Just those."

"Anybody phone and not leave a name?"

"No. Not that I know of."

"You sure there was no gruff voice that sounded long-distance?"

"No, Lilly. He didn't call." Of course he hadn't. Lilly always knew when Peter had called; it was something she felt. There was no call today, she was sure. Maybe this time she would just leave, just walk off the set and bypass Sandy altogether. She wouldn't do that, though. That would be too easy and she seldom missed any opportunity to hurt herself these days. She thought she had it coming.

George Sabberstein was waiting for her at the bar, that big mahogany expanse of tired journalists that was, despite the

19

impressive dining rooms, meeting rooms, and the endless boring newsletters from the club's current president, the real and perhaps only truly functioning part of the National Press Club.

The place was crowded for a Friday night. Lilly nodded to some reporters. Most of them were visibly exhausted, worn out from tracking down politicians and lies, words which had long seemed to Lilly to be redundant. The bar was filled with men and she knew the majority of them by name, knew them to be decent family men. Like George Sabberstein, a lot of them were married to women they could not stand going home to but whom they could not afford to leave. Suspicious of everything, they were emotionally mortgaged; time and events were disillusioning them even with their work. They knew the filth of politics, these complex men and women who drank too much and worked too hard. Like herself, most were cynics; only a few were whores. Lilly felt better just seeing them. They shared a standing joke at the bar: "If we drink to the truth, we'll go home sober."

George did not get up for her and only patted her back in greeting. They knew each other too well and too long for anything more.

"How was it tonight?" That was what he always asked.

"Fine. Just fine."

George nodded approvingly; he seemed unaware of the triteness of their exchange but his interest was real enough—Lilly's success mattered to him almost as much as it used to matter to her.

"You want to eat?" she asked, glancing at the clock over the bottles on the back of the bar. It was after seven.

"I guess. I'd like to get drunk first. You mind?"

"Only if I get treated equal." Lilly gently pounded on the counter top, determined to lighten her mood. She wondered how many times they'd had this same conversation in the past six or seven years. How many more times in the future?

"Tit for tat, Lil. That's the club's new motto since you pushy broads rammed it up our barstools. Now that we take women, we take'em any way we can." Two AP reporters looked up and laughed; the AP and UPI always followed the other's lead.

"Even in your forced liberation, George, you're still a bosom man."

"Well, I like to keep abreast." George's humor was like that; the rest of him was fine.

20

"Could I have fifty dollars for the ladies' room, please?"

He gave her a dime for the telephone, the way he always did, and she was reminded again that they knew each other altogether too well.

Maggie answered on the first ring; at fourteen, she was getting faster on her feet to respond to the phone.

"Mags? It's Mom."

"I knew it would be you. I called the station and they said you were gone for the night. Which means you aren't coming home for dinner and I have to feed the beast, right?"

"You should be so smart in school. Look, I won't be too late. George and I are having a drink. Shall I bore you with the nutritious values of peanut butter, or will you kindly feed Teddy and I'll be home in time to put him to bed?"

"What are my alternatives?"

"None."

"Mom, there was another rape in Georgetown. It was on the news tonight."

"Hang in there, Mags. Your turn will come."

"Mother!" She drew out the word in exasperation.

"Your mother is *off duty*. This is a recorded announcement. Your mother will be home by nine. Feed your brother and she will see you later."

Lilly hung up and went into the rest room marked HENS. Only the male press corps could come up with such a banality. For years they had voted down female membership in perfunctory little ceremonies that took no more than five minutes. When they could no longer exclude women, they had indulged themselves in hours of discussion about the installation of a new powder room. The word went around that the *Times* bureau chief had led a thirty-minute argument for additional urinals as the only sanitary conditions necessary for Washington's newswomen. UPI's senior woman assigned to the White House had given him a bronzed toilet seat when he was transferred to the Paris office. Lilly grimaced at the recollection of him wearing it around his neck at his farewell party.

Looking at herself in the mirror over the washbowl, Lilly examined her face for those little lines and creases around the mouth and eyes. She had only started to take serious notice of them several months ago; now they were all she saw. She wanted to persuade herself that it was only vanity, but she knew better—the wrinkles were sure signs that the death process had begun, each little puff and sag warning her that there was less time left. These were the last of the good years and she ought to be doing something with them. Mags had noticed the face changes, too.

"Mom, you're getting old."

"How kind of you to mention it, Maggie, my dear. But it's not age, little one; these lines are you, those around the mouth are your brother. Actually, I'm a beautiful princess under the spell of a wicked obstetrician."

"Will I get wrinkles around my mouth?"

"Not if you can manage to keep it shut once in a while."

But the lines were there, and no matter how many jokes she made they would not go away. And no matter how often Lilly told herself she did not mind in the least that she was forty, she minded a great deal. Not so much when she was with Peter. No, when she was with him, she felt young and expectant. Most of the time, anyhow. She hadn't felt like that in a long while and it made her sadder still. Peter, she thought, come kiss the frog back into the beautiful princess.

Lilly lathered her face with soap to remove the camera makeup, careful not to smudge her mascara, the way she'd watched Clara do when she was still a child.

"There you go, dipping into the past again." Lilly spoke aloud to the mirror; this relationship between herself and her reflection was something new, too. It was no special conceit; it just seemed the safest time to visit with herself. Probably another bad habit; sometimes people caught her at it. Even now, she saw that the black attendant was putting down her magazine and asking if she needed anything.

"No, Gwen, thanks. What I need they haven't invented yet." Lilly immediately regretted the self-pity. Briskly she ran an expensive brush through her short curly hair.

"The French make better hairbrushes than movies." She had spoken aloud again.

"Beg pardon?"

"Nothing, Gwen. Just talking to myself. One of the prerogatives of the aged."

The girl laughed, the way women of any color laugh at the mention of age when they are still in their twenties. "You're only as old as you feel."

"I know," Lilly said, "that's the part that scares me."

Walking back toward the bar, Lilly thought again of the exchange earlier in the evening between herself and her director. Gene Riggs was only being nice; he was a good kid; she'd no right to be so sharp with him. But the way he'd come bounding down the circular iron steps after her taping session had annoyed her unreasonably. So much energy and youth and enthusiasm. It was not the day for such ebullience, not when it was directed at her.

"Hey, Lil," he'd said. "If you've got a minute, I'd like to rewind that tape and show you what I've done."

"You mean what I've done, don't you? Is something wrong?" In her current state of mind she was sure she'd made some dumb mistake.

"No. You were great. It's the camera angle that's different. I had Gus and Tommy back off and shoot you from further back. Softens up the frame. You look ten years younger. Wait'll you see."

Her delicately controlled nerves frayed quickly. "Goddammit! Who the hell asked you to make me look ten years younger! I don't recall making any such request. I happen to be a film critic, not a movie star."

"Well, excuse the hell out of me. I only thought . . ."

"That I'm showing a little too much age? Think on your own time."

"I said I'm sorry." He was very hurt; her own body sagged from the outburst.

"I know, Gene. It's me. Off my feed lately."

"Yeah, I've noticed." He turned and climbed up to the control booth and Lilly had simply not had the strength to call him back. She was very disturbed by the tantrum, though—it really wasn't like her. But it *was* like her lately, a lot like her, and she didn't understand. Or didn't want to. She had analyzed the incident carefully in the cab ride to the press club, insisting to herself it wasn't insecurity about her appearance; she looked better now than she did at twenty. No, it was something else, something deep inside, some frightening warning to get ready to be old and finished. She related the story to George when she took her place next to him at the bar.

"Why'd you make such a fuss? He wasn't exactly shooting you through cheesecloth. Besides, you look great, Lil. The best. Everything about you is in good shape. Your work. The kids. You got the best damned legs in television."

Lilly smiled. "Couldn't you use the old bosom bit? Just to cheer up a pal?"

"Legs, kid. You wouldn't want distortion from a vigorous free press, would you?"

"As a matter of fact, yes. I'd also like a very dry vodka martini. On the rocks and with a couple of olives." She waited for him to make the obvious connection between her chest and the olives. Instead, he was unusually serious. "I mean it, Lilly. You're the best damned woman I know."

Lilly laughed, embarrassed. "Since when do you know anything?"

But the appreciation in his big, broad face was genuine; she relied on it so.

"You know something, George? Lately I think that if I didn't see myself so brilliantly reflected in those smiling Jewish eyes of yours, I might not actually exist."

"It's good to know what you keep me around for."

This was as close as he would come to exposing his uncertainty about her and they each looked quickly down into their glasses, uncomfortable at the mention of the lack of romance between them.

"Too bad, huh?" he said.

Startled, Lilly answered without looking up, "Much. Much too bad." The finality of their words made her think again of Peter and she drank the rest of her martini in silence.

When the third round of drinks came, Lilly borrowed another dime. The phone took longer to be answered this time.

"My working mother has abandoned us. This is the sister of a helpless brother speaking. We are alone and unprotected."

"Mags, how did you know it was me?"

"I didn't. I always answer the phone this way."

"Well, stop it. You'll give working mothers a bad name."

"What about us working kids, don't we count for anything?"

"Look, nut, where's your brother?"

"Locked in the bathroom."

"Oh, God. Not that already. He's only ten."

"Mother! You are evil as well as negligent. He's in the tub for a change. He's got the Sony in there with him. Says he'll be out when the late news comes on."

"If the cultural cretin doesn't electrocute himself, will you take a whip and a chair and force him into the bed for me? I'm going to be later than I thought. And Mags? There weren't any phone calls for me, were there?"

"Nope."

"Maybe someone called and Teddy . . ."

"He didn't call, Mom. I'm sorry."

Lilly hung up and thought of Maggie. Maggie—the little girl who could have been Lilly—no delusions, no coquetry, no self-effacing and ingratiating seductiveness. Maggie will say what she means and mean what she says. And probably still end up waiting around for someone like Peter to call. But she won't hate herself because of it. Please God, don't ever let Maggie hate herself.

They got very drunk, she and George—Lilly quiet, he talkative, the reverse of their usual outings. Abruptly George returned the conversation to a personal level.

"What's bothering you tonight? What's the matter with you for the last couple of weeks, in fact? Some guy again?"

Lilly lifted her head, a little surprised. Since she had started seeing Peter, almost an entire year now, she'd been very careful not to mention him to George. Some inner instinct, she guessed, but she knew enough not to talk to George about Peter. Not this time around.

She shook her head. "I don't know what's wrong, George. I just can't seem to shake the feeling that I'm approaching some kind of showdown. Something I can't stop and I'm not ready for."

"Since when aren't you ready for anything?"

"Since maybe all my life. I just didn't know it till recently. It's like there's someone inside me trying to get a message across and I can't figure out what it is. The thing that scares hell out of me is that I think it's something I really ought to know, some vital piece to a puzzle that I can't go any further without. It's about to drive me nuts."

"For God's sake, Lil!"

"Leave God out of this. He's never around when you need Him, anyhow."

"Since when are you admitting God is a he?"

"I'm really very serious, George. Never more serious in my life. The whole thing's been closing in on me for months. All day, for instance, I've felt like I'm about to explode. It's as though something is going out of me, or worse, it was never there in the first place." Lilly put one hand protectively over her chest; she tightened her other hand around a fresh drink.

"I don't know," she went on, "I don't seem to believe in myself anymore—if I ever did. Nothing seems good. Or at least, nothing seems good enough. Oh, I don't even know what I'm trying to say. Everything is so empty and pointless."

"What you need is a good man."

The pig will out, Lilly thought; even in the best of them it's there. For only a moment she considered telling George about Peter and how her last encounter with him had left her feeling so inadequate, so empty. It struck Lilly as funny to be able to pinpoint this emotional down-sliding precisely to that last weekend in New York with Peter only a handful of weeks ago; funny only because she hadn't figured it out sooner. It was so obvious. Well, it was nice that something was obvious. She asked the bartender for more ice, then turned again to George. It was annoying to have him say she needed a man.

"I've considered running an ad," she said. " 'Independent woman of an age, has own identity and income, but wants good man. Only qualified need apply.' I thought it would read better if I leave out the part about my sharp tongue and the two smart-mouthed kids. I wasn't planning to give the year model either."

"Why do you have to make a gag of everything? A woman like you does need somebody. We're meant to board the Ark in pairs, baby, only you won't give in to it."

"What is this from you? Of all people, you're telling me now about going off in twos? You're the one who always talks me out of my conquests. Remember?"

"That's because you make such lousy choices. And for God knows what reasons. Face it, Lil, you're hitting the time in life when you need someone around, someone solid."

It occurred to Lilly to lift her drink and pour it over George's head; it also occurred to her that he probably didn't have a clue that he deserved it.

"Come on, George. Who says that Ark will float anyhow? I've done that before. Care to count the times?"

"You mean Harry?"

"For starters. Yes. He's the only one I married. I doubt he'd give me a reference. And what is all this stuff about a solid man. Except for you, it's been so long since I've seen one I wouldn't recognize the breed on or off an ark." That's not true, she thought. There was Peter. He was solid. At least he started out that way. For a moment Lilly felt she might actually cry, that maybe she ought to. Just burst into tears and tell everything to George and let him rationalize all the pain away, the way he always did. And then what?

"There are plenty of good men around, Lil. You just keep going to the zoo for yours. One bad marriage and a few misguided romances doesn't mean it's all over. Somebody will come along and make you happy."

"Happy! For Christ' sake, George. What is happy? You sound like Hollywood. All my life some movie has been shouting for me to mate and be happy; be patriotic, pure and happy, in that order. I went out and did those things and it's all a hoax, a giant bloody hoax."

Lilly sat forward a bit unsteadily and put her elbows on the bar, warming to the topic. George was leaning back, staring at her; she was, of course, not addressing herself to the subject at hand but he was pleased to see something of her usual spirit.

26

"I planned my life by those gargantuan contraptions called movies and what has it got me? Happiness? Happiness was dreamed up by brilliant Jewish immigrants who came to Hollywood to pump out the 'joy' that started a whole generation of us on an impossible search for it. The Great Love Story! It's paid off for everybody except those of us who sat in the dark swallowing every word of it."

"You've managed to cash in on it pretty good."

She had overstepped; George was rankled by the Semitic reference. His anger rose as he spoke. "Those Hollywood Jews have put you to work."

Lilly ignored the warning in his voice; she wanted to fight tonight, to scream and to accuse someone of something. Anything. "You bet your ass they've put me to work, and I've paid for it every step of the way. The sons of bitches crammed that whole happiness routine down my throat in about two million reels. And for what? To look around at forty and wonder why I can't see a tidy ending coming up? I believed it when I didn't know any better, but I'm not about to hear it from you." She was actually shouting, striking out at him along with everyone else. She was going to have to control herself; after all, George only meant to help, like Gene, her director. Was that what made her so angry? The help? She could only muster the smallest smile.

"Anyhow," she said, "it's not personal. My single best friend is Jewish." And so is Harry, she reminded herself. And my children. And Peter. Her smile grew more natural; George accepted the tacit apology by ordering more drinks.

"I don't know what's got into you, Lil. I always think of you as knowing what you want."

"Me, too. Maybe that's the problem. Maybe what I really want is the happy-ever-after stuff I've just denounced." She stared into her drink for a few seconds and then abruptly changed the subject. "George, I found out something this afternoon. I'm a certifiable cynic."

"Bullshit, you're the most incurable romantic I know."

"Maybe that's what makes me so cynical." They both laughed. "Lately," she said, "I've thought of selling out but I honestly don't know what for. I'm not feeling particularly marketable these days."

"That's a crock and you know it."

"I'd like to know it. I *need* to know it. But I'm better at bullshitting everybody else than fooling me. That much I do know. These last weeks, it's that, well, I'm just not sure who I am. I'm at the age where I'm supposed to pass painlessly into middle life. I think the expression is 'to mellow.'" Lilly paused, frowning at her own dramatics. She leaned over to George and put a hand on his shoulder. "My problem is that I can't seem to get on with the business of growing up. There's this young girl inside me who won't turn herself over. She doesn't trust me and I can't say as I blame her."

"Come on, baby. You're better than this."

"Wrong, George, *wrong*. I'm just like everybody else. I've been so busy playing a game that I haven't noticed that time's closing in. Right now, all I've got is a little bravado; the script calls for courage." She took a large swallow of her drink; she might as well say it all.

"Those two children at home? They're mine and I love them. But nobody asked me if I wanted them. One morning I was throwing up and I've been somebody's mother ever since. And I'm responsible for them, them and the house they live in and me and the work I do to pay for it all.

"I'll tell you what's wrong with me, I'm tired and I'm scared and I'm lonely. Half my life is back there somewhere and I don't know if I've salvaged enough from the chaos of it to get me through the rest." Lilly paused only long enough to light a cigarette. "Jesus, George. I'm ready to get the hell on that Ark. It would be terrific to turn myself over to someone. But there's nobody out there I want. Nobody I want that wants me. Anyhow, I'm all I've got right now."

"There's someone out there for you. Trust Uncle George on that."

"Sorry, Uncle, but I just may have priced myself right out of the going market. Who needs a woman of *any* age who's not sure who she is, never mind one who may be too old to make the necessary emotional compromises?" Lilly was suddenly flooded by thoughts of Peter; everything kept coming back to him. Somehow, she thought, I've lost control of my life again. It's slipped away when I wasn't looking. She felt a wave of nausea and stood up to leave, a little shaky.

"Let's go. I'm whining. My performance deserves a bad review."

"Lilly, if you don't have it all together, nobody does."

She shrugged. "Maybe in the final reel, somebody will save me."

Outside it was still sleeting but the street was not icy. George whistled for a cab and put her inside.

"We go our separate ways?" he asked.

"Story of my life."

"It doesn't have to be."

Lilly grabbed at his hand through the open window, not wanting him to say anything more. "Yes it does, George. It's the only honest ending."

He leaned in to kiss her good-night, almost precisely the way Peter had sent her off that last time in New York—goodbye, he'd said, and she'd asked if it was over and he had said nothing, only waved to her as the taxi pulled away from the curb. George was waving to her now, too. Someone was always waving in or out of her life.

The telephone rang later in the night. She was still sitting in the kitchen, her coat over the back of her chair where she'd left it, an empty glass before her.

"Lilly," George was whispering into the receiver from some downstairs extension in suburban Virginia. "I'm worried about you," he said.

"Me too."

"I'm here whenever you need me."

Her response was very faint. "Thanks."

"What are you going to do over the weekend?" he asked.

"I think I'll go back and grow up one more time. Look under each memory for that girl who won't turn into me. Spend some time with Clara. She's the only one who knows how I'm meant to turn out."

There was a long pause on the other end of the wire.

"Lilly, honey. Your mother's dead."

"I know, George. I know."

# 3

SUMMONING her mother was not easy; Lilly had two distinct sets of recollections. There was the early Clara with the curly dark hair and lively blue eyes, the one who loved Lilly and cuddled her close, the bubbly Clara who was so popular and who included Lilly in grown people's conversation, took her along to the beauty parlor and to her endless card parties, who let her sit at the same table with the adults at Sunday lunch while everyone else's children were made to sit in a separate place. This was the Clara who was still able to care about lovely things and gay excursions, the one to whom Lilly would come each morning to have the sashes of her hand-smocked dresses tied into special bows, the Clara who would spend hours brushing Lilly's thick curling hair with the silver monogrammed brush that had its own matching comb and mirror on the vanity.

"The other girls are so ordinary, darling, they don't have naturally curly hair like ours. We are very fortunate not to be like everyone else."

Lilly would go off to school persuaded that her sausage-like ringlets were a source of envy to her schoolmates whose own hair, in the fashion of the times, was mostly braided or poker-straight and tied back with bands of ribbon.

It was this gay and romantic Clara who made a ritual of wrapping Lilly in the marabou-trimmed silk kimono which had been part of Clara's trousseau and who propped her alongside her in bed on real goosedown pillows with exquisitely tatted lace edgings. The satin eiderdown tucked around them, they would play lady, giggling and waiting as Idah brought her mother's breakfast tray. Clara would dip a triangle of buttered toast into her coffee, holding one long polish-tipped hand under the offering for Lilly to devour it in a single bite. Together they would open the morning paper to the section marked SOCIETY AND HOME DOINGS and read aloud from the "In and Out of Town" column about who had just returned from a weekend in Atlanta, or who was having houseguests for the holidays. Lilly would snuggle close to that mother and listen as she read about older girls who had become engaged, or the others who had just had babies.

"Now, none of this is for you, Lillycake. Clara forbids you to be ordinary. My girl has better fish to fry than marry some silly boy and have babies every year."

Although they never spoke of what precisely kept Lilly from being ordinary, it was understood that she was special; that her drawings taped to Clara's triple mirror were the very best, her earliest poems showed genius; her vocabulary was precociously extensive, and that "Lilly, darling Lilly, can dance like an angel." Often Lilly read aloud from her library books to her mother's enthusiastic approval; her dramatic recitations and elocutions were productions Clara thought worthy of all luckless visitors to the household.

"Wonderful, wonderful Lilly," she would say, clapping her slender hands even before the finale. "You're just like your mother, aren't you, darling? Someday you'll do all the things that make me proud. I just know you will."

Lilly would stay hours next to her mother in the large, high bed listening while Clara talked on the telephone to Leyla or Mary Nell as they discussed endlessly the things they had done the day before or would do that afternoon. On those occasions Lilly held herself so still that an arm or leg would invariably fall asleep and the tingling would become so awesome that she was sure it could be heard through the receiver. Later she might help Clara dress for the day, following her about from closet to mirror, but never into the bathroom, for her mother was very modest and often told Lilly that it was common and unladylike to use the toilet unless both water taps were running full force.

Instead, Lilly would wait on the big satin hassock next to the dressing table, watching Clara as she settled into the small gilt chair and pushed up the sleeves of her dressing gown to fix her face. Fascinated by the ritual, Lilly paid especially close attention as her mother dampened the mascara cake and rubbed it with the tiny brush into a thick liquid which she stroked on each lash before curling the lashes carefully with a little pink-handled crimper.

Lilly loved Clara's giant dressing closets that opened with

double doors to show row upon row of shoes: red cobra ones with wedges and straps, brown alligator with open toes and heels, patent-leather pumps with bows, brown-and-white spectators, and the dozens and dozens of different-colored satin sandals with their high and pointed heels. For each pair of shoes there was a separate matching pocketbook whose contents Lilly lovingly transferred one to the other: the gold cigarette case with the diamond Scottish terrier in the center, its matching lighter and the powder case, tubes of lipstick, a silver mesh change purse, rattail combs, a leather-bound copy of *Goren on Bridge*, rolls of Tums, half-used packs of Raleigh cigarettes and Chiclets. Lilly would carefully remove the coupon from the cigarettes, and happily empty the purse of the loose tobacco as she chewed on some of the escaped gum.

From a perfumed velvet folder in the top dresser drawer, Lilly selected her mother's fresh handkerchiefs, chiffon squares for evening, white lacy ones for special days, and a seemingly limitless assortment of flowered and embroidered linens for regular use. One Christmas Clara had given Lilly seven little handkerchiefs of her own, each with a different day of the week stitched in the corner. Lilly kept them in her treasure box to take out and admire, but she could never bring herself to soil anything so splendid. Despite the number of times she was told that a lady was never without a fine handkerchief, Lilly would face every crisis in life without one.

There was also the other Clara who cared for none of her lovely things, who never left the house for days at a time, the Clara that Idah complained of when she had to keep Lilly with her in the kitchen all morning.

"Your mama's in a mood today. She's having one of her spells and you're not to pester, you hear?"

Together she and Idah would sit at the chipped enamel table playing fish, both of them waiting expectantly for the bell to jingle in the butler's pantry.

"Lord only knows what she wants now. That woman has the devil in her today."

It was not that Idah was mean. Lilly knew that. It was just that she had had a mean life. Tall and mostly bones, Idah's white skin was heavily freckled from outdoor work. She came from a farm in another county and had presented herself just exactly as Clara often related the story to Leyla or Mary Nell.

"My dears, she simply appeared one afternoon without a stitch of luggage or a sign of a reference. Came right to the

32

front door, *the front door,* mind you, and said to me as brazen as anything: 'My name is Idah, Ida-with-an-H. I don't drink or smoke and I keep a house as clean as my soul.' "

Idah had been there since Lilly could remember, her thin red hair always done up in green rubber curlers, her hands never idle, always busy, always red and raw no matter how much she used the bottle of Jergens lotion she kept on the window sill above the sink.

Over Idah's bed was a gold-framed picture of Jesus Christ on the cross; her other walls were covered with the religious pictures from the calendars that Quiggly-Humphrey Funeral Home sent each year. Her prized possessions were her two Bibles.

"One is for show and one is for go," she would explain to Lilly with a rare grin. The black pasteboard book was for every day and the white leatherette one, with "Idah Hennessey" stamped in gold on the left-hand corner, was kept neatly wrapped in a tea towel and brought out only on Sunday, when Idah would loosen her fuzzy red hair and go off to the Calvary Baptist Church to absorb the Lord's word from the Right Reverend Hinds Higgins during the course of his congregation's all-day worship. Her affections and earnings were reserved for "the Almighty," for Idah believed devoutly that if she took care of God's needs, He would surely see to hers when the time came.

"Jesus Christ, the Son of our Lord," she told Lilly, "is the only man I will ever give myself to. The rest are all dirty and filthy. A man wants only one thing of a woman but he don't mind taking her money along with it. A person sticks by the Good Shepherd and she'll be all right in this life and a heap better off in the next."

It was to this stern and loyal woman that the other Clara turned during the bad times, those interminable days when Lilly's strange and uncontrollable mother lay about her darkened bedroom all afternoon in a rumpled satin nightgown, not eating, not talking on the telephone. Idah would stay with Clara for hours reading to her from the Bible and when Idah finally came out of her mother's room, Lilly would know that everything was all right once more and that the real Clara would reappear soon.

On one of the bad days when Idah was elsewhere in the house, Lilly had gone into her father's bedroom and crawled on her hands and knees through the connecting bathroom to stare at her sleeping mother. Clara's arms and legs were

33

thrown carelessly over the covers, her mouth, turned down into a bitter expression, was smeared with red lipstick. She had awakened and found Lilly there, calling her close and gathering her to her, squeezing Lilly breathless and moaning to her over and over. "Oh, my poor Lilly. My poor baby. Don't look at Clara now." Lilly had tried to push away, but the grip was tightened. "Clara's here with you always, baby. Do you love Clara? Tell Clara you love her."

Then she would push Lilly back sharply. "Being alive is a misery, a horrible punishment. It's better to be dead in the ground while you're beautiful—not to grow old and ugly." And then she was smothering Lilly again with naked arms, stroking her face and rocking her, crooning to them both. "You're going to be the best, the very best. You'll make Clara proud. I know you will, won't you, baby? Promise Clara."

Her mother had squeezed Lilly's cheeks, forcing a pout of her mouth, and had kissed her full on the lips. For the rest of her life the smell of liquor on someone's breath would remind Lilly of that afternoon.

Over the years the Good Clara disappeared with an almost predictable frequency, and Lilly existed only for her return, cherishing each hour with her, growing more and more dependent on affection from the woman she determined to believe the true Clara. During the other times, Lilly lived a fantasy, pretending that her real mother was away on a holiday and would soon come back to swoop her up and love her all the harder for the absence. She waited patiently for the good days, for the special afternoons when Leyla or Mary Nell might come to visit, almost holding her breath for them to say the words she needed to hear: "Why, Lilly is the spitting image of you, Clara. The two of you could be sisters."

Which is how they came to see themselves, two beautiful and loving sisters, one a complement to the other, separated only on Clara's "little holidays." On the sad days Lilly stayed mostly to herself, reading the books that Clara liked to hear recounted or storing up little paintings and poems and bits of amusement that she could surprise her mother with. By the time she was twelve, Lilly believed she could grow up to be Clara, convinced that if she was very, very quiet and made no trouble at all for anyone she would turn into the good Clara and they would never be separated again.

At times her father, gray and distant, would try to explain the strange woman who was pretending to be her mother. Lilly listened politely to him as she always did, but the things he said were really meant for someone else, just as her father seemed to belong to some other child. She would nod and say "Yes, sir," eager to back out of his study at the first opportunity. Once he spoke of that long-ago summer at Myrtle Beach, and although she sensed that he was telling her something important, Lilly truly could not remember and did not understand what he was saying. She only knew that she and her father made each other uneasy; it was their single common feeling.

Lilly and the good Clara were best friends, and Lilly came eventually to replace Mary Nell and Leyla in her mother's life. The best days were when it was only the two of them. She would rush straight home from school to find her mother dressed in a beautiful robe, propped on pillows on her chaise longue, waiting, eager to hear every single detail of Lilly's day.

"Darling girl, tell Clara everything you did. Were you wearing the prettiest dress? I know you were the smartest one, weren't you?"

Lilly would spend hours inventing elaborate stories in which she always won the spelling bees, scored all the points at whatever game was played at recess; her artwork took first place, her geography maps won the most stars, and it would always be she who recited her part in the play with the most emotion and to the greatest applause. Sometimes Lilly invented herself such roles of glory that she even convinced herself that she was indeed an extraordinary prodigy, one who often found herself confused and indignant that not everybody accorded her the kind of praise she had come to imagine she deserved.

Their evening meal was always taken on identical trays, both Lilly and Clara seated before the fire in Clara's room listening to the radio as they ate, chatting and commenting on Henry Aldrich and Boston Blackie as though they were all great friends of long standing. Clara would tell Lilly all that had happened that day to Pepper Young's Family, and bring her up to date on the travails of Mary Noble, Backstage Wife. Several times each month, large boxes would arrive from New York filled with the dresses and coats they had selected after hours of pouring over the Best & Company catalog. Clara would make Lilly try on each purchase, telling her how beau-

35

tiful she looked and describing in the most minute detail all the places Lilly would go, the people she would meet, the clever and witty things she would say.

Once there had been a young girl's outfit for horseback riding: twill jodhpurs, checked jacket, knee-high brown leather boots, a derby felt hat and an imported English riding crop. At Clara's insistence the costume was worn so often that even Idah came to believe Lilly was actually riding to hounds every day. In truth, Lilly seldom went anywhere in those days other than to school. Not until she was thirteen. That was the year Clara developed an insatiable passion for movies.

They went many times a week, sometimes to two in a single afternoon. Both of them would become so involved in a film that for days they might discuss a particular plot, each taking the role of one or the other of the actors and reenacting the story endlessly. After seeing a re-release of *Gone With the Wind*, they spent an entire week creating final reels where Scarlett got Rhett back, or—and more to Clara's preference— glorious endings where the heroine went on to "better things than just hanging around Atlanta." These were the wonderful times, and even when Clara was unable to get out of bed, Lilly continued to go to the movies alone, carefully remembering every scene to share with her mother when she returned. Then she would describe each costume and setting so meticulously that Clara might sometimes become confused as to which films she had actually seen, versus those Lilly had only drama- tized for her.

"You will probably be a great actress, darling," Clara would say to Lilly. "You make everything come alive. Why, I can even believe you are Miss Bette Davis and Jezebel all in one."

When things were better, the two of them would sit to- gether in the darkened movie theater exchanging whispered comments on Joan Crawford or Judy Garland; later they would emulate the women on the screen so well that Clara thought of herself as actually being Jane Wyman or Claudette Colbert, talking as they did, using their gestures, once even cutting her curly hair into bangs that would not stay flat on her forehead. Clara would only see films that were pleasant and she believed deeply in all the good things on the screen. She liked to remind Lilly that a person had only to make the right choices in life to be happy, the way they did in her favorite old movies.

"You see how nice things turn out? A girl keeps herself pure and the right man comes along, Lilly. Not some silly boy, but a real man like Henry Fonda or Jimmy Stewart.

They'll know you've saved yourself. Just stay clean, honey. A man has no respect for you if you don't. You listen to Clara and you'll find a wonderful man to make you happier than you can imagine."

# 4

LILLY shifted her weight in the kitchen chair, jolted back to reality by the sound of Maggie coming down the back stairs. She had been sitting there, smoking and drinking coffee since long before dawn. Hastily she emptied the full ashtray in front of her, blowing at the tobacco grains on the pine table. Both children thought it their duty to object to her smoking. It was the one commendable message they received from television, the one Lilly appreciated least. She pulled her robe closer about herself, and with unconscious concern, ran her fingers through her uncombed hair. Forcing a smile to her face, she held it up for Maggie to graze with a careless kiss.

"Hi, pal."

"Morning, Ma."

"Could I be either Mother or Mom, Mags? It's Saturday and I feel too much like 'Ma' to be addressed as such."

"What's bugging you?" Maggie asked, pointedly inspecting the cigarette stubs in the trash.

"What makes you think the grinning head of this half-nuclear household could possibly be troubled?"

"Whenever you talk like there's an audience, I can tell you're making an effort not to look worried. And since when are you up this early on Saturday unless you can't sleep?" Maggie did not pause for a reply, but rubbed her stomach. "Can I have a fried egg sandwich? You owe me. I cooked last night." The girl turned the *Washington Post* to the entertainment section.

"Margaret, my dear, you are a smart-ass that only a mother could love."

"Truce. I'll drop the 'Ma' if you'll cool the 'Margaret.' "

"Deal." Lilly broke an egg into the skillet. "What are your plans?"

"It's a White Slave Saturday. I go to Dad's at ten. My part

of the divorce agreement, you may recall." The sarcasm was heavy.

"Mags, an occasional weekend at your father's is hardly cruel and unusual punishment. Besides, you're getting too long in the tooth for white slavery. They want them younger. And less mouthy."

Lilly turned the egg over and pressed two slices of bread into the toaster. "Mayonnaise or butter?"

"Mayonnaise, please. My mama's Southern and I never learned better."

For about the thousandth time in the last few weeks Lilly was feeling uncomfortable with Maggie's glibness. In the six or so years since the divorce, Maggie had been deliberately brought up as an equal, treated as an adult maybe sooner than the child could handle. Maggie had adopted Lilly's own flippancy as though by osmosis and it not only annoyed Lilly to be bested, it made her uneasy that such sophisticated jargon might be placing the girl into a social situation beyond her maturity. Worldly behavior made Mags good company, a convenient place to unload responsibility, but was it right?

"Maggie, I think you should show more respect for your father. Be grateful he isn't like most divorced men who forget the old children once they've got a new family."

"Mother! How would you like to spend a perfectly nice weekend chasing a baby brother who's not even housebroken for a stepmother who is only ten years older than you? It isn't easy to be ordered around by someone six inches shorter who wears training bras. That woman thinks stepchildren are indentured servants, for Christ' sake."

"Cinderellas are not profane, Maggie. Cursing isn't ladylike." Lilly smiled at her use of the very words that Clara had so often directed at her when she was young. Maggie caught her expression and flashed a "home free" look. Once again, the child seemed to have the upper hand and, once again, Lilly felt the nagging concern that her permissiveness might be coming home to roost. She put the sandwich on the table and stroked Maggie's long, straight, sun-bleached hair, feeling an enormous affection for her. Leaning down, she kissed the top of her head; Lilly had to clear her throat before she could speak.

"I love you very much."

"Me too."

They sat silently, a little embarrassed by the emotion between them. Lilly stole several quiet looks at Maggie busily studying the movie section and licking mayonnaise from her fingers. She's all right, Lilly thought, the good stuff is there. She is beautiful, beautiful inside and out, and goddammit, I need her more than she'll ever know. The great lump of sadness resettled in her chest, bringing with it the familiar anxiousness to beg the child not to leave but to stay, stay and give Lilly a sense of purpose, a reason for being alive. This new desire to clutch at the children was frightening. Lilly shook her head to dislodge those thoughts and looked toward the refrigerator at the greeting card magnetized to the door:

It's nice to believe when the going gets rough
That your friends will come running to make things less tough,
But you'll find you are the strongest when standing alone
And the help you rely on is solely your own.

She had bought the card months ago for Maggie, who was then going through the first of what would inevitably be a legion number of adolescent concerns with the opposite sex. Scrawled under the rhyme, in Lilly's own hand, was another message: "But you can always count on me. XXXXX's, Mom." The card had found permanent residence in the kitchen but what Lilly had intended to be an amusing comfort to her child had, instead, become something of a personal taunt. She wanted Maggie to lean on.

Lilly was reminded again of Clara and cautioned herself. I will not use this child. I will not do that to her. I have to let go, free her of being a full-time daughter—the way I've forced her to free me of becoming a full-time mother. She reached into the pocket of her robe for a cigarette. Maggie watched her, frowning darkly.

"Oh, for God Almighty's sake," Lilly said and lit the match anyhow.

"Profanity, Mother dear, is most unladylike."

They were still laughing when Teddy came in. The only male in the house, he was given to entering rooms without advance notice. At ten, he sensed a feminine conspiracy and was wont to secretly monitor their conversations, fearing in some way that the women in his world were bent on liberating him from what he considered his rightful place of superiority.

"No matter what, I'm not going to do any favors for anybody today and that's final." He spoke with a forced gruffness. Pointing at his sister's plate, he said, "I'll have that, too."

Without otherwise acknowledging his presence, Maggie slid her empty dish toward him. "We are only sex objects. Male chauvos fry their own eggs around here."

Lilly walked over to the boy, gently folding down the extended middle finger he offered his sister; she patted his thick, curly dark hair so similar in texture and style to her own.

"Mayonnaise or butter, Little Pig?"

"Both. And bacon."

The women's movement was passing Teddy by, and no matter how much conversation was made about sexual equality, he believed that females were meant to serve him. *Trouble is,* Lilly thought, *that's exactly what I do.*

"Try 'please,' " she said to him.

"Please."

Maggie was outraged. "Boy, is this kid in for a surprise when he starts looking at girls who aren't in the centerfold of *Playboy* magazine which certain kleptos I could name have been stealing from Doc's Pharmacy."

"Your brother's interest in the female anatomy is normal, natural and healthy." *That's what Peter had said when she told him about Teddy's precociousness.*

"Mother! Tell that to Mr. Justman, whom you so thoughtfully made me wait around for all yesterday afternoon in order to show him this pigsty that he is going to paint next Thursday for a hundred and fifteen dollars."

"You didn't tell me he'd come."

"You didn't ask."

"That sounds high for a coat of paint."

"He says he'll have to replaster the hole this toad knocked in the wall between his room and mine. Mother, he's a regular Peeping Tom."

"I'm *Teddy,* you dummy."

"Whatever your stupid name is, I call you a sex-a-maniac."

Teddy again stiffened his middle finger in his sister's direction.

"Stop it, both of you. Just precisely what did the painter say?"

"That he couldn't get to it till Thursday; that it would cost one hundred and fifteen dollars. Mom, he took one look at those naked centerfolds glued to Teddy's walls and asked if my brother was away at college. I told him he was riding his tricycle at the playground."

"I do not ride a tricycle anymore and if you say that again I'll bust your butt."

"See, all he thinks about is my body, the shoplifting little pervert."

Silently Lilly turned the bacon, remembering every word Harry had said when they were married—"Everyone should have two children, a boy and a girl. First the girl. We practice up on her, and by the time the boy's born we've already made the mistakes that Spock says are inevitable in rearing first children. They should be spaced by three years so there will be no jealousy."

Well, it wasn't deliberate, but that's how it worked out. Girl, boy, three and a half years apart. Only, both children spent part of every waking moment stalking each other with blunt instruments. Harry blamed her for their rivalry, insisting in accusatory conversations that it was Lilly's "fucked-up notion of some kind of half-assed sense of equality" that was causing the friction. Maybe she was at fault. She seemed anxious to blame herself for everything else lately, why not this? She sighed, leaning herself against the edge of the stove. You do the best you can, she told herself, pour whatever you have into them whenever there's time. The rest is chance.

Suddenly tired, Lilly put Teddy's sandwich in front of him, feeling his grubby hand pat her behind. I love this one just as much, she thought, and Lord forgive me, I like his physical interest. If he thinks all women are meant to fall over him, it's because he knows I do. At any goddamned age, *they know*. Gently removing his hand, she placed a paper napkin in it and smiled down at his greasy face. "Teddy, stealing from Doc will grow hair on the palm of your hand."

She turned to Maggie, sensing the girl's indignation. "Look at it this way, Mags, given his early lust, we'll never have to fish him out of gay bars, will we?"

Swell, she thought, the Voice of Reason. A forty-year-old stand-up comedian, a smash in her own kitchen. Two egg sandwiches, four fast jokes, and a couple of children who have no idea how much they're needed. She glanced again at the greeting card on the refrigerator door: *And the help you rely on is solely your own.* Well, fuck that, she thought. Fuck Dr. Spock, too. And Harry. Abruptly Lilly laughed, remembering that fucking Harry was one thing she never had to do again. It was among the few supposedly resolved things in her life that had not come unraveled. At least, not yet. As she rinsed the dishes, the idea of being quit of any conjugal responsibilities to Harry continued to amuse her, lifting her spirits. Goddamn it all to hell and back. With happy thoughts like that and a little unladylike profanity, it was just possible that she might make it through the weekend.

The children finished eating and left the table, and Lilly sat down to smoke another cigarette. It was nine-forty, she saw by the clock. Just as punctually as he did everything, Harry would come to collect Mags and Teddy at exactly ten. That left her twenty minutes to decide whether to be upstairs when he arrived or to change into her clothes and face him down. Thinking of herself as taking the bull by the horns, she went up the steps, two at a time, grabbing at random in her closet and pulling on a pair of gabardine trousers.

The bull was as analogous of Harry as anything. Before they were married she had delighted in his assertiveness; it had made her secure that he was so positive, so dead certain of what he would do with their lives. That was what had attracted her to him in the first place, wasn't it? Certainly it wasn't sex; the bull association did not extend to that. The thought made her laugh. No, sex was never a driving force between them. Only after the divorce had Lilly discovered that sex was not the meaningless nonsense she had supposed. Something else to change her attitude about and adjust herself to. Another fucking loose end. She grimaced at the poor humor. She hated bad jokes. Life with Harry had been one long joke, ten laughterless years of a bad joke she had played on herself.

Lily continued dressing, carefully, out of some perverse need to show herself to Harry in the fastidious manner he admired. She thought that "fastidious" was another good word for Harry. He had been that kind of lover, almost clinical. She had known so little about sex that she thought that maybe tidiness and efficiency was all there was. Neat and quick and be done with it. Well, that was something else again, something else she had learned later in life than she should have.

Her first experience hadn't been much different either. Clara had said she was a late bloomer and it was so. Without ever soliciting male attention, it had come easily enough. Boys appeared to take her to football games, dances, even the movies. They never called until well after her mother had retired, for it upset Clara whenever Lilly was out of the house. Lilly would say good-night and pretend to go to her room, and would wait there until Idah came to announce her guest. Boys were a matter of some indifference to Lilly and she kept them waiting in the hall, and then, with no eagerness and with a certain formality, she would descend the stairs, nod in casual recognition before taking the young man into her father's study. An introduction to her parent had nothing to do with filial respect; it simply served to remind the caller that Lillian Bellingrath had a sense of propriety. She was, as Clara often said, a little too extraordinary for these silly local boys.

Her father would be covered by the evening paper and

would lower it just slightly to acknowledge Lilly's friend. Both males would regard one another with discomfort, the older man fingering his paper impatiently, the younger one awkwardly shifting weight from one gangling leg to the next. Never able to address her father directly, Lilly would speak to him only when she was certain of his attention.

"This is my friend . . ." she would say levelly, adding the young man's name. Invariably, her father would conclude the ceremony with a detached suggestion that she take her little friend into the kitchen for some ice cream. He never said good-night to her, and never once had he told her what hour to return—a source of some envy to Lilly's more carefully supervised contemporaries, but a permissiveness Lilly guessed to be based on indifference rather than trust.

Actually, she disciplined herself more carefully than anyone else would have dared. Her behavior was flawless. With that one foolish exception. He was called Hose Nose, of all things, a tall lanky boy who liked to explain his nickname by pointing to his large nose, saying that he had kept it out of other people's business and given it a chance to grow. Lilly had not particularly liked the boy but she had gone with him that night to a party in a nearby park where other couples were already rolled up in blankets, sitting around a fire. All but Lilly were drinking a mixture of gin and grape juice. Something called Purple Jesus.

"Come on, Lilly. You're being a cube. Try some." Hose had pushed the offering at her and she had shrugged it aside, gesturing that he should have her share. It had not taken long for him to become drunk; his heavy arm over her shoulder became a dead weight, his speech slower than usual.

"Just one swallow, Lilly. You'll like it. It'll make you feel good."

He had become sullen when she declined again and had moved further to his edge of the old army blanket, staring petulantly at the others around them who were swallowed up in the silent darkness. From over his shoulder he spit words at her. "Just because your mother's a lush doesn't mean a few drinks will turn you into an alky, too."

Had he doubled his fist and struck her in the stomach, it could have been no worse. Lilly almost fell forward. She leaned over and took hold of each of her saddle shoes, resting her head on her bent knees; it seemed that she was frozen into this pose, unable to think of anything to say, aware of nothing except that he knew about Clara, this stupid boy with his stupid name knew about her mother. His words sounded over and over in her ears. How did he know? How many of the others knew? Did they all talk and laugh behind her back? How had Clara let this happen to her? Let her be humiliated and hurt like this?

And then Lilly had quite calmly sat up and reached for Hose's paper cup and finished what was in it; when it was refilled, she emptied it again. The boy had anxiously given her more and more, nodding approvingly as she drank it down, then began to nuzzle her neck. But Lilly was thinking only of Clara, hating Clara for letting her down, hating her and screaming inside her head that Clara had betrayed her. Lilly was angry, more furious than ever in her whole life; her chest was pounding with rage even as Hose eased her backwards onto the blanket. She was dimly aware that he was fumbling now at her breasts, whispering that he loved her, that he would respect her. Lilly did not pull away. Her head was too full of Clara, of her need to strike back, to punish, to hurt Clara as Lilly was hurting. Yes, she had only to close her eyes and commit the unpardonable sin, the sin against Clara's belief in Lilly's purity.

Lilly fixed her attention on the boy's giant nose as she lay beneath him, fascinated to see it come so close to her face, then move back, come close, retreat, come close again. There was no pain, really no feeling at all, and just as suddenly as the motions of sex had begun, they were over. She heard a low groan followed by the sound of Hose drunkenly vomiting into the grass. Absently, Lilly listened to him retch and then she had handed him a tissue from her purse, casually, much as she would have ministered to a sick stranger. She stood up, slowly straightening herself, and began to walk back toward the car. It was funny but she wasn't thinking of Clara anymore, nor was she mad, not even the least bit. What she thought about was *For Whom the Bell Tolls*, about Ingrid Bergman, about what nonsense it was to expect the earth to move.

Lilly finished dressing and touched her mouth with lipstick, glancing critically at her reflection. It did not trouble her to remember that night anymore; the memory did not even bring a frown to her face. Instead, she concentrated on her hair; she was never particularly confident of her appearance whenever she viewed herself as Harry would. She turned away from the mirror, resigned. He never approved anyhow, no matter what pains she took.

Back downstairs, she quickly tidied the kitchen. Harry never approved of her housekeeping, either. Well, what the hell difference did it make what Harry thought? But it mattered. Whatever the reasons, Lilly thought, I'll never be free of a need to impress him. She wiped off the counters and tossed the damp cloth into the cabinet beneath the sink, then hurriedly collected the debris of daily life, caps, gloves, sweaters, comic books, a broken tennis racket, baseball cards, one lone sneaker, a green and white hockey stick with the name of some other child marked on its tape-wrapped handle. She stuffed everything inside the antique pine cupboard, kicking with her foot to close its crudely fitting double doors. Guiltily, she pressed the large number of cigarette stubs beneath the other garbage, feeling like some kind of an ax murderess secreting the weapon. Harry did not smoke, but he knew her habits and it would not do for him to see the evidence of her current confusion. No, if she had to fall apart at this late date, she would not give Harry Shawcross the satisfaction of spotting the clues. A quick spray of Lysol would cover her tracks; he would find her serene, maybe in the rocker in front of the television. Lilly sat down and flipped the channels nervously. Cartoons on every station. Saturday! Snapping off the set, she grabbed the editorial section of the *Post,* rehearsing a look of interest.

He came through the kitchen door without knocking and she could only stare at him mutely, her composure slipping away, just as always. Goddamn him, she thought as she carefully folded the paper, the unused prop. Half a dozen years since the divorce and he could still reduce her to total foolishness without even opening his mouth. She sat helpless and still, feeling herself fill with loathing. Not for him. For herself. For Harry, she no longer felt any emotion as definite as hate.

"Kids ready?"

A shouter by habit, Lilly made herself walk casually to the phone, press the intercom button and buzz Maggie on the third floor.

"Dad's here." It was all she said.

Replacing the receiver, she turned to Harry, and not knowing what else to do she gestured toward a chair. He declined to sit and so she stood also, increasingly ill at ease with his indifference.

"Looks like a nice day for a change," she said, then shrugged at her stupid remark.

Harry nodded and checked his watch.

Lilly was having trouble fighting down the inanities his silence could prompt. She was thinking that here before her was the man with whom she had lived, eaten and slept for ten years, the father of her children, and she had more rapport with the laundryman. At least when she handed over the dirty sheets they managed to communicate. Maybe she ought to toss Harry the dirty clothes and send Mags and Teddy off to the wash. It was hard to control the nervous laughter that was pushing its way up to her throat; she jammed her hands into the pockets of her cardigan and stared out the kitchen window. They stood there in total silence, she and this person who was once her sole source of identity. Now, she thought, our single common bond is the children, and they are taking their precious time getting themselves down here to connect us.

"Listen, creep," Maggie was saying over her shoulder to Teddy as they stumbled down the stairs, "either that two bucks turns back up in my jewelry box or I'll break your head."

"You and who else?" Originality was not Teddy's strength in debate.

Flashing Lilly an "It's your fault" look, Harry greeted the children with a warning. "Let that be the last of this kind of talk for the weekend. It may be tolerated around here but not in my house. Is that clear?"

Each child glared murderously at the other. Wordlessly they kissed Lilly good-bye and followed their father out the door. The latch clicked as they left.

Lilly sagged against the countertop as though the breath had been knocked from her, then turned to watch through the window as they got into the car. The old jealousy that the children might prefer Harry to her had long since been replaced by other fears. First guilt, now anxiety. Those angry voices rose within her shouting for Mags and Teddy to stay, not to leave. Not today. Or tomorrow. She could vanish if they didn't keep watch.

Sternly Lilly reminded herself of the times when she couldn't get rid of Mags and Teddy fast enough, days when she thought she knew who she was and where she was going and was damned glad to let Harry take them off her hands for a while. She did not feel like that anymore; she felt afraid.

She fumbled in the drawer for a fresh pack of cigarettes and ripped it open, lighting one so quickly that her throat burned from the match's sulfur and tears smarted her eyes. Her chest hurt with complicated emotions she could no longer control and she leaned her head against the glass windowpane and began to cry. Right now, she thought, no matter what I think later, right now I want Harry and Mags and Teddy. I want us to be a family again.

She stood at the window for a while longer, her arms tightly wrapped about her, her lower right lip pinched between her teeth to stop the crying. Disgusted, she tossed the unfinished cigarette into the wet sink and listened for it to sizzle, then tore off a paper towel from the rack, crossed to the antique mirror that hung between the pots and pans on the pegboard and wiped at the running mascara under her eyes; she blew her nose and glared at her reflection.

"You dumb bitch. You've had your chance at it both ways and nothing works." She blew her nose again and continued: "Listen, lady, I'm running out of patience with you. You're forty years old. Remember? And I'm sick and tired of your vacillations—you and your stupid-assed discontent. You deserve to be alone. It was you who did this to us in the first place. And it's you who'd better figure some way to get us out of this or we'll end up on the funny farm with the rest of the crazies." Lilly looked levelly into her own eyes and for a moment she considered calling Peter. He could either help her through this or make it worse. Probably worse. Well, she couldn't bear that again, not now. The gamble was too great. Irritably she reached toward the refrigerator and snatched up the silly greeting card, angrily reading the last line aloud: *The help you rely on is solely your own.* Quickly and purposefully she ripped it into halves, into quarters, into tiny pieces. Then she filled a glass with Scotch, added ice, and sat down at the table to try to sort out the shredded fragments of the card. Nothing fit. She could make no sense of it. Sadly Lilly brushed the scraps of paper into a neat pile with one hand, sweeping them into the open palm of the other, and dropped them all into the trash. Nothing could be made whole again once it was deliberately torn apart.

# 5

IT WAS the early part of the 1950s that she remembered so clearly. She had, she supposed, become what was considered in small Southern towns something of a spinster. Not yet twenty-one, but still unmarried, rather unusual among her school friends, most of whom had had grand weddings with bridesmaids and flower girls and gone away on storybook honeymoons. They had all settled quickly into early matronhood with small babies, some of whom arrived considerably short of the acceptable time period. Each of the girls seemed to have given up on their romantic illusions and their figures a good many years before they could vote, a constitutional prerogative easily by-passed in the hassle of housekeeping.

Lilly had not gone away to school. Instead, she was taking courses in English literature at the state college in a nearby city, driving the thirty-odd miles each way several afternoons a week. It was not as though anyone actually insisted she stay home; it was just understood that the mother would cease to be if the daughter was not there. Nor did Lilly question the arrangement. She questioned nothing in those days; she accepted everyone else's clichés just as she lived one herself.

Her schoolwork consisted of a good deal of outside reading and she attended only a few classes, where she listened to the other students discuss the works of classical and contemporary writers, occasionally submitting her own views in carefully written essays. When she was not in the library, she was at the movies, bringing home to Clara the stories of the books and the films. Over their supper trays, Lilly would, as always, entertain with lively reenactments of *Jane Eyre* or *Eugénie Grandet*, in both the novel form and the movie version. Clara would listen raptly to each rendition, always insisting that the plots of the motion pictures—as altered from the fiction— were by far the best.

Actually there wasn't anything else Lilly chose to do. Her life was easy. Uncomplicated. Being with Clara was as meaningful as anything at hand. Sometime earlier that year, their roles had reversed: Lilly became the dominant figure; Clara, the child. It was now she who read the newspapers to her mother or took her for an occasional automobile ride to point out the changes in the quiet streets of the city. Lilly tried to interest Clara with word of her old friends and neighbors—embellishing all the local gossip to the acceptable degree of pleasantness—but Clara scarcely listened anymore.

Lilly routinely combed her mother's hair each morning and often shopped for the negligees and bed jackets that now comprised her wardrobe. With great ceremony, a large blond-wood console television was installed in her mother's bedroom; a sizable antenna had to be attached to the roof. Clara was instantly addicted to the fuzzy screen and was hardly able to contain herself until evening, when the single station available to the area went on the air. From six o'clock until sleep came, all time in the household was measured by half-hour game shows and quiz shows. Clara would not watch the news, which was all right with Lilly, for a little of the outside world went a long way with her too.

Several young men still came to escort Lilly to various social functions. Most were what Clara called the hicks, the unclaimed leftovers from the early marriages that had taken away the more desirable boys. She went with them to backyard cookouts, and to the holiday dinner dances at the Country Club, disliking the ordeal of separating to one side of the room with her married girl friends to hear their endless complaints of neglect, of idle days and active toddlers. Lilly's frame of reference in such matters was limited.

It was depressing for her to see that the lives of her friends were spent in clusters: in the homes of one or the other; small children playing in the backyard by day; husbands grouped in rowdy camaraderie by night. From their constant cups of morning coffee her friends progressed to evening cocktails, and always, always, the endless droning gossip, much of it, she suspected, centering on Lilly herself. Oh, her friends welcomed her, wanted her; she represented an unthreatening alternative to their own existence, as though they needed her spinsterhood as a reminder that they had struck the better bargain. None of this troubled Lilly, for, in truth, she too supposed they had chosen the wiser course. It was not that she envied them; she knew she had only to be patient. The right man would be along soon, the right kind of life.

Returning one afternoon from class, Lilly was surprised to find her father's car in the drive; he was seldom home before dark. But it was old Dr. Royster who met her in the front hall.

"Lilly, dear, I'm afraid I have bad news."

"Clara?"

"Now, Lilly, come in and sit down. This is not going to be easy for anyone. I want you to be very brave."

"Where is my mother?"

"We took her to Memorial a couple of hours ago."

"Idah. Idah!" Lilly's voice sounded as if it came from elsewhere, but she did not remove her eyes from Dr. Royster's face.

"Lilly, please sit down. Miss Hennessey is not here. She has gone to take the things they need to get your mother ready."

"Ready? Ready for what?"

"Clara has—ah—passed on. It happened around three this afternoon. We tried to find you. I did everything I could."

He reached to console her, but Lilly pushed past him, almost knocking him down, and ran up the stairs, stopping abruptly before she entered her mother's room, slowly, reverently. The bedcovers had been stripped away and the fire had gone out. For some reason, this was the greatest shock. For the last dozen years apple logs had burned day and night, winter and summer, and now the cold hearth gave off nothing but a musty smell as though death had always been present and only the crackling of the burning wood had staved it off so long.

Both papers carried short obituaries. "Clara Ann Baldwin Bellingrath is dead at 43. The late Mrs. Bellingrath was the only child of banking executive Charles Allen Baldwin of Little Rock, Arkansas, deceased; and the late Margaret Lillian Whitehead of near-Clarksville, Tennessee. Mrs. Bellingrath came to South Carolina as a bride where she was early active in local theater groups and contributed to many civic functions in the area. Bedridden for many years, Mrs. Bellingrath expired on Tuesday of natural causes. She is survived by her husband, Theodore Edgemore Bellingrath, 59, local merchant; and one daughter, Lillian Baldwin Bellingrath, 20, a student at State College. Services will be held Friday at 10 A.M. at Quiggly-Humphrey Funeral Home. Interment will follow at Whitelawn Presbyterian Park."

Dr. Royster said that Clara had suffered a liver attack. "The poison went straight to the brain, Lilly. She had no pain."

Idah insisted differently. "It was her heart, Lilly. It just gave out."

Lilly didn't know about any of this. She knew very little about anything, only that Clara was gone, that finally she had left Lilly behind just as she had always known she would. She could feel nothing, no resentment, no sorrow, only that strange twisting sensation in her chest, like a pair of long, thin hands inside her, wringing themselves quickly and nervously, over and over. Lilly could almost hear the dry sound of skin rubbing against skin. She was able to stare straight ahead and still see the hands moving inside her.

People came to the house out of custom and curiosity. Many of them Lilly had never seen before, but they came in streams, bringing cakes and fried chicken, bowls of potato salad and pies and casseroles. And so many hams. The food was placed on the massive mahogany dining table, which was extended by its three seldom-used leaves; stacks of china plates and linen napkins were placed at each end; Clara's best flatware was lined into precise rows. For three days Lilly was aware of nothing save the perfume of flowers and the sound of idle chatter. Mary Nell and Leyla were there, hugging Lilly and telling her that, my, she had grown and didn't she look just like a young Clara? And then they would dab at their eyes and go into the front room to ask the other callers to sign their names in a leather guest book.

Idah, in black, kept a stern vigil over the food, replacing the deviled eggs and adding fresh coffee to the large silver urn on the sideboard. Lilly's high school chemistry teacher came also, and he walked awed from one large room to the next, taking her aside on the sun porch to say between mouthfuls of creamed rice and turkey that she was a brave girl, a very brave girl indeed.

Her own friends stopped by in groups of twos and threes, assuming shifts to sit with Lilly as though by some prearranged schedule. It seemed a conspiracy that she not be left alone. There was always her father, gray and solemn in the entrance hall, shaking hands, unsmiling, but nodding to each new arrival, thanking those departing and acknowledging by a bow of the head the many phrases of sympathy.

"A good woman."

"So young, Mrs. Bellingrath was, to have suffered so much."

Her father's bookkeeper, in tears, clutched at him. "You were a good husband, Mr. B., none better. You gave her everything a woman could want. The Lord knows you were a loyal Christian man, Mr. B."

Lilly viewed it all with a detached curiosity, but she was

making mental notes. She had to be ready to describe it all to Clara later.

Not so many people were at the burial. Lilly knew a few of the pallbearers by name, a few by face. There was a small awning set up and the freshly dug earth was covered by a rug of artificial grass; folding chairs lined one side of the red-clay hole and wreaths of flowers and satin ribbons on wire stands banked the other. Lilly was seated in a shroud-draped chair next to her father, their seats slightly separated from the rest; they were Clara's only living relatives.

A minister, unknown to Lilly, offered the usual praise of the "dear departed" and read aloud from the Scriptures, enjoining all to bow in prayer as the flower-draped coffin was slowly lowered into the ground on wide black straps. A single shovel of dirt was symbolically tossed into the grave and then everyone was touching Lilly's hand or her sleeve before they went away.

In the back seat of the limousine that returned them to town, Lilly and her father sat silently as they drove down the familiar streets. She gazed out the window, taking special notice of each landmark they passed, and was rather surprised when the car turned into the long drive that led to the empty house. For a moment she wondered why they had come there; there was no one home anymore. Lilly stared dumbly at the big old house, noticing curves to the roof, odd little porches here and there, things which had not caught her eye before. She gave a small start when the uniformed driver came to open the door for her. Her head nodded him away; she could not get out of the car yet, it was too soon, all of it over too soon. The driver went around to the other side of the automobile and she watched as her father reached for the strap which dangled over the rear window. He seemed to be making an enormous effort to heave himself forward, then paused and turned back to Lilly. She saw that his face and his hair were all of one pale shade. He was speaking to her.

"What?" She lifted her hand to push back the hair from her forehead.

"I said you'll probably be going away now."

"Yes." She had answered without any sense of having made a decision. "Yes, I suppose I will."

Some friends came to help her pack. They all had suggestions as to what she should do with her life, even set to bickering among themselves as to whose advice she should follow. Lilly stared vacantly at the chattering, arguing girls, dazedly wondering why they were in her room, handling her clothing, touching her possessions. It was only the rubbing sounds of hands that she heard, those hands wringing in her chest so loudly that everything else was drowned away. Confused, she would wander into her mother's empty room, surprised to find it vacant, puzzled as to where Clara could possibly have gone. And then she might forget everything for whole days at a time.

The afternoon she was to leave, her father spoke briefly to her about money; Idah followed her from room to room reminding her about God and the evils of a Yankee city; everyone was speaking to her at once, talking, warning, directing, deciding. It was nice that she could close out the voices, tune them so low that the people around her seemed like characters in a film with no sound. Perhaps someone cried that afternoon, maybe one of her friends wept and made her promise to write or to come back soon to visit. If they did, Lilly did not hear, could not remember.

When she arrived in New York, it was the beginning of a particularly hot summer. She handed the cabdriver the piece of paper on which was written the address of a hotel-residence for women. She could not recall now who had suggested this particular place for her to stay; in fact she had only the dimmest recollection of the long train ride, the bumping, jerking motion of the track as she lay, fully clothed, in her berth for the overnight trip. This inability to remember things was not frightening. There was no pain in a vacant mind.

At the hotel's entrance, Lilly pushed through the revolving doors, its rubber flaps making a strange sucking noise, a comforting whooshing sound that matched the one inside her head —sealing her off from whatever had gone before.

It was a gloomy lobby, the kind of room Clara would call low-down, as if someone had hoped to preserve an earlier splendor and failed. There was a whirring electric fan behind the frazzled gray woman at the reception desk; the woman had a little silver fountain pen attached to a cord that was clipped to her blouse; she pulled at it to fill in Lilly's registration card.

"By the week or month?"

"Oh. By the month, please."

"Wanna see it?"

"I beg your pardon?"

"The room, honey. You want to look it over?"

"No. No, thank you. I'm sure it will be fine."

"Well, it's your money."

The woman hit the palm of her hand rapidly against a small round bell and slid forward the key that designated Lilly's quarters, a room she supposed was nice enough, considering that the only other hotels she had seen were in movies. The wallpaper was pleasantly faded, its pale roses on arched trellises barely discernible. The white furniture was recently painted; two beds, a desk, dresser, bureau, nightstand; pink chintz of another dull pattern covered a chaise that matched an armchair. On the wall, over the twin beds, hung reproductions of Gainsborough's paintings of "Blue Boy" and "Pinky" —Clara had a double deck of playing cards with the same pictures and it was nice to see their familiar faces.

The room had three large screenless windows that looked out over the street eight stories below, the highest Lilly had ever been. It was very warm and she went immediately to let in some air, the sound of honking horns jolting her. She sat down on the ledge of one of the windows to watch the traffic, pulling her knees protectively toward her chest.

For several days, she wandered about the city on foot, touching with her mind the classic New York landmarks, Radio City Music Hall, the Empire State Building—Clara always called it the *Entire* State Building and that did seem to Lilly the more apt name; there was no part of the city from which it was not visible, like a lighthouse.

She ate at no special hour, just as she felt hungry. Sometimes in the Automat, sometimes at the big delicatessens, but she liked the small, cozy restaurants best, those funny little places tucked into the bottom of the large dingy buildings— they had brightly checked cloths and served foreign foods she'd never tasted. But it was the people seated at the other tables who delighted her, their overheard conversations sounding so intimate, their faces glowing pleasantly from dripping candles stuck into fat, straw-covered wine jugs.

Some mornings Lilly walked up and back past the shops and stores, maybe going inside one of the larger ones to ride the moving stairs or to finger the items of clothing displayed on endless counters. With the help of a newspaper, folded to the movie listings, she learned which theaters were nearby and which ones she would have to travel to by taxi. She saw a different film each afternoon and would emerge into the hot sunshine to find a convenient place to eat. Alone at a table or at the counter, she would check the paper to select a film to see that evening. Sometimes she had to eat quickly in order to be at the movie before it began but often she would spend a long while over her food so that she would not have to pass time wandering in the streets.

On her way back to the hotel at night she usually stopped at a sandwich shop and returned to her room with a brown bag of new tastes—corned beef, pastrami, liverwurst, kosher hot dogs with sauerkraut. She developed a passion for cream soda and Danish pastry and kept a supply of both on the sooty window ledge.

For an extra charge, the lady at the desk sent up a mahogany-boxed television whose tiny screen received several different channels without obstruction and Lilly thought how much Clara would like this. In fact, she would think about Clara most of the time if she did not watch herself. When she was at the movies, she did not think of her mother at all, but when she was lying on her bed reading paperback novels and eating her sandwiches, the loneliness would envelop her like a sudden heavy fog, and Lilly would find it impossible to swallow the hard edges of the rye bread.

Once in a while, she spoke aloud to Clara, maybe to describe a movie she had just seen or maybe to read to her from one of her books. When she realized she was alone, she would cry for a long while until she fell asleep or until the tears gave way to a suffocating fury and there seemed to be no air in the room. Then Lilly would rush over to one of the opened windows, curling herself into a ball on the ledge, wondering why she was in New York and what in the world she was meant to do.

Slowly, she came to recognize some of the hotel's other female residents, the ones she saw in the elevator. Maybe in a few weeks she might invite one of them inside her room when they came in friendly curiosity on the pretext of borrowing shampoo or a pair of stockings. But not yet. These girls were somehow *different* and a little ordinary; Clara would not approve of their bleached hair, their gum and cigarettes, their coarse language.

The first time Lilly went a whole day without thinking of Clara she felt very guilty and punished herself by withdrawing from all pleasure—no movies for a while and only a little time watching television. Instead, she would read aloud as if to Clara, almost imagining her on the faded chaise longue across the room.

There seemed no pattern to these emotions. One day she would wake up relieved to have her mother's lingering presence; the next day she might find herself hostile that Clara would not go away and leave her in peace—those moments made her sad and contrite, but still Lilly continued to become unreasonably antagonistic toward Clara and she would dress herself in a manner that she knew her mother would have found distasteful. Such defiance could last all day, but at night Lilly would often wake drenched in sweat and overcome by an unbearable longing to be with Clara and to do all the things that pleased her. More than anything in the world, she wanted another chance. She would be so much nicer this time if only she could start all over again. On the nights Lilly could not go back to sleep, she would sit on the window ledge watching for the first signs of daylight, sit there and sit there until her muscles ached to be stretched and she would finally get up and fall back across the bed until the day was safely started.

# 6

LILLY was embarrassed whenever she remembered Loretta, but she touched at the recollection much as a tongue that cannot stay away from a hurtful tooth. When she thought of Loretta, she was reminded of how her friend was always hungry, always stretching for something that was a little out of reach. Tall—very tall, in fact—Loretta was a large-boned girl, a bit too heavy but with an open, almost handsome face, a voice that was breathless and husky, yet clear and completely audible despite the flat accent of the Dakotas. She had very short red hair, styled in what Clara would call a bob, but she did not have pale skin—she had very lovely olive skin with no freckles at all. Loretta did not care about clothes and always wore trousers and an old sweater, even at night. She told Lilly she was a photographer's model when there was work. She was the most honest and the least puritanical person Lilly had ever known, and it somehow seemed all right when Loretta said that she generally posed without any clothes at all.

Loretta shared everything about herself. It did not matter that the confidences were not invited, nor was she slighted when the intimacy was not returned. It was as if Loretta saw herself as being somehow in charge of Lilly—usually speaking for Lilly to the other girls in the hotel as if Lilly were not able to do so for herself. They seemed always to be alone with each other; Lilly felt herself much like the younger sister and made no objections to being treated as such.

At first Lilly had been slightly uncomfortable with her new friend, feeling that she ought to be doing something to earn Loretta's attention, but it had been easy enough to relax, to let Loretta take her over and to shower her with unstinting affection. It was so decidedly un-Southern, so blessedly un-Southern not to have to parade and rely on one's lineage, on relations and connections; to have a friend of one's very own who did not connect her as Clara's daughter, someone who knew little and cared less about her previous life.

Loretta never tired of praising Lilly, and although occasionally the lavish compliments made Lilly feel a little uneasy, she offered only the smallest protest, for in some strange way the things Loretta said were Lilly's only clues as to what she must appear to others to be. Lilly had no idea what sort of person she actually was, but she came to believe herself as Loretta saw her, strong and brave, enormously elegant and feminine. It pleased Lilly to be so clearly and pleasantly defined, and when Loretta found Lilly's conversation amusing, even outrageously funny, Lilly indeed saw herself as humorous. The more Loretta laughed, the more Lilly tried to be deserving of her friend's attentions, becoming perhaps a bit of a clown, striving to entertain her friend just as she had tried to do for Clara. Loretta often talked of their moving into their own apartment and maybe becoming famous and sought after for their wit and talents. Other times Loretta could become moody and depressed and say that Lilly would probably leave her because some man was bound to come around to take Lilly away sooner or later. Lilly would jolly her up by making little jokes and promising solemnly that it would more than likely be later than sooner.

Loretta was twenty-five, almost five years older than Lilly, and it seemed natural that she should do so many thoughtful things without ever making equal demands. Still, Lilly felt the burden of a response. Just to look into Loretta's open face made Lilly wish hard to return her candor and warmth but somehow she could not let herself go. For one thing, she did not know how. Also she could not help feeling that a strong relationship between two women was only for marking time, that friendship with women lacked a certain dignity, and that such things were a little peculiar, a second-best arrangement. Women only made do with each other until they found a man to be with. Lilly could almost hear Clara tell her that time spent with other girls was time wasted.

Loretta was always in Lilly's room. She was plopped on the bed one afternoon peeling tin foil from a handful of candy kisses, holding the chocolate to one side of her jaw to speak. Her words sounded belligerent. "How do you spend your nights when I'm not around?"

Uncertain of the implication at first, Lilly looked puzzled, and then she laughed, kept on laughing, unable to stop, the way people do when they have not laughed much before.

"Are you suggesting that I'm like Vivien Leigh in *Waterloo Bridge*? A woman of the streets?" Lilly was delighted.

"Yeah. I guess you could put it that way. You do keep funny hours for a girl with no real job."

Loretta peeled more candy as Lilly continued to laugh. "What's so funny?"

"I don't know. It's just funny, that's all." Lilly did not add that she was somehow flattered.

"Well, it's not so funny if you have to do it for money."

Lilly was shocked and could think of no clever retort.

"Honey," Loretta said, "you kill me. People do that, you know?" She put several more chocolates into her mouth, studying Lilly with her eyes and rolling the tin foil into tiny balls as she talked. "I've done it." Her voice was defiant. "Only I don't much like it, money or not."

Lilly was aware that her own mouth was hanging open.

Loretta shrugged and said that doing it for money was at least better than being married and having to do it for your keep.

Such an unthinkable statement made Lilly's question come in a rush. "Is that what you think being married is?"

"What else?"

"A lot else. You do it then because you love your husband. You want to."

"Is that what you want? A husband?"

The question was posed so disdainfully that Lilly could only combine a nod with a shrug, hoping the subject would pass. When it was obvious that Loretta intended to continue, Lilly asked just what else was there. What did Loretta want instead of marriage?

"Oh, I don't know. I guess I'll keep on doing what I like, mostly. And that doesn't include belonging lock and stock to some man." She thought a moment. "Maybe just live by myself. Yeah, that way nobody owns you and you only stick around because you like to."

Loretta was tossing the little balls of foil now from one hand to the other. "When a person loves you, they love you. Man or woman," she said. "If they don't, they go away anyhow. Why not make it easy?"

"Because," Lilly answered levelly, "when two people care about each other, they should get married and stay married." She was embarrassed by her own vehemence and took up another sack of candies and threw it playfully at Loretta.

"Listen," Lilly said, "married or not, nobody has to—you know—do it for money."

"For what, then?"

"Love."

"Money lasts longer."

"That's because you've never been in love."

"And you have?"

"No. But I intend to be. And you're just talking this way because you've never been in love either."

"Don't you be so sure about that." Loretta giggled as if at a private joke. Lilly waited to hear more, but for once her friend was strangely silent.

In the months that followed they went everywhere together. Lilly often tried to press money on Loretta, the way she did the other girls who were "down on their luck" or those who needed "a touch to get through to payday." Lilly became quite popular with them, never bothering to keep track of who borrowed what, not concerned if or when the debts were repaid. But Loretta would accept nothing; it infuriated her that Lilly gave money to the others. She even brought Lilly small presents and stubbornly insisted on paying the bill whenever they ate in a restaurant. This seemed ridiculous to Lilly, this insistence of Loretta's that she pay; just as it made her feel silly when Loretta insisted on helping Lilly in and out of taxis or holding the doors open for her, as if Lilly weren't capable of managing for herself. They had been good-naturedly arguing over a dinner check one night when Loretta became quite angry.

"What's wrong with my money?"

"Nothing. Nothing at all," Lilly had said. "It's just that my father sends me so much of it and it seems only right to use his and not yours."

"I am perfectly capable of taking care of both of us."

Lilly had been incredulous. "Loretta, it's not like it's my money, that I earned it or anything." But her friend had been very remote as they walked the six or eight blocks to the movie they were to see, and when Loretta insisted on buying the tickets, Lilly had made no protest. Inside the theater, Loretta had asked if she wanted popcorn or maybe some candy and Lilly started to say no, but catching the look of disappointment on Loretta's face, she had quickly changed her mind and accepted a large box of popcorn. During the movie, Loretta had reached into her own purse and brought out a Kleenex and given it to Lilly to wipe her hands. Later, Loretta had fallen asleep, her head at first resting against the back of her own seat and then, suddenly, she had put her head against Lilly's shoulder. Lilly thought the position must be uncomfortable for Loretta, her being so tall and all and having to crunch over at that peculiar angle. Lilly had giggled. She was plenty tall herself, but next to Loretta she felt so small, so protected by her friend's large body.

Toward the end of August, Loretta kept bringing up the subject of Lilly's getting a job, of settling in permanently.

"You got to do something."

"But why?"

They were stretched out on Lilly's two twin beds, Loretta reading magazines and Lilly reading one of her endless novels.

"For one thing, you're liable to get bored and go home if you don't go to work."

"I don't need to work."

Loretta pulled herself up on her elbows. "Honey," she said, "I don't know the things you do. About books and all. But I do know that it isn't right that a girl like you should just hang around the picture show and read all the time."

Lilly closed her book, first marking the place, and rolled over on her side to face Loretta in the opposite bed. "But I'm perfectly fine this way," she said.

Loretta got up and came to sit next to Lilly; she began to rub Lilly's back and Lilly had to lie flat again to get out of her reach.

"You see, Lil, if you don't work, you're liable to get restless and then you'll be too quick to take up with some probably ridiculous guys to pass the time. Or you might even want to leave New York." She was pushing Lilly's hair back over her ears, talking reasonably as to a child.

"You are the most beautiful girl I've ever seen," she said. "You ought to do something with what you've got. Go on television and sell something, maybe model. Yeah. You'd be about the best model there is. You've got those long legs. And you're so thin." Loretta put her hands around Lilly's waist, squeezing her; Lilly moved slightly to get up but Loretta was blocking the side of the bed.

"You really are beautiful, you know. And bright and funny. Elegant, Lilly. That's what you are, elegant."

For a moment Lilly felt she was hearing her mother speak and she closed her eyes; it was so nice to be stroked and told lovely, encouraging things. But she felt sad, a sadness for Clara that she had not dared let take her over for a long time, and when she opened her eyes, tears rushed down her cheeks and there was Loretta's warm and loving face above her, nodding and smiling, urging her to go ahead and cry. Crying was good for her, Loretta said. Go ahead and weep because Lilly was sensitive and perfect and beautiful, so beautiful. She had every right to cry.

"I don't have what you have, Lilly. I'm not like you. You have it all. Everything a girl could want. You're going to do right with it. I know. You're going to make me very proud."

Then Loretta leaned down to gather Lilly in her arms, hugging her, patting her hair and rocking her and telling her to cry some more. At that moment Lilly loved Loretta more than she had ever loved another person, and for no more than a second she understood how it might be possible for one woman to surrender herself to another, to want her and to love her back. The thought, at first pleasant and somehow reassuring, grew suddenly shocking. It was disgusting and nasty for women to care for each other and to hold each other, terrible and frightening. Loretta was pulling her very close and kissing her wet cheeks, whispering again that she was so lovely, so very lovely. Lilly's body went rigid with shame. She pushed herself away from Loretta and ran into the bathroom and was sick. Thereafter, Lilly stayed deliberately away from Loretta and hid in a doorway when she saw her in the corridor. Once they chanced to be in the elevator at the same time and Loretta had very coldly asked how Lilly was and Lilly had only been able to nod and mumble that she was fine, thank you. She had very nearly not made it to the bathroom to be sick again. After that, Lilly did not use the elevator at the times she thought it likely she would run into Loretta. Instead she told herself it was normal to be lonely and that she did not miss Loretta's company at all. She also told herself that maybe it was time to find herself a job.

Lilly's hand shook as she reread the ad in the *Times:* "House model. No special experience. Small salary, good benefits . . ." For a moment she considered telling the taxi to drive on, but she paid the fare and got out onto the street. The building was tall and dirty, hardly distinguishable from the ones next to it. Seventh Avenue was a whole lot more than a cab ride from the East Side. Lilly looked up to check the street number over the heavy glass doors. People jostled past her as she stood there. A hard-eyed young man shouted her out of the path of the long rack of identical dresses he was steering down the sidewalk.

The offices listed in the ad were on the eighth floor, directly opposite the elevator opening. Lilly pushed her way out and walked to an enclosed square cage where a squat lady ladened with scarab bracelets and ropes of pop-apart plastic pearls was busy at a switchboard. Without otherwise acknowledging Lilly, the woman pressed a loud buzzer with her knee and pointed toward the door to the showroom.

Lilly very nearly collided with a slender young man who had a tape measure hanging from around his neck.

"You applying?"

Lilly was caught off guard and the man seemed irritated by her slowness. "For the job?" he said.

"Yes. I'm Lillian—"

"Tell it to Bertha. Over there."

He indicated a smaller room, off to the right, and went out through another door which, Lilly could see, led to the actual factory—men and women were bending over broad tables fitting patterns and operating loud whirring machines, steam was rising from the large presses.

Lilly followed the terse directions to the woman who was Bertha, an ample-chested black person who spoke in a Northern accent. She instructed Lilly to pick an outfit from an open rack and told her to choose from the shoes and accessories heaped on a table.

"Go on in the main showroom when you're dressed." Bertha aimed a thumb over her shoulder and bent back to the sewing on her lap.

Lilly put on a three-piece tweed suit and selected a pair of black alligator shoes that were too small; she walked into the showroom with tiny, uneven steps.

There, in the middle of dozens of identical French chairs, were three seemingly identical balding men of medium build, paunchy men, dressed in dark striped suits showing wide white shirt cuffs and enormous jeweled links; the stones flashed as they lifted cigars to and from their mouths. No one spoke to her directly, but one of the men gestured for her to walk in front of them, back and forth. They studied her silently, blowing out great puffs of bluish smoke. A harsh voice ordered her to remove her clothes. Lilly hesitated only a moment and then began to disrobe, taking off each item until she stood barefoot in her slip. Still another voice said that she should stand on a little raised platform in front of the wall of mirrors.

One of the men came and measured her with a frayed cloth tape, her dimensions noted aloud.

"Everything's in the right place," he said. Lilly was fascinated that he could talk with a cigar clenched between his top and bottom teeth.

"Let's see your mouth, sweetheart. You can smile, can't you?"

Then he took one of her hands and examined it. "Finger-nails are lousy. Why d'you bite them? Don't you get enough to eat?"

He did not wait for an answer. Instead, he took his cigar and dropped it into a nearby vase of wilting yellow and white chrysanthemums and turned toward the other men. They nodded.

"Honey," he said, "if you get past Lazlo, the job pays eighty-five a week. No set lunch hours and twenty percent off samples. What say?"

Vincent Lazlo made no effort to disguise his homosexuality; he seemed almost to flaunt it. Thirty, maybe thirty-five, he was extremely handsome in a disarmingly masculine way, impec-cably dressed, and, Lilly noticed, his hands were beautifully manicured—perhaps the loveliest hands she had ever seen. He tapped a sterling silver yardstick against the shin of his crossed leg as he watched her settle into a deep chair opposite him.

They were in a chrome and fur office, the far wall covered by a startlingly bright and very large abstract painting; heavy gray wool draperies shut out the noise from the street, making Lilly feel comfortably removed from the boisterousness of the garment district.

"Those three out there"—Lazlo waved gracefully toward the other room—"they don't know from peplums but they put up the money and have the headaches. I'm the artist. You're the body. Not a fancy model, honey. Just a body."

He paused to lift a fat crystal lighter to his cigarette. "You ever model before?"

She shook her head.

"Good. No bad habits to unlearn. I'll teach you what you need to know."

He leaned back and smiled for the first time. "Two things we get straight right now. You don't make dates with buyers and you don't get pregnant."

It was easy to lose track of the season. In the fashion busi-ness, you worked on the spring line even though it was only September and it seemed to Lilly as if she lived in the fitting room, as if she had always lived only in that one cavernous building.

Her working day was spent on an elevated, carpeted circle in front of many mirrors and under very strong lights. She was always in her underwear. Several of Lazlo's assistants were kept busy draping fabric around her, pinning it here and scissoring it there. When they fought over a neckline with the cutter or when the young men argued shrilly among themselves for one type of cloth over another, Lilly stood silently, waiting for them to settle the dispute and return to her.

A garment was molded to her body as if she were a live dressmaker's dummy and then it was taken to the workrooms where the rough sample was transformed into a master pattern. No one bothered with her otherwise and she was there for weeks before seeing Vincent Lazlo again. When he finally began to work with her, he only shouted, calling her Sandy, the name of the last house model, who had left abruptly to marry a wealthy vacuum-cleaner manufacturer. Lazlo was easily angered and Lilly was more than a little nervous in his presence.

"Over here, Sandy. Now walk about three feet, pause, turn around again, pause. No. No. No! You're not slopping hogs, honeychile, you're showing off a dress. Try to get that into your head, will you? That's better. Now turn with some style this time. Jesus Christ, not like that. Don't you know anything?"

It surprised Lilly how easily she could become angry. She was not accustomed to losing her temper. Her voice shook. "Mr. Lazlo, when you hired me, it was for my limited experience as well as my limited proportions." Close to crying, she rushed to finish her say. "For eighty-five dollars a week, I'm not supposed to be Suzy Parker. And, if you would like to know, my name is not Sandy. It's Lilly. And, if I knew anything, anything at all, I wouldn't be here, I can tell you that."

She stepped abruptly from the ramp and walked to the dressing room, furiously unzipping the sample garment and telling herself that this whole stupid idea was dumb—dumb and stupid. She didn't have to work anyhow and it was just as well; she couldn't do anything and she didn't want to. She bit down on her lip not to cry.

"Mr. Lazlo says when you get changed he will take you for some dinner." It was Bertha.

"You kindly tell Mr. Lazlo that my hog-slopping days are over around here."

Lilly was buttoning up her own dress as he walked into the dressing room, not bothering to knock. No one did.

"Now what?" she said.

"Now we eat."

He gave her a boyish smile. "You can't walk out on me this close to a show."

"Give me one good reason why not."

"Two." He grinned. "The really talented models think they're too good for this kind of work, and besides, not one of them is flat-chested enough to wear the samples."

Lilly smiled in spite of herself and looked at him through the reflection in the mirror as she tightened a wide belt at her waist. Her brow crinkled with indecision.

"Well, this is your lucky day," she said at length.

"How's that?"

"My appetite is bigger than my ego." She smiled slowly. "I'm starved."

"All right then, Sport. Let's go." He took her by the elbow and reached to open the door.

"The name's Lilly."

"You don't mind if I call you Sport, do you?"

Lilly paused to consider. "I guess not. What do I get to call you?"

" 'God' would be all right with me."

"As in 'Goddamn you'?"

"Honeychile"—he bowed deeply—"you may not have so much to learn after all."


Lilly was happy, even eager for Vince to take command of her. With him she was strangely calm, almost serene. It was as if Vince were in control of her nervous system, as if he could look into her mind and know what she was thinking or wanting before Lilly herself had any idea of it. She needed no one else as long as there was Vince—no friends, no life of her own; he and his world were enough and would be enough for a very long while. He told her she wished to be the very best manufacturer's model in New York and, of course, he had to be right, that was what she wanted. And he was teaching her something new every day.

"Look at it this way, Sport," he would call to her as she went through her paces on the runway in the empty show-room. "It's on-the-job training. Other than doctors, who else gets to practice up on a live audience?"

He permitted her to wear very little makeup and only the simplest of clothes, saying she was so wholesome she ought to be advertising bread and that he would keep her that way as long as he could. When she expressed uncertainty about anything, Vince put his arm around her shoulder and squeezed her to him and she was sure. Their months together melted into a year, and Lilly was beginning to see that beneath the assumed European mannerisms and the sometime-British accent, Vince was just an Indiana boy who cared deeply about the evolving American fashion industry. The way she cared about him.

Every day since they became friends someone told her how lucky she was to work with Lazlo. He was becoming the most noticed young designer in ready-to-wear, wasn't he? Certainly, they said, anyone could plainly see that he was something of a celebrity in his own right, lionized more and more by the trade journals as well as by the society columnists. Absolutely, there was no question that he was the anointed darling of his private clients and much the status symbol of out-of-town buyers. They had said all along that she should be very grateful to Vincent Lazlo and she was.

It became their habit to dine each night in one of the elegant restaurants at which Vince thought it profitable to be seen. Vince's mannerisms altered appreciably in any social or public situation and it was a curiosity to Lilly to watch him change roles so easily.

"What is this split personality of yours anyhow?" She asked this as they were settling themselves into a restaurant's red leather banquette—she, starved and anxious for the menu; he, keyed up and happily waving and nodding to some of the other diners.

"Don't interrupt when I'm doing my Pope on the Balcony number," he told her under his breath, still bowing and fluttering his long, graceful fingers toward an adjacent table. When he turned to her, it was in his regular, unaffected manner. "Now what was that pedestrian remark?"

He signaled the waiter for two glasses of vermouth before she could respond.

"Sorry, your Eminence, but I was just wondering why you go into your suave David Niven routine for everyone but me."

He seemed taken aback that she would ask. "Because I trust you. And I respect you." He called for menus. "You see, ducks, those rich ladies who have no more on their minds than what goes on their backs become very insecure when they have to deal with people who don't look and talk the way they do. It throws them. So I give them what they're comfortable with."

The waiter brought the menus. Vince studied his as he spoke. "Besides, I like playing gentleman. Somewhere inside me is a regal princeling of a fellow—a closet aristocrat. I bring him out when it amuses me."

"I see," she said sarcastically, "and I get the Terre Haute special? The real you?"

"The genuine article, Sport. Now, if you were rich and famous, I'd give you the full treatment. But if you were rich and famous, I wouldn't be feeding you every night. What will you have?"

He was giving his entire attention now to the large white card the maître d' placed before him.

Lilly affected her most rural South Carolina accent, knowing it amused him. "Some of that skinny fried fish."

"One goujonette of sole?"

"And a side dish of them pommes de terre, if you don't mind."

Vince laughed. "And to wash it down?" he asked.

"How about an RC Cola?"

"What vintage?"

"Any day this week will do right nice."

Vince ordered both dinners in flawless French and dismissed the hovering captain.

Lilly turned to him, suddenly serious. There was so much she wanted to know about him.

"What was it like in Terre Haute, Vince?"

"Pretty middle-class. My dad sold insurance five days a week and worked Saturday and Sunday in his Victory garden, even after the war. Grew the best vegetables on the block."

He paused to be sure she was really interested in what he was saying. Lilly urged him to go on.

"My mother sewed for other people. Damned good at it, too. Followed patterns, made up some of her own. All with a pedal Singer machine. Till the day she died, her calves were firmer than mine."

"And when she died?"

"I was free. I would never have left otherwise. She was a wonderful woman—wanted me to get married and bring home some grandchildren more than anything in the world."

"Did she ever guess why you didn't? I mean, did she know?"

"About me? About being gay? No. Never. The old man, though, he knew; I think he always knew. But he loved her as much as I did and he never let on. Must have been hard for him to carry around the burden of my sexual peculiarities all those years, never talking it over with her the way he did everything else. We didn't discuss it, but somewhere along the line, when I was fifteen or sixteen, we both knew and we had an unspoken agreement that she was not to find out. It would have killed her."

"And your father?"

"I don't know. He never talked much. Used to tease me in

front of her about being a lady-killer, though, staying out late and all that. Once I was engaged for a while but couldn't go through with it. My mother asked my dad why I had broken off with such a nice girl. You know what he told her? He said, 'Peg, that boy is looking for someone as fine and wonderful as you and it's going to take time to find her.' I don't think I ever loved him so much as when I heard that. One of these days, I'm going to tell him that I got to be the way I am all on my own, that it didn't have anything to do with him or her. They never let me down in anything."

He paused to taste the wine, then bowed his head to the wine steward to fill both glasses.

"Except I believe the old man would rather not hear the truth. He is the kindest person in the world and I think he likes to think that I'm still just looking for the right girl."

"Do you hear from him?"

"All the time. He used to send me a little money each month. Now I take care of him. Still has his garden, he says. Funny, but I always think of him on his knees pulling weeds. Just a few weeks after my mother died, I went out back and said I wanted to talk to him about something important. He looked up and said was it that I was wanting to go away? I nodded and so did he. Then he said, 'It has to be what you want, son. I'd keep you with me forever if I could but a man has to make his own way.' So you see, Lillysport, you are indeed getting the best part of Vince Lazlo."

"Oh, Vince"—she was almost tearful—"I know that. I just wish there was something I could do to help."

"Help what?"

"You. You know!"

"I *know*. It's you who doesn't. I like the way I am; being homosexual isn't a bad way to be. No shame, no guilt. You see"—he drank some wine—"I don't feel like damaged goods. I like myself and if I happen to prefer boys to girls, I don't think that's anybody's problem. Certainly it's not one for me. Like most people, you have some silly notions that all of us want to be straight and that some wicked fairy—you should pardon the expression—changed us against our wills.

"In some funny way, I always knew what I was, and except for a few smart cracks in high school, and a lot of biased laws, I was never hounded like some of my friends. No daddy kicking the shit out of me. No pampering mother tying me to her emotionally. I really have no complaints."

He lifted his glass in her direction. "Of course, my chosen

field of endeavor precludes blackmail and social outcasting." The thought made him laugh. "Can't you just picture some guy walking into my office and threatening to expose me if I don't hand over the secret dress designs?"

He was quiet while the captain poured more wine; Vince never spoke personally in front of waiters.

"If everyone in the fashion business stopped talking to homosexuals, you could hear a pin drop on Seventh Avenue. And if they outlawed us, the garment district would fit quite comfortably inside a phone booth. No, I'm safe. Safe and unashamed."

"Is there anyone special for you?"

"There has been. May even be again. But I'm no more desperate for a man than you are. Probably not as much because I love my work. What you have to understand, Sport, is that homosexuals are as selective and as particular as straight people. Maybe more."

"Why do you spend so much time with me?"

"Because I like you, Lilly, for God's sake. You're a breath of clean air. I hope that's the same reason you're with me. A man and a woman can enjoy each other without sex, you know."

He wiped his mouth delicately with the stiff white napkin.

" 'Course, now"—he smiled—"if we keep meeting this way, there is likely to be some questioning of your motives. All I stand to lose is my girlish reputation." He turned to stare at her curiously. "What are your motives, by the way? How come a beautiful girl like you doesn't have men hanging on her every word?"

"I don't know any men." She laughed. "How is a girl supposed to find a husband in the fashion business, anyhow?"

"Is that what you want?"

"Sure. And some kids."

"Holy Christ. At least I don't have to consider the children." He giggled, taking more wine. "You really want a husband?"

She nodded, self-consciously.

"Why?"

"Who knows why? I just want someone to love and love me back. I had such a funny family myself that I think it might be nice to try one with a happy mommy and a nice daddy and some pattering little feet." She tried to shrug aside the emotion in what she was saying.

He looked incredulous. "You really mean all this, don't you?"

"Of course I mean it. You act as if I were Joan of Arc asking for a suit of armor—a husband and children is the norm. You make it sound wild and unusual."

"Well, if that's the way you want it, we have to be sure to find one with big money. If I have to lose you, I want it to be to some rich bastard who can afford to buy my clothes without the discount."

He was studying her closely now, as if she were someone he didn't know quite as well as he'd thought.

"There's no rush," she said. "And he doesn't have to have money."

"It's just as easy to love a rich man as a poor one."

"I don't think so, Vince." She was nervous talking this way, twisting a cocktail stirrer as she spoke. "When a man has money, he expects everything his way."

He laughed. "And how would you know?"

"Well, my father is kind of like that."

"Bossy?"

"In a way, yes."

"And rich?" He seemed surprised.

"Sort of, I guess."

"Good God, Sport. You got a rich papa? What the hell are you doing with me?"

"We like each other, remember? And he's not all that rich." Lilly thought maybe they should change the subject.

"Well, well, well." He stared at her. "Vince Lazlo with a rich mannequin. Why didn't you say so?"

"I didn't think it mattered."

"Maybe not. But it sure makes things easier."

"Easier for what?"

"To get a husband who can afford you."

"How's that?"

"It takes money to attract money."

"I told you. I'm not looking for that."

"You don't know what you're looking for. But leave it to me. It might be fun, you know?"

"What?"

"Finding a husband."

Lilly felt an acute stab of discomfort, as if she had started something she had no wish to finish. She gathered her gloves and purse to go to the powder room.

"Just keep me posted on the wedding date," she said, hoping the discussion was over.

"Yeah," he said. "The ceremony wouldn't be legal without you."

The subject of Lilly's future did not come up again, not for several months, and then only because of Vince's insistence that she take an apartment of her own. He had, he said, found the perfect place only that morning.

"Between Park and Lex, Sport. We don't want to look like a bloody heiress. Draws the wrong sort."

"Wrong sort of what?"

"Husband."

"Whose husband?"

"Yours."

Lilly made a small face at him.

They went to look at the apartment; Vince insisted she call it a flat and it was, she had to admit, very lovely—two main rooms, a small kitchen, a nicely landscaped rectangular garden. The bedroom and bath were to the quiet side, with long rows of windows reaching from the floor to the high ceiling. He had her sign the lease that very day.

At first he consulted her about the decorating; eventually he took full charge. On Second Avenue he found an oversized antique canopied bed and immediately set about finding the proper person to make the mattress. In fact, the perfection of the furnishings became near-obsessive with Vince; it was all he spoke of when they were together. Sometimes he brought swatches of fabric to work with him, not for Lilly to select, only to admire. He would tell her that the drawing room— "Only yokels says 'front room,' Lilly"—was to be done in white, two white damask sofas covered with brilliant red and pink down pillows; an ornate French armoire and bookcases were to be installed on either side of the double folding doors and there were Italian bergère chairs intended to pull into what Vince called "conversational groupings." Lilly did not ask who would comprise the conversationalists or what the conversation was meant to be.

Vince even showed her different stains for the floors, saying as he waved the samples quickly in front of her that, of course, the darker the better and didn't she agree?

Shortly before she was to move in, they went down to Madison Avenue, where Vince steered her quickly through several antique shops, rather as a housewife might breeze through a supermarket, selecting that Oriental-import lamp, those three Lowestoft platters, a set of Meissen bowls to be used as ashtrays. Later that afternoon he arrived at the apartment with a Bloomingdale's shopping bag filled with pieces from his own eclectic collection of small table items, silver snuff boxes, ormolu framed miniature paintings on ivory, carved tortoises.

Arranging them to his satisfaction on a small round table, Vince stood back to admire his handiwork.

"These are only On Loan from the Lazlo Collection," he said, thoroughly pleased with his humor and his taste. Lilly scarcely troubled to look at the small objects, preferring not to let herself become attached to things that could be taken from her.

Glancing about the room, Vince asked if she had any personal photographs. "No pictures of you and mums riding to hounds or whatever it is you crackers do for jollies down there?"

" 'Fraid not. Mums didn't go in for horses. If she had, there wouldn't have been any money left for this dollhouse."

Vince was openly offended by any reference to his extravagance, completely indifferent to the fact that furnishing the apartment had taken a sizable chunk from her mother's trust fund, which had matured on Lilly's twenty-first birthday. A goodly part of the check her father sent each month would now have to go for rent and upkeep. A rich husband was taking on an additional and irritating urgency, but Lilly smiled to put Vince at his ease. He smiled, too.

"Old things," he said, "are a good investment. Expensive old furniture and rich old men. You can trust me on that."

The day she brought over her few possessions and her clothes, Vince was on an aluminum stepladder in the drawing room, hammering away. When the nail was firmly in place, he tore brown paper from around a large gold-framed canvas. Done in the early 1930s, the painting was of a beautiful golden-haired young woman in a flowing soft dress sitting on a gilt armchair, a feathered boa draped around her slender, bare shoulders. She wore a long strand of matched yellow pearls which were only slightly lighter in shade than the small pug dog in her lap. Lilly had to help him lift the portrait up over the mantel. When it was in place, Vince backed down the ladder and drew her to the far side of the room, looking from the painting to Lilly and then back again, artistically narrowing his eyes.

"Well, it's not rubber-stamp perfect, but it will do." He gestured palm up toward the painting. "Lilly, my dear, meet your old mums. If anyone mentions the difference in coloring, just say you take after Poppa's side of the family."

Happily he clasped his hands beneath his chin, delighted by her surprised expression.

"Happy! For Christ sake, George. What is happy? You

And then there was the party. Vince made it sound so essential, as if there were no earthly reason for a nice home unless it was for a party. He had brought up the subject very matter-of-factly—had, in fact, only casually torn some pages from the back of his little leather notebook and handed her the neat columns of names, thirty of them.

"You've met them all at some time or other," he said, then opening his desk drawer, he brought out a manila folder. "Study these photographs so you can match the names to the faces. I've jotted down the essentials about each. The important thing is that we do not appear pushy or obvious. You do your homework and leave the rest to me."

Later he went over the dinner menu with her, emphasizing what he termed "our plantation theme." An enormous Negro woman was to be imported to cook.

"Just think of her as an old family retainer and so will everyone else."

There were to be thin slices of Smithfield ham, crab Maryland, buttered grits soufflé, fruit, salad, cheese, tiny beaten biscuits and delicate pecan tarts, the recipe for which Vince would later insist had been passed on to Lilly by her black mammy on her deathbed. On the geranium-strewn terrace an elegant black butler with snow-white Uncle Remus whiskers would be standing ready to mix drinks in frosted silver mugs and to pass hot cheese straws. When Lilly finally saw him, she was convulsed with laughter and asked Vince if the butler was any good at singing "Swanee."

"For God's sake, Sport, don't dare have him open his mouth. He's from Trenton."

"Then who's responsible for these Old Dixie splendors? You ever spend any time down there?"

"Philadelphia is as far south as I ever care to go. But ole Vince has done some research." He tapped his right temple to indicate the source of his genius. "You just be a good little belle and don't ask so many questions."

The night of the party, Lilly was wearing a long marquisette Lazlo gown with a deep ruffle hanging from the shoulders, and she felt more than a little silly in it, standing next to Vince, waiting with him for the guests to arrive. She said nothing.

"Miz Lillian," he said, "Uncle Vince has a coming-out present for you."

She opened the velvet box and there on the sculptured white satin was a long strand of yellow pearls identical with those in the painting over the mantel. Vince kissed her forehead and moved her around to face the portrait. "Mums would have wanted you to have these."

Lilly felt tears start to sting her eyes and she turned away from Vince quickly, asking him thickly to please fasten the clasp at the back of her neck. He was humming "Camptown Races" as he adjusted the pearls and just listening to him made her smile again and feel better. She wanted now to tell him so many things, about how much she loved him and how much she always wanted them to be together, but before she could speak, there was the bonging sound of the chimes and Vince was before the mirror smoothing down the lapels on his velvet dinner coat and adjusting his black bow tie. He waved aside the butler and went to open the door himself, both arms extended in an effusive greeting.

"How darling of *you all* to come. Lilly! Of course, you know Tot and Marty!"

Lilly smiled and held out her hand the way Vince would want her to do, but there was a sudden heaviness in her, a strange and disturbing uneasiness, that things were already too far out of her control.

She had known there could be no stopping Vince after the successful party. He became more Southern than a Mississippi planter, even took to wearing vests with a white suit and referring to his bewildered business partners as "Yankee profiteers." Every day he was smoking long thin cigars as he worked. Lilly protested only mildly about his blatancy, even laughing a little at his unsubtle public references to her as a textile heiress.

"Just fun and games, Sport. A lovely charade. Life is like that. You dream up what you want to be and you be it."

"I suppose so. Only I'm not sure what I want to be. It's so phony, Vince."

"To move among phonies is to beat them to the draw, or drawl, as the case may be."

"Trouble is, I feel like the one who's phony."

"You're real and they aren't. It's that simple. In this big bowl of hamburger you are steak tartare. The single genuine article."

He looked straight at her.

"And I love you for it, Sport. Sometimes like a sister, and sometimes"—he lifted his chin to gaze directly into her eyes—"well, sometimes like the wonderful girl I might have been. I expect great things of you."

Unexpected anger flooded through her and she opened her

mouth to let it out. But she did not know what to say, did not know what it was that had caused the anger to rise. Shivering, she felt disgusted by her moment of disloyalty to this man who had just said he loved her, the only man in her life who had ever spoken those words to her. She had to cough before she could answer.

"I love you, too, Vince."

He hugged her very close.

And then she persuaded herself that she really should do as he thought best, that exaggeration was, after all, only a minor vice. She told herself that maybe people were just figments of someone's imagination. Maybe that's what life really was.

Now they spent only a few evenings alone, but they were the best, those quiet nights when he instructed her in the preparation of the perfect martini or quizzed her on wine vintages and cigar brands. They listened to Bach and Mozart until she learned to distinguish one from the other, and after dinner they would curl up on the couch and Vince would take out his little leather notebook to go over the list of men he considered eligible prospects for Lilly's hand.

"There's a Whitney coming on the market. Divorce. I've made some discreet inquiries. We don't want to look interested in him until it's official. Can't afford to let anyone see what we're up to, can we?" He moved on to the next item on his list. "What about that Greek we met last week? Any flares?"

"None. I can't understand a word he says. His English is awful."

"His credit is superb."

Her patience was thin on the subject. "I can't spend all my time in Cartier's, Vince." She began to file her nails irritably.

"What about the Liquor King? He's a trifle bald, I admit, but he keeps his body in shape."

She continued filing. "He's more interested in you."

"Oh? You think so?" Vince marked the man's name with a star.

"As a matter of cold, hard fact, Vince, they're all old and boring."

"As a matter of cold, hard cash, they're blue chip to the core. The very rich are always boring. That's why they need us."

Annoyed by her lack of interest, he went on checking names in the book, moving his gold pen methodically up and down the list. Lilly could tell he was offended and would sulk, she knew, if she did not show some enthusiasm. He was like Clara that way, withdrawing from her if she was disobedient. It was so hard to say no to them.

"Why can't I just keep on working and maybe meet some nice young man whose English is as good as his Dun and Brad?"

"Because those things don't come together." His tone was very curt. "And because you deserve the best and you're going to get it if I have to cram it down your dainty throat."

# 7

SOME months later at a publication party in the wine cellar at Delmonico's, Lilly met Harry Shawcross. She was ill at ease in crowds and was relieved to be engaged in conversation with anyone.

"You a friend of the author?" he asked.

"No. The friend of a friend."

"Whose?"

"His."

She pointed Vince out in the crowd. He was standing with two of his fashionably dressed clients, using his arms in flamboyant but graceful gestures. His exuberant party voice seemed unusually shrill; it carried all the way across the noisy room.

"You part of that?" he'd asked.

Lilly was not as blasé about Vince's homosexuality as Vince was. "If you mean are we friends, yes. If you mean anything more, no."

She turned to walk away but he grabbed at her sleeve.

"Sorry," he said, "it's just that sometimes women who hang out with queers are not very interested in real men."

"Well, I assure you I like a real man—if and when I run across one."

"Well put. I guess I asked for that," he said. "What do you do?"

She disliked the sound of the question, as arrogantly put.

"I'm a hundred-dollar-a-night hooker." She smiled acidly and walked away, thinking that he had asked for that, too. She caught sight of him later and followed his movements curiously for a while before dismissing him.

Several days later he telephoned her at work, explaining that it had taken a good deal of ingenuity to track her down.

"I've only got seventy-five dollars but can we spend three-quarters of an evening together anyhow?"

It took Lilly a moment to follow him; then she remembered her flippant remark about being a call girl.

"I've doubled my price." She laughed, embarrassed.

"Then how about a seventy-five-dollar steak?"

"I'm awfully busy."

"I'm awfully patient. At Yale I learned that you may as well go ahead and do the things you're going to end up doing anyhow."

She thought him over. He did not especially appeal to her but his aggressiveness was different, different from the jaded passivity of the older men she met through Vince.

"Are you rich?" she asked, almost hoping to insult him.

"I intend to be."

"I guess your teeth and hair are your own?"

"Yes. But the best part of me was shot off in the Argonne Forest."

"You saw the movie!"

Lilly smiled into the receiver when he said he had, and unconsciously she raised her hand to smooth her hair. "Well, all right. Lady Brett accepts." She expected to feel an immediate regret; she usually did when she acted impetuously.

"I'll pick you up at eight."

"I live on Seventy-third—"

"Between Park and Lex. I know."

"How?"

"Something else I learned at Yale. It's called sociological research."

He hung up.

Lilly dressed elaborately as she usually did for an evening in New York, but it was to an out-of-the-way neighborhood bistro that he took her. They had to wait for a vacant table. Once seated, Harry ordered for both of them, not asking if she preferred a cocktail but telling the waiter to bring two glasses of wine. Lilly had not realized wine was ever served by the single portion.

With Vince and his friends, Lilly had felt anxious to fill the lulls in the conversation with nervous chatter, usually asking the kind of flattering questions that Vince would arm her with before they went out. Well, she needn't be bothered by silences this time; Harry Shawcross never stopped talking the entire evening. Not that she cared to remember too much of what he said but it had only been necessary to listen—maybe a nod or two, a yes or a no now and then, a smile. It was easy just to sit there and be spoken to and not care at all if she was making a good impression. It was strange that she should feel a little tired when he finally took her home.

He asked to see her again; she'd been expecting it and had planned to make some polite but negative reply. She was also expecting him to make some romantic overture and was pleasantly relieved when he did not. It was good not to have to do anything at all, especially not to have to fend him off. Still, she was surprised when she heard herself agreeing to see him for dinner the very next night; this surprise was something she never quite got over as she continued to accept his other invitations. Dinner. Lunch. A play. She did not mention Harry to Vince until some weeks later when, as she was about to leave work and was saying good-night to one of the fitters, Vince called to her from his office, saying that he would pick her up that night at eight-thirty.

"For what?" she asked, a frown creasing her forehead.

"Dinner. The Ludlows. Remember?"

"No."

"Thought I'd told you. Never mind, just wear the lavender chiffon from the spring line. I'll fill you in later."

"I've got a date, Vince."

"A date? Who the hell with?"

"A friend. Someone I met a few weeks ago." Lilly was edging toward the door, hoping to leave it at that. Vince came out of his office to where she stood.

"You have a date?" He spoke in an accusing manner.

Lilly felt her temper stir as she nodded.

"Who is he? What does he do?"

"His name is Harry Shawcross. He works in films."

"What's he after?"

"My charming company, I guess." Her voice sounded more sarcastic than she realized.

"My ass," Vince replied. "He's after what he probably thinks is your fortune. Just exactly what does he do in films? How old is he, anyhow? Shawcross? I don't know any Shawcrosses." For a strange moment Lilly felt very young, almost like a girl again, backed into a corner and Clara was about to find out something she had been hoping to hide. Lilly very quickly turned around and hurried out the door and into the elevator. The next day she avoided Vince and went to lunch without him, keeping distance between them for over a week when, as she was sitting in the building's ground-floor coffee shop, he joined her unexpectedly, saying nothing but handing her a neatly typed sheet of paper:

Harold Alvin Shawcross. Born in Hollywood, California, 1931. White. Jewish. Circumcised. Father was H.A. (Buddy) Shawcross, Hollywood director. Created low-budget series of murder mysteries. Married to sometime actress Nadine Silverman. Professional name: Nora Sanders. Some scandal involving studio executive prior to marriage. Father committed suicide in 1940. Shot in mouth. Mother remarried in 1943 to Calvin Kling, only son of Massachusetts textile family. Killed in Pacific in 1944. Mother married Hollywood screenwriter Grant Peters in 1952. Divorced that same year. Goes by name of Nora Shawcross. Currently living in Holmby Hills, California. Subject of report twenty-five years old. Never married. Attended small private school in Santa Monica. No military service. Studied Political Science and Communication Technology at Yale University. Graduated in 1952. Summer apprenticeship to Edward R. Murrow at CBS in 1953. Employed by Sach Brothers Productions, makers of documentary films for television. Currently residing at 128 East 91st Street, New York. Voter registration unknown. Religion: None. No outstanding debts. Annual earning placed at $18,000. No record of arrests or sexual deviance. Subject is 5'10", brown hair, medium build, wears glasses and is left-handed. No other distinguishing physical scars or characteristics. Considered Group Three credit risk.

She tore the paper to sheds. "You bastard. I hope this cost you plenty!"

"It did. I also know you've been seeing him behind my back several nights a week this last month. I also know you haven't slept with him."

For some reason this bit of intelligence angered Lilly the most. Her cheeks burned pink.

"Lilly, for God's sake, you can do better than some dumb kid in a Yale beanie who doesn't have enough ambition to get laid."

She forced herself to speak quietly, looking down into her coffee cup. "Harry thinks it's better to wait." There was defiance in her voice.

"Wait for what?"

She looked straight at Vince now, daring him. "He wants to marry me."

"You bet your sweet, stupid ass, he does." The accent was all Indiana. "You think he hasn't read all that heiress crap

Uncle Vince has been pitchforking out to the gossip columns?"

"I say he loves me."

"He loves what he *thinks* you are. I'll tell you what he loves, the Lilly Bellingrath I created. From your underwear to your lipstick, Sport, you are *mine*. He sees only what I've given him to see."

"Then you've oversold your product, and you better find yourself another toy. No more Henry Higgins with Lilly, Vincent Lazlo. The rain in Spain is over."

As surprised as he by the outburst, she broke into tears. She cried so easily these days.

"Oh, Vince, just meet him. Give him a chance. Don't do this to me. I'd never be any good with all those fat, old men who hire wives. I'm almost twenty-three years old and it's time for me to be serious. Harry loves me and he'll take care of me."

Vince insisted on a restaurant, calling a public place "neutral territory." It was small and quiet and obviously expensive. Lilly was nervously laughing to fill the awkwardness between the introductions. The battle between the two men began immediately.

"A negroni?" Vince appeared to be speaking only to Lilly. She nodded.

"And yours, Mr. Shawcross?"

"The same," Harry countered. "But with vodka, if you please."

Point for Harry, Lilly thought. Vince did not like the smell of gin; he said it was the drink of vulgar people.

"I suggest the vitello tonnato." Vince signaled the waiter. "Have you a wine preference, Mr. Shawcross?" Vince seemed determined not to use Harry's given name.

"House wines don't travel well. I'd prefer a bottle of soave, wouldn't you?"

Harry looked to Lilly and she moved her head to agree.

The game continued, marked and scored as in a tennis match. Fashion, movies, grand hotels, barbers, politics. Point here. Point there. Vince considered politics a pedestrian subject and it seemed to Lilly that he was becoming a little sullen.

She spoke up quickly. "Harry, tell Vince about your new project."

"He wouldn't be interested."

"Yes, he would. Wouldn't you, Vince?" Lilly pleaded, turning from one man to the other.

"What is your project, Mr. Shawcross?"

Harry needed little encouragement. He began to outline at length his plans for some new form of commercial advertising that could be disguised as mini-documentaries. He talked extensively of major oil firms, of their needs, their products, the advantages and liabilities of public opinion, saying that he had been in conference with several of their presidents and they had been very receptive to certain of his suggestions. Several times Harry mentioned how very quick company executives were to see the merit in all his ideas.

"I'm sure they are." Vince answered as if to terminate the discussion.

Harry seemed oblivious to Vince's lack of interest. "It's something I've been positive about for some time now." he went on. "And I think I have a real contribution to make. I see it this way . . ."

The waiter interrupted to serve the first course, and when he left the table, neither Vince nor Lilly encouraged Harry to continue. Harry lapsed into a rather petulant silence.

"Harry," Lilly offered cheerfully, "you really should come to Vince's next collection. He is a genius. I'm convinced he'll win the Coty this year."

"The what?" Harry asked, a certain archness to the question.

"The Coty Award. For fashion."

"They give out prizes for stuff like that?" Harry said.

"Stuff like what?" Vince charged.

Harry lifted both hands in a gesture of disparagement. "Fashion," he said.

"Yes. They do. Do they give something to people who do commercials?" Vince hated television.

"I hardly find the two things analogous," Harry snapped, "and I don't actually do commercials. I'm in documentary filming."

It made Lilly uncomfortable for men to be so petty; they were carping at each other the way jealous women do, she thought. Why couldn't they be friendly and talk and enjoy each other? She tried several more times to find some common ground, but both men set aside each topic with only a few clipped words. Lilly was more than a little relieved when the meal was finished and she saw Vince motion for the check.

"Signor Shawcross has made the bill when he came in," the proprietor said.

Vince glared and stood up abruptly; he nodded toward Harry, showing his teeth in what was meant to pass for a smile. "That was very kind of you, Mr. Shawcross. But unnecessary."

"Any friend of Lilly's is my guest."

Vince walked around to the back of Lilly's chair and began to help her into her jacket. Harry put out his arm and pulled the coat from around her. For an instant it seemed as if they would tear the garment in two.

"Lilly and I are not ready to go yet, if you don't mind," Harry said.

"I always drop Lilly off on my way home," Vince answered.

She had come with Vince straight from work but she shook her head in confusion, glancing from one to the other. Neither man was looking at her. It was as if she were not there. Vince pulled at her arm to help her up.

"I said I'd see to Lilly, thank you." Harry's words were hissed. The two men stared angrily at each other for a long moment until Harry extended his hand to Vince and said good-night. Vince gave only the curtest kind of bow and walked out the door.

She continued to see Harry at night and to work with Vince during the day, but the strain of not talking about the one to the other was taking its toll; she was tired much of the time. Sometimes Lilly felt herself a pawn, torn between their demands of her and some ill-defined desires of her own. With Vince it was different; he never spoke of Harry. It was as if he did not exist. Harry, on the other hand, never missed an opportunity to make a caustic reference to Vince.

"Where is Daddy Longlegs tonight?" he might ask. "Buggering the boys in the back room?" Harry made Vince's homosexuality a special target, despite the fact that he could see this infuriated her. He kept at it as if to berate Vince made Harry somehow more manly and desirable.

"Vince isn't like that and I don't want you to talk about him that way."

Harry knew enough to let the subject drop—for the time being. "Then I'll move on down the agenda. Why don't we get married? In, say, about an hour?"

"Can't eat that fast," she responded. She was not yet ready to say yes or no to Harry's proposals. "Tell me what you're working on," she asked, easing to a new topic.

"You," he said.

Lilly laughed; she was not at all unhappy with his persistence.

At other times it might be she who would circuitously bring up the subject of marriage.

"When you were a boy, did you ever think about having children?"

"No. But I thought a little about what you do to get them." He grinned.

"Be serious. Surely you had some ideas of what you wanted when you grew up."

"The usual. A nice girl, nice house. Mostly I always wanted to go to an office. I've managed that part," he said. "I'm pursuing the rest right now, in case you haven't noticed."

Lilly was pleased; she had never felt so desirable.

"What about you?" he asked. "I guess you played house when you were a little girl?"

"As a matter of fact, I didn't," she said. "I sort of assumed I'd get married someday, but I don't remember preparing myself to keep house or anything." The admission came as a surprise even to her. "I was always with my mother," she explained. "We played lady a lot but we never played housewives."

Lilly paused to collect her thoughts before continuing but Harry had begun to speak.

"I wanted to be like my father until I was nine and he died. He killed himself, you know. Nothing to copy in that."

He drank from his glass, his face becoming dark and brooding.

"The son of a bitch. He didn't even have the courtesy to blow his brains out in a hotel. Right in the bathroom. Nora—my mother—sent me to look for him. I found him, all right."

Lilly hurt for him and put out her hand to cover his; Harry did not brush the sympathy aside. It was nice that he needed comforting.

"My father—" she started, but Harry was talking again.

"So for the next ten years, I hated him," he said. "When I came East to school, I told people my father died of influenza. Some imagination, huh?"

Lilly wanted to tell Harry about Clara, thinking that if she told him about her mother's death it would make him feel easier about his father.

"My mother was kind of—"

"God, don't bring up mothers. I think I spent those ten years planning how to get away from mine. She never had any time for me, except to nag and criticize. The woman I marry will be different, I can tell you that. Nora thought of one person all her life, herself, and she hasn't changed. I used to call her to talk over everything I was doing but I always seemed to catch her when she was having company or getting a divorce. She came to town once when I was working with Murrow. I told her what a terrific job it was and how well I was doing. Know the one question she asked?"

Lilly shook her head.

"She wanted to know if Murrow was married. No other interest."

Lilly reached to touch him; again he did not pull away. He really needed her understanding. Never had she felt such tenderness, such protectiveness toward another person. She hoped her feelings showed in her eyes.

"Look at me, Harry Shawcross. People can be better than what they came from. You'll never be like your father. I can tell. You are special and talented and if your mother doesn't see that, I do."

She went on talking with unaccustomed fierceness, making him believe her, believing it herself. "When I have children, I intend to care about everything they do," she said. "And even if I don't know you that well, I know you'll be the same way. You'll be the most wonderful father in the world."

"You'd have been a perfect mother for me."

Lilly looked at him and smiled at what she thought was a joke.

But it was a solemn statement. Harry was not one to joke about the things he thought important; he seldom spoke humorously, not of himself. This seriousness was one of the things she liked best. When something really mattered to her, she tried to be funny about it—to hide how she felt. She thought it her most frivolous trait.

Later, when he had taken her home and she was alone, Lilly would let her mind go back over the evening's conversation and she would tell herself that Harry Shawcross was certainly a solid no-nonsense young man of integrity and determination. She told herself that it did not matter that they spoke only of him; if they were to marry, there would be plenty of time for talking about herself.

More and more she thought of marriage to Harry in terms of *when* rather than *if*. In the early mornings, alone, curled into a warm embrace with her pillow, Lilly would lie very still and encourage good thoughts of Harry, thoughts of how he was the kind of person who would make sense out of his life and perhaps of hers, too. It was when she was by herself like this that she liked Harry best, and she might stay in bed for a very long while and press onto her vision of him all the better bits and pieces she had collected from the night before.

At those times when he sank into his dark moods, she insisted to herself that they were no more than moments of sensitive introspection. If he became unreasonably irritated by a waiter or a taxi driver and seemed to lose control, Lilly argued that it was because he was so intelligent that any inefficiency affronted him. She found it especially romantic that he did not insist on making love to her—So gentlemanly, she thought, so respectful and considerate, the way love ought to be. Pure. Everything in its own time and place. Sometimes, if she concentrated hard enough, her heart could turn at the sound of his name, and sometimes, when she wasn't tired, the touch of his hand might almost be too pleasant to bear. Lilly was convinced that she was very happy, that surely this was love.

Which, of course, did not explain why she did not just go ahead and marry Harry. He was very impatient with her ambivalence and was insistent that they should drive to Maryland that very Saturday, be married that afternoon by a justice of the peace and return to New York on Sunday. He would, he said, move his things into her apartment on the following Monday.

"Your fairy godfather will never let go, Lilly. You've been trying to bring him around for weeks, haven't you?"

She looked down, not wanting to meet his gaze.

"And he insists you can do better, doesn't he? He thinks I'm not good enough." Harry's face became ominously red.

Lilly still did not speak.

"Answer me, goddammit."

His sharp tone jolted her but she was rather excited by the command in his voice and nodded to him.

"It's now or never," he said. "I'll rent a car. If you're not ready to go Saturday afternoon, he wins and I lose."

Lilly felt the sudden panic of indecision grip her. "Vince is the only family I have, Harry. Try to understand."

"I have tried. If we get married, I'll be all the family you need. It's up to you. You can have me. Or you can hang around a bunch of café socialites until you turn into one. They're takers. Inheritors." He spat the word at her. "Is that what you want?"

For some unexplainable reason she started to cry. "I don't know what I want."

"Then come with me, Lilly." He was gentle now. "I need

you. There are so many things I want to do and I want you with me."

They were standing in the hall of her apartment, near the door.

Harry stroked her head as she held it against his shoulder. "Come on," he whispered soothingly, "it's time to play house."

"We don't know each other very well," she said haltingly.

"Look at all the time we'll have to get acquainted once we're married."

He was smiling, sensing her confusion and taking advantage of it. He lifted her away from him, holding her at arm's length. "I'm asking you to be my wife. Is that something to cry about?" He was suddenly very gay; his moods shifted so easily.

Lilly moved closer to him once again; she was comfortable when she was held, so safe and certain.

"I know. I know," she said. "Let me just talk to Vince once more. We'll see about Saturday."

She gently eased away from him only to rush back for him to hold her once more.

"Tonight, Harry—" She was crying now. "Let's go right this minute. I can get a few things and—"

"I've got an important meeting tomorrow. Saturday. We'll wait until Saturday."

Lilly smiled, wiping at her eyes with her sleeve. "Not very romantic of you."

"We've got forever to be romantic."

"Yes," she said. "Yes. I'd like that more than anything."

She did not go to work that next day but lounged moodily about the apartment in an old chenille robe, feeling as if she had an important errand to run but could not think of what it was. Her mind was a mess, cluttered with vagueness and indecision. Around two she telephoned Vince.

"Can we have dinner tonight?"

"The Yalie have a fraternity meeting?"

"I need to talk to you, Vince."

"I'm meeting some people at Elmers. Can we meet there?"

"El Morocco's so noisy. And the food is dreadful."

"I thought you wanted to talk, not eat. Can't be too serious if you're thinking of food."

"O.K. I'll see you there. What time?"

"Nine."

She needed to recall their old closeness. "Aren't you going to tell me what to wear?" she asked playfully.

"I thought you were doing your own thinking these days."

"I wish I were better at it," she said and laughed.

"I do, too, Sport. I really do."


It was only a little after nine when her cab pulled in front of the night club. As if for battle, Lilly drew her coat close around her and went quickly up the few steps to the entrance; the doorman greeted her familiarly. She declined to check her wrap, and asked instead to be taken to Mr. Lazlo, following the captain into the large black and white room to a prominent table on the right, conspicuous but pleasantly distant from the dance floor. The best.

Vince rose to greet her, kissed her casually and began to introduce the others; one was a movie producer—an old acquaintance of Vince's who he had once told her made "those dreadful spear and sandal films where the lions eat all the Christians." Lilly had never met him before and half-heartedly studied him as Vince helped her out of her coat.

Aged and weathered, the man sat Buddha-like next to a twenty-year-old girl in a sequin dress who was holding his hand and rubbing the back of his neck. Next to her there was an Argentinian Lilly had encountered before; his rumored homosexuality did not compromise his desirability as an escort. Tonight he was with a wealthy, older woman whom Lilly recognized from seeing her picture in the newspapers; her mouth was already slack from too much wine. Beside her was another man of about thirty, a stranger; he completed the group. Lilly nodded to them all and asked Vince to order her a Scotch.

"We were just talking about Greece," Vince said. "We have an open invitation from Mr. Rickles here, Lilly, to go around the islands on his boat anytime we like." Vince bowed his head toward the movie producer.

"How nice," she said politely. "I hear they're beautiful."

The man grunted in agreement but said nothing. The girl beside him was now stroking his thigh and dipping her finger into her glass for him to lick it; there seemed to be no light behind the girl's eyes and Lilly shuddered, realizing that the girl was only a little younger than she. She wondered how long before the light would go out of her own eyes? She shivered again and Vince lifted her coat around her shoulders, thinking she was cold.

"Stuart here"—Vince was gesturing to the strange young man—"is very interested in fashion."

The man smiled anxiously, quick to pick up where Vince left off, but it was difficult to follow him; his speech impediment was very pronounced. Lilly had to lean closer to understand him and was grateful to be distracted by the waiter who brought her drink. She seized the interruption to whisper to Vince. "Can we dance?"

"Terpsichore calls," he announced gaily to the table, holding back her chair. They inched out onto the crowded dance floor.

"I'm sorry to come at you this way," she began.

"I'm sorry I couldn't shake free. Stuart, the one with the lisp? Well, he's thinking of incorporating me. Expanding into furs, luggage, bed linens. Maybe a men's line." It was what Vince had wanted since she had known him.

"That's wonderful. You didn't tell me."

"Well, we haven't talked much these last weeks."

"That's part of what I want to see you about."

The band changed beat; the music was Latin. They both despised it.

"We can stick this out or go back," he offered.

"Let's fake it. I can't talk in front of those people."

"All right. One, two, cha, cha, cha. What's up, cha, cha, cha."

"I'm thinking of marrying Harry on Saturday."

"And?" Vince seemed indifferent.

"And I don't know."

"You here for a blessing?"

"I don't know that either."

"You've got as much business marrying that martinet as I do dancing to this spic music." He stumbled as if for emphasis.

"Harry's not a martinet and don't say 'spic.' "

"I thought you came for advice, not to give it."

The rhythm changed to a tango but they continued to cha cha.

"This damn music is what killed Valentino," he said.

"Vince. Listen. I think maybe I ought to marry Harry and I want you to talk to me about it."

"What's to say?"

"Something keeps telling me that maybe I ought not."

"That *something* and I have a lot in common."

"You see"—she bumped into a couple of dancers and mumbled an apology—"I'm wondering if my hesitation is because of you or what?"

"The 'what' being your good common sense?"

"Why do you say that, Vince? You don't really hate Harry. What is it?"

"First off, I don't want to let you go. Purely selfish. It won't be the same without you. Mostly, Sport, I don't think he can make you happy. He's a humorless kid who's out for himself. Do things his way and you'll be welcome along." The music changed again and they adjusted to it. "I just happen to think you need more. When you're older—and you're getting there, kid, you know—you'll want something besides a demanding and insecure little man who is neither tall enough nor generous enough to measure up. Imagine ten years and two kids. It'll be too late then. Whatever it is you see in this guy now—if you see anything, that is—will be lost in the shuffle. You'll be trapped. Trapped and wasted. And too old to do anything about it."

Lilly was enraged. "So I should marry some blithering old fool who can afford to paw me over?"

"I never said my way would be bliss. But your emotions will be intact." He looked at her hard. "You could still have the kiddies and the marriage license, but when you find out that none of it lasts, that not one bit of it is worth a rat's ass, you can take the money and run. In style. You won't have been really involved."

"But I want to be involved! Don't you understand that?" She was shouting to be heard over the loud music and the band stopped abruptly, allowing her voice to carry. Lilly looked about, embarrassed; she lowered her voice and continued. "I want to be a part of something. Not a toy."

"You want to be involved, Lilly, O.K. But involved in something that has to do with you. Not this kid. You don't see it, but better things are coming. You can do or be anything you want; only, you refuse to take a chance on yourself."

The music was softer now; they began a slower dance.

"And what is that supposed to mean?" she asked.

"Anything you want it to mean. That's the whole point."

Lilly felt dizzy and nauseated, her confusion worse than before. She looked up, dismayed to see the sleek Argentine standing next to them, tapping at Vince's shoulder, grinning stupidly at Lilly; the fool wanted to dance with her.

"My turn," he chirped.

Lilly stared at him blankly, and then let go of Vince and walked quickly off the dance floor. At the table her chair was occupied now by the older woman; she was considerably drunker than before; her head was rolling slowly from side to side. Lilly sat down in a different seat, next to Mr. Rickles, and reached across the table to retrieve her drink. The young man, Stuart, was talking animatedly but Lilly did not even try to pick up the pieces of his conversation. Distracted, she nervously twisted at a book of matches.

When she realized a hand was on her knee, it did not particularly surprise her; that sort of thing often happened to her in night clubs. Calmly she turned to the puffy, yellowish man beside her and tried to sound reasonable, humorous.

"Mr. Rickles, I'm much too old for you." She patted his pudgy hand and returned it to his own lap.

The room seemed to close in around her, noisy and crowded with elaborately dressed women, all escorted by the kind of men who seemed always to be staring at the younger girls who moved in and around the packed dance floor. Observing the girls, Lilly shivered again; how often had she overheard them in the powder room, even been sorry for them. For an instant she felt envious; at least these prowling girls seemed to know what they were after.

Sounds and smells were about to suffocate her. Lilly looked quickly at the vacant-faced girl still dutifully caressing Mr. Rickles; over her shoulder she saw Vince making his way back to the table, happily chatting as he advanced, and she was gripped by a terrible urge to get out of the room, away from these people, from Vince and his kind of life.

She grabbed her purse and ran up the curving stairs to the ladies' room, where an attendant in a black uniform and a white apron handed her a fresh towel. Lilly wet a corner of it, dabbing at her forehead, wondering if this was how people felt before they fainted. She fanned herself with the towel. The mirror over the basin reflected her frightened eyes, stranger's eyes. Quickly Lilly put a dollar bill onto the attendant's plate for tips, and took out a single dime for the pay phone.

Harry answered rather irritably.

"It's me, Lilly." She was trying hard not to cry.

"Is everything set for tomorrow?" he asked.

"I'll be ready." She started to cry anyhow, but quietly. "Harry?" she said. "It's going to be all right, isn't it? I mean, you really do love me, don't you?"

"How many times have I said so?"

"Yes. I know. I know. I'm sorry. Just jittery. I love you, too, Harry."

"You can show me by being on time tomorrow. O.K.?"

Lilly avoided the stairs and went back down to the main level by the small elevator and walked straight out the front door, standing with her arms folded about her for warmth as the doorman hailed a cab. She had left her coat at the table. Well, never mind. It wasn't really hers. Like everything else she was leaving behind, it belonged to Vince. Part of the Lazlo Collection.

# 8

ALL brides are nervous. Harry had said that each time she shifted and fidgeted on the drive down to Maryland.

"Don't men get scared?"

"Some do."

"But not you?"

He patted her knee. "I know what I want." He withdrew his hand and concentrated on driving.

Lilly lay down on the seat, her head propped precariously against Harry's right thigh; she could feel his muscles tense as he applied pressure to the accelerator. He drove very well, she thought; it was the first time she had been in an automobile with him at the wheel. It was a day of many firsts.

Lilly smiled and closed her eyes; she ought to sleep if she could, but strange and uninvited visions invaded her: she saw herself in a wedding dress—perhaps it was Clara's, she supposed her mother had one; they never spoke of such things—but she imagined herself in it, nonetheless, coming down the wide front stairs of the old house at home. The image brought an unexpected surge of longing. Longing for what? She shifted positions again and sternly reminded herself that giggling, leaping girls throwing rice and straining to catch the bride's bouquet was commercial nonsense, the epitome of corniness. Still, it might have been nice, something pleasant to remember when she and Harry were old. She should not think of them as old. She should think instead of the night ahead.

They really knew so little of each other, she and Harry. Sometimes, when she was with him, she could feel a bit inadequate and she wondered if she would feel that way tonight.

For two months now, they had done little more than exchange affectionate embraces, some kisses, of course, but not much else. She guessed it was right that they not grapple with each other like adolescents—that was how Harry had put it—but it was peculiar that it had been so easy for them to wait. Just what was it they were waiting for? Lilly closed her eyes again; her mind inventoried the few things she had in her overnight case. There wasn't even a new nightgown. Vince had been the one to see to her wardrobe, but what she had worn to bed had been of no interest to him and very little to her. Well, probably too much importance was placed on the glamour of the wedding night, anyhow. Idly she began to stroke Harry's leg, feeling his muscles grow tense.

"Better sit up," he warned. "The traffic may get heavy and I might have to stop suddenly."

Lilly sat up and moved close to him, adjusting the rear-view mirror so that she could straighten her hair; she was startled by her pallor and did not object when Harry reached over and returned the mirror to its normal position. At its regular angle she could see his reflection; quietly she studied his precise, handsome face and a surge of pleasure rose within. Well, it's not exactly erotic longing, she thought, but that would come later. She smiled to herself when she remembered the old nightgown.

"Where are we spending the night?" she asked.

"No place special. We'll find something."

With her head against the seat, she indulged herself with thoughts of quaint country inns and fourposter beds, maybe a fire and a cold chicken. Cold chicken was somehow romantic. She felt quite cozy at the prospect of Harry and a cold chicken —delighted, in fact—but still it worried her that Harry might find her inadequate. He'd known so many women. At least, she assumed he had. Sex was certainly not Harry's favorite subject for discussion and whenever she asked questions about girls he'd been with, he could become very evasive, wonderfully private. Well, such conversations were best put off till later; she'd manage the night ahead somehow.

But the growing insecurity was making her irritable and she mentally argued with herself that it was the man's job to know about sex; the woman was only supposed to be chaste. Lilly frowned at the thought of the boy from home—Hose Nose— and that night so many years ago; the boy's name was about the only thing she could still remember. No, that night simply did not count. After all, it was only fifteen minutes—was it even that long?—yes, a quarter of an hour of youthful nonsense. It would be foolish to bother Harry with that ancient history. Not that he had exactly said so, of course, but Harry would expect her to have kept up her end of the deal, to be a virgin. She wondered if he'd be able to tell she wasn't. Nonsense. Men couldn't tell and it was really very silly of her to be thinking this way, borrowing trouble.

Slumped low on her side of the car, Lilly encouraged her thoughts into more pleasurable channels. She was doing the right thing, she told herself. Boy meets girl, they embrace, he sweeps her away, the music swells meaningfully. The End. The Happy End. It would be just fine, damn it, just fine. She fell asleep only a short while before they reached their destination.

"Wake up, Lilly!"

Harry shook her; for a moment she was unsure where she was.

"Take your pick," he said. "The chapel of your dreams."

Lilly was a little repelled by what she saw. The signs in front of the one-story, almost identical little bungalows were much alike: DERWOOD JONES, J.P.; HAPPINESS HOUSE; VOWS EXCHANGED, NOON TO MIDNIGHT. It seemed a midway. For the dumbest moment, she wanted Harry to turn the car around and take her back. Back to what?

Their knock at the door was answered by a small thin woman in a housedress. She spoke through the screen. "You got an appointment?"

"We were told it wasn't necessary."

Lilly could hear the edge to Harry's voice and her stomach knotted involuntarily.

"Well, the hubby's out back, but I'll call him. You come on in."

They were ushered into a musty parlor and neither she nor Harry said anything more until the angular man approached, smiling obsequiously; he did not halt his banter as he pulled on a dark-blue suit coat that did not match his trousers, and knotted his tie.

"Nice day for a weddin'," he said. "Happy is the bride the sun shines on, you know? We have a ring, of course? Our neighbor sometimes plays the Hammond, but only when you give notice. The wife here and her sister will witness. Ella! Sarah, go get Ella. No corsage? Have a few in the icebox on

97

the back porch. Have to charge for 'em, though, you know? Now, just stand right here. Wait a sec till I pull this shade. More like a church, huh? Now, we'll just take your names for the book. Might as well pay, too, and get it out of the way. This is my wife, Sarah. You met, didn't you? And Miss Ella? Girls, meet what is about to be the Shawcrosses. Heh. Heh. Marry in haste and live a long and happy life, you know? Heh. Heh. Right here. No, a little closer. Join hands, please. Ella, better you take the phone off the hook. Dearly Beloved—that's not really part of the ceremony, you know, but I kind of like to say it if you don't mind—Dearly Beloved . . ."

Back in the car, Lilly voiced her doubts about the abruptness of the ceremony.

"It's binding," Harry assured her. "No matter how long it takes."

Lilly groaned. "It's a regular cottage industry here," she said. "Wonder they don't take American Express."

"This is not the time for making jokes, Mrs. Shawcross."

"Then feed me. Where do we hold the marriage feast?"

"Anywhere your heart desires."

Lilly had hoped he had made a plan.

"There doesn't seem to be much around here," she said, "maybe we could drive to Baltimore."

"It's a lot out of the way. There's bound to be something closer, I'll stop and ask."

He turned into a service station and Lilly got out and walked to a rear door marked LADIES. It was locked and she went to get a key.

The rest room was filthy; she wondered why in the world anyone would bother to lock it. Probably to isolate the germs, she thought, and then resignedly she spread some facial tissue from her purse over the toilet seat and playfully began to draft a wedding announcement: "The bride was ravishing in her double-breasted yellow checked Lazlo suit. First stop on the Shawcrosses' honeymoon agenda was Herzog's gas station . . ."

Harry was already back in the car when she came out. She called to him through the window. "Any luck?"

"He says there's a Howard Johnson's about eight miles off the main road."

Lilly's face crumbled.

"And"—he held up his hand to stop her from speaking—"a pretty good seafood place less than twelve miles back. What'll it be?"

"Need you ask?"

She got in and sat very close to him; when they were out on the highway, he put an arm around her shoulders.

"Any regrets?"

"Aside from the local toilet facilities? None. Oh, Harry! Let's have a lot of wine and talk and talk and talk."

"Plumbing isn't all that's in short supply around here. It's a dry county."

"Shades of the old hometown." She was trying to conceal her disappointment. No white veil was one thing, but no champagne was another. She had so wanted the day to be gay, memorable.

"How do we christen the ship?"

"Among my meager possessions," Harry said slowly to tease her, "there is a bottle of Scotch. I thought it might come in handy."

"Something for your nerves of steel?"

"Actually I was worried about snakebite."

This was how she liked him best and she hugged him so that he would know. It would not matter about the restaurant. Nothing would matter anymore.

They stayed in the back booth until well after dark, the Scotch bottle in a canvas satchel on the floor beneath the table.

"More strong drink?" Harry offered, and then added to her glass, putting in some extra ice cubes.

"And fast music," she said, taking three more of the quarters stacked on top of the paper-napkin dispenser. She went over to the jukebox and took her time making the selections.

Harry toasted her as she sat back down. "To the little woman."

"All sixty-eight inches of her," she said. They clinked glasses.

"You don't mind my being so tall, do you, Harry?"

"Only for as long as we avoid hand-to-hand combat."

"I'll never beat you."

"Love, honor and obey?"

"So that's what all that fast talk was back there."

"Translated, it means you're stuck with me forever," he said.

"Who's complaining?"

"Not I, said the spouse."

"Any more bad jokes and I'll change my mind about the fisticuffs." Lilly laughed all the same; it really was going to be just fine.

"We must never quarrel, Lilly," Harry said and reached for her hand. "My mother did enough of that to last me. I want you on my side every inch of the way."

Lilly wished his moods would not shift so unexpectedly.

"I plan to dog your every step." She smiled to lighten his seriousness; it seemed to have come from nowhere.

"I'm going to be the best damned producer of documentaries this country has ever seen, I promise you that much."

"Of course you will." She laughed and saluted him.

He withdrew his hand from hers. "Don't laugh. I mean it."

"I'm not laughing. I'm just agreeing with you, that's all."

But there was no softening of his features.

"Harry, you're serious, aren't you?"

He nodded mutely.

"Listen, I do believe in you. You'll be the best thing going. I know it."

He relaxed, visibly.

"But not till Monday," she said, flirtatiously checking her watch. "That gives you approximately thirty-six hours to devote yourself solely to me."


The motel's neon sign flashed through the bedroom window and made everything look green. Lilly nervously twisted the gold ring on her finger and went to draw the wide striped curtains that matched the spreads on the twin beds; it was like a room in a college dormitory except that there was none of the personalized clutter. With her nightgown over her arm and a few essential cosmetics in her lap, she sat down on a straight chair, waiting, smoking a last cigarette and wishing for another drink. The average fidgety bride, she thought, one with only an old nightgown and no bedroom slippers. The mental picture made her giggle, and suddenly everything about the entire day seemed very funny and she began to laugh out loud, laughing so hard that she slid down on the plastic chair cushion, holding her stomach, her legs sprawled before her. She was still slumped there laughing when Harry came out of the bathroom wearing a new pair of boldly printed pajamas.

"What's so funny?"

"Me. You. All of this." She looked at him, waiting for him to laugh, too.

"Haven't you ever seen a man in a pair of pajamas?"

"As a matter of fact, no."

It was really terribly funny now and Lilly was bending double in uncontrollable roars.

"Lilly, there are certain things you don't make fun of." He was jerking back the bedcovers.

"I'm not making fun of you, Harry." She rushed to sit on the side of his bed to reassure him, but he turned his head away. "Look at me, Harry. I swear to God. I'm not laughing at you. I was only thinking how silly I feel about this old nightgown." She held it up. "I'm just laughing at me, Harry, honest."

He turned to look at the gown and she put her hand to his face.

"I'll only be a minute," she said, and ran into the bathroom, sorry that there was no time for a bath. She splashed some water over her face instead, pinching at her cheeks for color and wondering if she ought to put on some lipstick. No. It would be better to sneak back in the morning to fix herself up. Quickly she turned out the light and came back into the now-darkened bedroom and stumbled over Harry's shoes. Such an entrance! Immediately her laughter started up again.

"What now?" Harry asked.

"I'm such a clod. I was wondering if I should brazenly jump into bed with you or get into my own bed and let you come to me."

She sat down beside him, still laughing. When he did not respond, she got under the blanket with him, aware for the first time of how very tall she was; they were equal in length and she wanted to somehow make it up to him.

"I love you, Harry."

"I love you, too."

She began to giggle again in spite of herself.

"What are you thinking about?" he asked.

"About how I'm not Lilly Bellingrath anymore. I'm Mrs. Shawcross."

"As it should be," he said and pulled her nearer.

Lilly held her face up to be kissed. She liked to be kissed, and it was pleasant to be lying so close, to feel so secure, to touch and be touched. She started to whisper to Harry how she felt but he said that she ought not to talk—

"Not now, Lilly. Not now."

There were so many things to tell him, to share with him, but she said nothing; she did not want to take the chance of hurting his feelings again.

# 9

SHE rather liked being married. It seemed that she had so much to do: Harry had to be awakened every morning, his breakfast made, his pajamas put away, things like that. On nice days she walked him to the corner; at other times she waved him out of sight from the front window. Usually she had a second cup of coffee and read the newspaper. Sometimes she went out to have her lunch, or maybe to shop or to pick up something for dinner at the grocer's or at one of the delis in the neighborhood. The day the cleaning woman came, Lilly stayed in and made afternoon tea for them both, following the woman from room to room and visiting with her as she did her work. Frequently they watched a couple of the daytime serials on television. The cleaning lady was always promising to teach her to play pinochle but they never got around to it.

At first, she phoned Harry at the office every day around noon, saying it was just to hear his voice.

"Hi! It's me."

"Me who?"

"Me Shawcross. Can we have lunch?"

"Can't leave the office today, hon."

"You breadwinners have all the fun. What are we deductions supposed to do?"

"Be grateful. Listen, Lilly, got to run. See you at seven."

A couple of times during that first year, she had gone to a take-out shop and bought a carton of chicken salad, Harry's favorite, and put it in a small bag with some cheese and some very thin slices of pumpernickel bread and dropped in at his office. The last time had been especially fine. She'd brought some wine and had got quite high off only one paper cup of it and had wanted to stay with him all afternoon, maybe even go to the park and sit in the sun.

"Not today, Lilly. This is very cute of you but I think these little picnics are going to have to stop."

Before she knew it, she was back on the street and had wandered into the first movie house she came to.

On the nights Harry worked late she enjoyed browsing in the department stores that stayed open until nine, buying a lot of things for Harry; everything she saw was in terms of how much or how little it would please him.

Occasionally Harry might ring up in the middle of the afternoon to suggest they meet for dinner and she would spend the rest of the day washing her hair and trying on and discarding different outfits until it was time to leave. As a rule, she arrived at the restaurant before he did and would select the table, a quiet one with just the right lighting; the wine would be open and ready when he got there and Harry would be full of talk about his work.

"Tell me," she would interrupt, feeling playful and romantic, "what attracted you to me in the beginning?"

"Lilly. I was trying to tell you something very important."

His face would darken and she would quickly say she was sorry and would he please finish his story, but she would be hurt by his attitude, even angry; it was not always easy to hold on to her temper these days. Her temper, in fact, was becoming very troublesome as she got older. At this rate she wondered what in the world she would be like by the time she was twenty-five.

A lot of nights Harry stayed downtown till eleven and would have eaten before he got home. When he saw that she had waited dinner for him, he would apologize, telling her that time had gotten away from him and, anyhow, the switchboard had closed at six.

"I'm sorry, hon. I meant to call. I'm really sorry."

"Sure." Lilly was learning to pout as he did; she liked his efforts to bring her around.

Some nights she was already in bed reading or watching television when he came in. He would be tired and not have much to say and, of course, she would not say anything to him at all. Instead she would stay awake half the night to see an old movie and would punish Harry for his indifference to her by sleeping late the next morning, letting him go off to work without any good-byes. Other mornings he would try to make love to her before she was fully awake and she would push him away. Lilly would feel guilty about her behavior all day long and would be especially nice at night when Harry finally came home. Sometimes she tried to explain her feelings to him, but when she tried to discuss personal things with him they never quite came out the way she intended.

"I'm not a machine, Harry. I want to be awake and to talk to you once in a while before we make love. I mean, we could visit for a minute before we make love."

He had such unpredictable responses. "Is it too much for you to understand that I work my ass off all day and when I'm home I don't have much interest in recounting your innumerable charms? Christ Almighty, Lilly, it's hard to be a hand-kissing Lothario when you work on a nine-to-five schedule."

"Since when are you home at five?" Her disposition was starting to match his.

"That's not the point and you know it. You expect too goddamned much."

"For you, any thought, word or deed that does not have to do with some boring television documentary is beside the point."

"That's the way I was when you married me. You knew what you were getting."

"I thought I was getting a husband."

"Well, I'm tired of your demanding a lot of hearts and flowers."

"And I'm tired of not getting them."

They would turn to their separate sides of the bed and pretend to sleep; the coolness between them might last for several days and she learned to wait for Harry to make up to her. It was easy enough to tell when he was about to thaw, for it was generally preceded by his voicing some insecurity about his work.

"Frank Gattis is a fool." That was how he began. "Gattis thinks my ideas for the housing development film are too avant-garde for the taxpayer."

Lilly would speak on cue. "Since when does Frank Gattis know anything?"

"He's got a couple of the senior partners on his side this time. If they junk this footage, I'm going to quit."

"Maybe that's what he wants. With you out of the way, he could put out any imbecilic thing he wants."

Lilly would watch for Harry's eyes to soften, then she would give him what he wanted to hear. "You're the best there is, Harry. And if they don't know when something is good, then it's their own stupidity."

On nights like that they would probably make love and Lilly would be happy to sink into the cozy warmth of being held, wrapping herself in the security she craved. The delicate balance of the relationship would be even for days, even weeks at a time, and no amount of later examination could pinpoint precisely when this bartering of their needs ceased to work.

The next year of their marriage was uneventful; each day passed much as the one before it, politely, calmly. When he was expansive, Harry would say that behind every successful man there was a good woman like Lilly. But Lilly had a growing sense of being cheated; she could only wonder when Harry was going to get around to making something special of their lives, the way he'd promised. Sometimes she would sit in the living room of the apartment and watch him read through the papers he brought home from the office; she would study him covertly, concentrating very hard so that maybe her thoughts would, by telepathy, be transmitted to him.

*I want you to do something exciting, Harry. Something fun. Something to make me happy.* She would think that over and over. Once he had looked up and asked if there was something bothering her but she had only shaken her head, annoyed that he could not read her mind.

In bed one night she had felt strangely aggressive and had brazenly moved close to him, taking his hand and placing it on her breast, whispering in his ear, telling him the things she wished he would do to her, how he should touch her. Harry was very tired, he said, and had only leaned over and kissed her forehead. "You are a terrible little dreamer, aren't you, hon?"

Then he had gone quickly to sleep and she had lain there in the dark, her face flushed with embarrassment, telling herself that it didn't matter, that, after all, sex was not that special. What was it, really, besides another of her trivial routines, another household duty like the marketing or sending out the laundry? They had not been married quite three years when Lilly persuaded herself that sex was just another boring chore and that she was indeed fortunate that the kitchen linoleum required her attentions more often than her husband did.

She and Harry agreed on very few things. They argued especially bitterly whenever he suggested she reestablish communication with her father.

"At least write and tell him you're married."

"I can't do that."

"He's your father, for God's sake. He's entitled to know. He just might raise your allowance."

She had known he would say that. Harry was not at all embarrassed that they lived mostly on Lilly's income.

"Harry, I get a check every month. That's it. That and my mother's trust fund. No card, no note, just the check. I don't even like taking that."

"You have a ridiculous amount of pride."

"More than I can say for you."

He would slam the door when he left.

The next time she received her monthly check she sat down and wrote a note to her father's accountant explaining that she was married now and that her name was changed. Almost by return mail there was a check for ten thousand dollars with a covering letter from the bookkeeper saying that Mr. Bellingrath hoped that his daughter would be very happy and that she might perhaps find some use for his gift. She kept the correspondence secret for several weeks, and when the subject of money came up again she went calmly to the desk drawer for the letter and check and dropped them wordlessly into Harry's lap.

He policed her use of money very carefully. When she began to grow slack about housekeeping duties, Harry would throw her extravagance up to her, telling her that she was certainly overindulged, staying home and doing nothing all day but lying around a cluttered apartment.

"I do my share," she would counter defensively, but his accusations began to bother her, made her find fault with herself privately, made her guilty that she was alive by accident, surviving by means of inheritance and inertia. It got so that she wasn't liking herself very much and she wasn't really liking Harry any better either.

Quite without knowing it, the two of them arrived at a dull arrangement whereby they continued to live in mutual deception, reassuring the other in the vacant and offhand way of people who need to be reassured themselves. Each of them was impatient for the other to change. In no way were they so matched as in their silent demands that the other should take the initiative.

Harry assumed that when a woman said one thing she meant another, and that if he just kept on arguing she would change her mind in the end and come around. He told Lilly she was confused, a child-woman who needed his badgering to grow up. When she tried to explain herself—something she seemed so often called upon to do—he would brush aside her complaints of unhappiness and restless boredom with references to things like biology, hormonal chemistry, the wrong time of the month. Once she had been exasperated enough to ask why a bad marriage was supposed to be better than no marriage at all? Harry had thrown his napkin at her.

"Do you want to leave? Is that it?"

Lilly was frightened, afraid Harry might be trying to force her to do what he lacked the courage to do himself.

"You'd love that, wouldn't you?" he said. "Yes. Yes, you would. You think you can just take your daddy's money and walk out. Well, you're not going to have the pleasure of hurting my career, and you'd better get that straight. Divorce does not go down on Harry Shawcross's record."

"Oh, Harry!" Lilly was smiling nervously to cover her unease; she'd never seen him so hostile. "It's 1958. Divorce happens these days," she added, only making matters worse.

"Not to me, it doesn't. I grew up with it and I won't have it. I've seen what happens. But not to me."

Lilly was strangely reassured by the outburst and even managed a laugh.

"That's as close to renewing our marriage vows as we've come," she said.

"I'm sick of your sly jokes, too. Sick to death of them. And I'm tired of this damned delicatessen food. If I'd wanted to eat blintzes, I'd have married a Jew. If you can't cook, then buy American food. I never want to see another container of sour cream as long as I live. Do I make myself clear?" He shoved aside his plate and walked out of the apartment.

Lilly remained at the table, picking at her food. She had not seen Harry so angered since that night they were at an office party in some dreary little restaurant. Lilly disliked the people Harry worked with, especially the wives—or those who wanted to be—all of them talking in side whispers of the very mundane things Lilly wished to escape, the men speaking only of their work with narcissistic intensity, constantly haranguing about television trends and consciousness! That night she had interrupted Harry's discussion of "the Semitic pursuit of money over excellence."

"But, Harry, *you're* Jewish."

There had been a long silence in the group and she and Harry had left shortly thereafter. In the taxi going home, Lilly had felt that Harry might strike her.

"For as long as we live together, I never want you to say the word 'Jew.' " He spat it out distastefully, through clenched teeth. "Do I make myself clear?" he said.

He had certainly made himself clear and, ever since, Lilly had avoided the subject, wondering if there might actually be something physically wrong with being Jewish. In fact, she learned to avoid the intimacy of any kind of argument. Instead, she began to hold Harry even more at arm's length in all conversation—keeping him at bay long enough for her to subtly maneuver once again into the role of victor, leaving him to pout and smolder and to collect petty grievances against her until the situation was reversed.

Oh, there were occasional good days, scattered here and there, days when they would cling to each other and say "I love you" when they did not, nights when they had a need of each other and she would tell herself that things weren't so bad between them after all and that maybe she and Harry were actually not so very different from anyone else. If she should happen to pour herself a strong drink or two late in the afternoon, then by the time Harry came home she could even convince herself that they had things in common, things to talk over, a whole lifetime ahead of them.

When Nora, Harry's mother, came to pay her only visit, Lilly had felt especially sorry for Harry, almost protective. Like conspiring children, they had taken refuge in each other in the dark, as if they were in alliance against that dreadful woman. They had made love on those several nights of her visit, and when Nora finally left, Lilly had thought that perhaps the situation between Harry and herself might be improved or, at least, changed in some way for the better. What she had not counted on was being pregnant and she had been shocked to find that she was, shocked and sick and strangely terrified of being alone. She was also angry, with no idea what caused her fury. But it was anger nonetheless, anger and an awesome sense of complete and horrid self-loathing. Never once during that time did Lilly wonder just how far back her fuse for that anger had actually been ignited.

# 10

EVEN now, after all these years, Lilly realized it was difficult to look back at her marriage and be fair. She glanced around her kitchen, waiting for the familiar surroundings to bring some comfort, but she felt none. Surely, she reminded herself, surely there was a time when she loved Harry. The possibility that there was not caused her to shiver violently, made her feel cold all over. It would be unthinkable if she and Harry had never actually cared for each other, such an enormous waste of so much of their lives. Lilly shivered again, at once aware that her discomfort was mental—the kitchen was quite warm. Still, she felt chilled and pulled her cardigan closer. Was being cold another failing of the body? The blood running thin? Lilly went to the thermostat and turned it slightly higher, as if to persuade herself that the furnace, not her body, was to blame. It was annoying to do this; playing games with herself was the last straw, utter nonsense, all of it —especially this business of blaming age for all her problems.

She sat back down at the kitchen table, propping her legs up on an adjacent ladder-back chair, and without meaning to, she let her mind roam back to her last birthday, her fortieth birthday. They had all been gathered around this very table— she, the children, George Sabberstein. Lilly had insisted there be no fuss, but Maggie had baked a cake and Teddy had loaded it with as many candles as it would hold, dozens and dozens of them, many more than the required forty and one to grow on. It had very nearly taken all her breath to blow them out and she had laughed when she finally did, saying gaily to everybody that she was far too old now for so much exertion. Teddy had rushed to reassure her. "You're not old, Mom. You're just at the beginning of old."

She had laughed that night, but the truth of the remark was troublesome today—another joke gone stale. Lilly wondered if humor, like everything else she had relied upon for so long, was to desert her also. She glanced toward the kitchen clock and counted on her fingers, patting them on top of the table; it was only a little more than two hours since Harry had left and taken the children for the weekend. It seemed much longer, a lifetime. Hell, hadn't she been sitting here going back over the courtship and marriage of Lilly Bellingrath, a huge and important chunk of herself revisited, and it had covered no more than one hundred and twenty minutes. She sighed and looked again at the clock, frowning; the bloody thing seemed to be waiting for her to catch up. She poured another glass of Scotch and swallowed a mouthful as if it were medicine, hating the taste but needing the courage it brought, however false. With her free hand she reached up to her breasts, absently caressing each one; she often checked for lumps these days. Was she expecting them? Lilly looked down at her chest and it occurred to her that a lump might be an improvement. She wondered at what exact age women were faced with menopause.

Menopause! The word made her nose wrinkle. Clara once vaguely referred to it as the "change of life," but Lilly had only been eighteen at the time. It was funny she even remembered. When you were eighteen, you thought menopause was only something to do with old women. But when demolition companies tear down buildings, the first thing they do is turn off the pipes. Paint a white cross on the door: THIS PROPERTY CONDEMNED.

Lilly knew better than to be indulging in such morbid thoughts; if she were with Peter in New York, the way she had been on other Saturdays when the children were gone, she would not be feeling this way. She was almost never depressed with Peter, not about age and physical things, anyhow.

No, from that first night a little over a year ago when she met him in the Beverly Hills Hotel, she had felt a renewed sense of youth and excitement. She told him later that he'd come along just in time.

Peter was not somebody she expected to find in California, especially not in Beverly Hills, a place where she thought herself much like Alice Down the Rabbit Hole, so far from home and her sense of herself, a whole continent away from reality. She had felt disoriented when she walked into the Polo Lounge of the Beverly Hills Hotel that night, uncomfortable in that perennially dark room filled with those carefully exercised and massaged men in their silk knit turtleneck shirts, their sunglasses, even at night. Peter had later told her that most of them were shoe salesmen or real estate dealers—they are only pretending, he said, masquerading as movie executives in their navy blazers and ersatz crest rings; they were patent-leathered, gold-trimmed, silver-templed phonies.

That's how it always was for her in Beverly Hills, Lilly thought, everyone wanting something from somebody, having themselves paged by the hotel's liveried midget, pressing folded bills into the waiter's palm so that they could sit at good tables to drink and stare at the other pretenders. Oh, the Polo Lounge was not without a certain charm and, occasionally, a genuine celebrity used the place as convenient meeting ground, the way it had been in the old, vanished days of Hollywood.

Lilly had been over in California with several other film critics to tape the Merv Griffin show prior to the Academy Awards, and had gone into the Polo Lounge to ease her restlessness over a drink before going to her room to order dinner. Peter was at a table with a small group that included an aging director she had once interviewed. The director caught sight of her at the door and came to invite her to join them. Lilly was grateful to accept—Beverly Hills, despite its frenzied show of glamour, was a very lonely place for the outsider.

Another round of drinks was ordered—always there was another round of drinks—and the rest of the group separated into chatting couples, leaving her to Peter. She guessed him to be a little more than fifty; there was a lot of silver in his reddish hair and the combination of colors made him seem blond.

"You live here?" She had had to speak first.

"Intermittently," he said.

Lilly lifted her eyebrows.

"I'm a migratory scriptwriter," he explained. "No one can live here permanently and really write. It doesn't rain enough."

"I knew something out here made me feel funny," Lilly said. "But I thought the weather was supposed to be the best thing about the place." Knocking the West Coast was a favored pastime of Easterners but she liked to think herself above it.

"Genius"—he laughed in a pleasantly self-deprecating manner—"must have wind and rain and snow to survive."

"Like postmen?" she asked.

He nodded.

"What brings you here then?"

"Money. I forgot to mention its contribution to genius."

"Where does yours flourish when your pockets are full?" she said.

"New York. I teach there. At Columbia. You from around here?"

"Washington," she said. "Washington, D.C. It's every bit as Elizabethan a power corridor as this." She waved her hand rather disparagingly about the room.

"I would have thought it worse. Think they'll nail Nixon?"

"I sure God hope so," she said casually, not wanting to get into a discussion of Watergate. "How long are you here for?"

"Until nine-thirty in the morning."

"United's flight six forty-four?"

He nodded again in response.

"I'll look for you." She patted her purse to indicate a similar ticket of her own.

"What takes you to New York?" He seemed to inquire more from politeness than interest.

"A literary agent."

He looked mildly curious and waited for her to go on.

"Some publisher thinks there's a book in the changing role of women throughout the history of film."

"Do you?"

"I suppose. I'll know tomorrow," she said.

"It's a plausible idea. Some of my students would certainly agree. They think women have been badly handled by the camera and by literature." But he did not appear overly concerned; he did not appear overly anything except private. Very private indeed.

Lilly was ready to continue on the topic but Peter was finishing his cigarette, stubbing it out in the ashtray. He put his lighter into the breast pocket of his jacket, patting it.

"Are you first-class tomorrow?" he asked.

"Yes," she said. "All my life, I've paid for having long legs." She offered a broad smile and waited for him to say something else but he was ready to leave.

"Then we Fly United?" She asked this quickly, cringing a little at her silliness but wanting to say or do something that would keep his attention.

"Metaphorically speaking."

Then he said good-night to the others, including her in his good-byes, and walked away. She watched his tall frame maneuver between the other tables and wondered if he was married. Probably not. She thought him more the type to have some sort of loose but steady arrangement; he certainly did not look like the kind to spread himself thin with a lot of women. Perhaps she would ask him tomorrow, just come right out and say, "Excuse me, but are you taken?" Yes, that is what she would do. Unless, of course, he was traveling with someone—maybe a someone who was waiting for him at this very moment. The thought made her heart sink and she was surprised that his emotional status should be of such concern to her. Tomorrow, she decided. Tomorrow would tell the story. But she did not sleep well that night. She had not, in fact, slept particularly well any night since.

It was annoying to Lilly to remember all of that this morning; there were too many more pressing things to deal with. Irritated, she crossed the kitchen and poured more Scotch into her now empty glass, a little disgusted with herself for needing to drink.

"Keep this up," she said aloud, "and you'll end up like Clara whether you want to or not."

She added ice to the whiskey and continued speaking aloud.

"And while we're on the subject, just keep on talking to empty rooms like this and the men in the white coats will come to haul you off."

Defiantly she poured still more alcohol into her glass and opened a cabinet drawer for a carton of cigarettes, tucking it securely under her arm. She picked up the bottle of Scotch with her free hand and began to walk to the back of the house, toward the living room. When she passed the mirror, she stopped dead still, holding up the whiskey and the cigarettes belligerently, speaking directly to her reflection.

"If I'm going to die anyhow, I'm not about to sacrifice my pleasures before I have to."

She was only halfway out of the kitchen when the back doorbell sounded. Pausing for no more than an instant, she wondered who in the world would be calling this early on a Saturday; there was no one she chose to see and she continued on down the hall, calling aloud as she went, "Miz Shawcross ain't ta home."

"Lilly, it's me. George. Open up."

"I, George. Not me. Be grammatically correct when you invade my privacy."

Clumsily she shifted everything to the same arm and pulled open the back door.

"I'm lousy company," she said.

"Me too."

George walked past and into the kitchen, a quart of cheap blended whiskey in his hand. "No friend of Sabberstein takes a sentimental journey alone."

He reached an empty glass from the cupboard and followed her into the living room, where Lilly lay down on the couch, putting her bottle and the cigarettes on the coffee table near her drink, an ashtray on her stomach, settling in.

"This is no sentimental journey, George. I warn you. It's masochism on the march." She reached to pour more liquor into her already full glass. Some of it spilled over.

"Want some of mine?" he asked, pointing to the bottle between his feet.

"Thank you, no. My self-flagellation does not extend to stomach rotting." She held up the cap to the Scotch. "Try this?"

He refused. "Good booze is dangerous," he said. "It goes down easier. You drink more."

"Worried about your liver or your purse?" They were old hands at making this kind of conversation.

"Both." He eased back into the armchair, sliding the ottoman toward him with his legs, and putting both feet on top of it. "Are you up to the dirty parts of your life yet?" he asked.

"No. You're just in time. Shall I show slides?"

They sat silently for half an hour; the only sounds were the birds in the garden.

"Yappy bastards, aren't they?" he said. And then he told her to talk. "I'm not here to listen to them."

"I'm boring me, George. You deserve better."

"Just give the news, lady. Think of me as your friendly neighborhood exorcist."

She stared straight ahead, her mouth clamped shut.

"All right, your famous pump need priming?"

" 'Coagulating' is the word."

He was not deterred. "I was thinking this morning about the first time I ever saw you. We hadn't had our famous meeting at the time. I figure it was about eight or ten years ago, at a picnic. Maggie clinging to Harry's leg. You, my dear, looked like you'd swallowed a beach ball."

"Teddy!" She smiled and patted her middle, upsetting the ashtray.

"The three and a half of you hadn't been in Washington long. I remember thinking at the time how fresh and eager the Shawcrosses looked. The perfect young couple. New in town, ready to change the world."

"It got to us first."

"You walked head-on into that tight little group of New Frontiersmen, behaving, as I recall, like you were in a police line-up. You stole my heart, kid. One glance and I knew you could never make it. I said to myself, That one will have to toughen up or go under."

115

"I managed both."

"Ungracefully, as I recall."

"Most."

"Ever wonder what happened to those people who made life so crappy for you back then?"

"Only when I have to."

"They weren't so bad, Lilly. Probably just as terrified as you. Only they knew better than to expose their bleeding parts to the pack. Look at it this way, babe, you lasted them out. They're gone and you're still—"

"Nowhere," she interrupted, "beneath this glamorous façade, George." She was speaking in grunts, kicking off her boots and upsetting the ashtray again as she did. "Underneath all this, I am still that angry, frightened girl. The only difference now is that I'm the one who intimidates me. I do a better job."

She lapsed into another silence.

"I never liked Harry. Did you know that?" he asked.

"I didn't know anything. I'm glad you did."

"Well, he was a judgmental little bastard. The type's not hard to spot."

"Why weren't you around to tell me that before I swallowed so many beach balls?"

"Come on. Those two kids are the best going."

"Oh, for Christ' sake, George. You don't have to be a Pulitzer Prize-winner to know that." Lilly knew it annoyed him when she made any reference to his Pulitzer.

"Well, if you're intent on wallowing in self-pity, ole George is here to remind you that Mags and The Kid are the best possible arguments for population explosion.'"

"*Alors.* We agree."

George continued, more gently. "Those people got to you right in the beginning, didn't they?"

"Only because I let them. I was so stupid. I thought all you had to do was follow the instructions. God knows they were printed in big enough letters. Right across my chest. Harry saw to that."

"Harry. It always comes back to him."

"Him or somebody. All morning I've been thinking how other people have directed my life. But you know something, George, that's too damned easy. All right, I was malleable and young. But it's no excuse for letting others take control of me. I was lazy. Somewhere within that angry, lazy creature, I knew better. It was just simpler to go along than to work things out for myself. I think, my friend, that I have got from life precisely what I put in for."

She belched lightly, not bothering to apologize.

"Philosophy and self-pity are a nauseating combination," he said.

"I was about to come to the same conclusion myself." She laughed and he joined her, relieved to see she still knew how.

"Hey, Lil, do you remember the night Harry had the cocktail party, the one before the screening of his civil rights film? I still hadn't met you—or, at least, you weren't aware of me. You got drunk as hell and told him off. God, I loved it. I can see you now, mad as a wet hen you were. You turned to Harry and announced that a rotten hour documentary was not going to make up to black people for two hundred years of singing and dancing.

"I can still remember those politicians, their fat jaws dropping to here. Your exact words were, as I recall, 'Sixty minutes of prime time whining about social inequities is not going to help Martin Luther King. If you want to change things, try getting off your righteous behinds and rustling up a little legislation!' And in a Southern accent, no less. Harry jumped up—you remember?—embarrassed as hell, telling you between clenched teeth that things come slowly in Washington. 'Yeah, Harry,' you said. 'Everything but the promises.' It was a great exit line, kid. Until you tripped going up the stairs."

Lilly remembered. Too well. She could go back even further, all the way to the days before she dared to express an opinion, to 1960, to that year when they first moved to Washington. It was the time when even the myopic could see that future campaigns and elections were going to depend on television. The Kennedy-Nixon debate had started the political flesh market toward electronics; Harry had been quick to figure that one out, she had to give him that. And there they were, she and Harry and Maggie, settled into a Georgetown house, smack in the bosom of a fresh administration, part and parcel of the new blood brought in by a young President. Lilly was only twenty-six years old and had no objections to leaving New York. It was not as though she were uprooted; she had never really belonged there, either. Certainly she had not belonged with Harry, that much was apparent. But by the time she had come to realize it, she had Maggie. Poor little girl, accidentally conceived as some sort of truce between them.

Lilly thought back to her first pregnancy. It was such arrogance to undertake the responsibility for a new life when she had no idea of how it would turn out, especially when she didn't even know how her own life would turn out. For a while, after the initial shock of being pregnant had worn off, she had hoped against instinct that a child might bring her and Harry closer together, just by its mysterious presence. But the pregnancy had come to seem a willful loss of control that would ultimately usurp her last chance for freedom. When it was altogether too late, the idea of bearing Harry's child had angered her. Babies, she had found, lock you to a man, its father; you have to please and serve on pain of abandonment. Was that what she had wanted? A baby to bind her to her marriage because there was nothing else to be bound to?

Right after Maggie was born, Harry had gone away for several months to work in the Democratic campaign. When Kennedy was elected, Harry had stayed in the capital to be close to the new administration and had taken his sweet time in sending for her and the baby. Well after the Inaugural ceremonies, she remembered, almost spring—she had seen the season as an omen, a good time for a fresh start.

A month or so before she got to Washington, Harry had bought the house, allotting the rooms for his convenience; her clothes were already hung in the guest room, his in the master bedroom. Several dinner invitations had been accepted before the exact time of her arrival had been established.

"I'll have to go to these things without you."

He had taken her lack of objection for granted.

"People here do things pretty much according to number. At this late date, you'd only upset the table balance. Anyhow, you'll probably want a few evenings alone with Maggie to get her used to the new house. A strange baby-sitter would confuse her, don't you think?" And then he'd added meaningfully that she would want to be very calm and rested before she set about meeting these new people. She wanted them to like her, didn't she?

Lilly had tried very hard to be liked. Especially in the beginning, the first evening out, in that big country house in McLean, across the river, in Virginia. They had parked the car on the dirt road just outside the stone gates and walked up the gravel drive. Lanterns were dotted about the lawn and, over to the side, there were small round tables with flowered cloths reaching to the ground; down near the pool an orchestra was playing bouncy dance music. Lilly thought it all very lovely, and in a burst of enthusiasm she mentioned to Harry that even Vince would approve.

"Lilly, don't bring up that screaming faggot's name. Please.

If anyone asks you about yourself, just say you were in the fashion business. Don't volunteer anything. Don't, for God's sake, tell anybody you ran around half-naked in front of a lot of Jewish rag merchants. These people won't understand." He gripped her arm tightly as they went up the front steps. "Nobody will be interested anyhow."

The hostess had greeted Harry warmly and nodded pleasantly enough when introduced to Lilly; then the young woman took Harry aside conspiratorially, leaving Lilly to follow along behind. She looked around for the bar and tugged at Harry when she spotted it.

"Hold it a minute, honey," he had said to Lilly, disengaging her hand and patting it absently. "Just stay here a sec, I'll be right back."

She had leaned against the wall of the wide entry hall, unnoticed and annoyed about it. Several times someone glanced expectantly in her direction, nodded slightly, but then moved on. Lilly sensed immediately and with some bitterness that she was among people on important missions; they would have no time for her, not now, not with so many contacts to be made.

Several of the host's small children in matching pajamas and robes were sitting on the hall stairs and Lilly went over to them, gratefully. She did not have much experience at talking with children—Maggie was still too young to be communicative—but she selected the oldest, a boy of about twelve, and eagerly asked him where he went to school, his grade, his age, his hobby—anything to keep the exchange going. The boy led her to the basement to see his boa constrictor, and Lilly watched, horrified, as he took the reptile from its cage and allowed it to wrap around his neck. This made her think of Harry, which in turn made her giggle; she turned and ran quickly back up the stairs.

She saw Harry in the library and waved, starting over to him, but for some peculiar reason Harry shifted his position, placing his back to her and inching a bit closer to the man with whom he was speaking; he even put his hand on the stranger's shoulder to draw them more deeply into their private conversation. Lilly was incensed but it was too late to turn back; she was caught midway between Harry and nothing. Embarrassment always made her bold and she walked straight over to the two men and locked her arm through Harry's. The talk ceased abruptly as Harry told his friend that this was his wife; he did not call Lilly by name, nor did the man appear to expect it. He only nodded stiffly but politely and then excused himself. Harry seemed unduly annoyed at the interruption and Lilly nudged him toward the bar, saying that she would like a drink.

"Tell the bartender. That's what he's here for." Harry spoke irritably; his entire body exuded a strange coldness.

The bartender smiled inquiringly and she repeated her order in a louder voice than she had intended.

"A vodka on the rocks, please. In a large glass."

Harry looked around, alarmed, as if she had shouted an obscenity.

"Women here don't do much drinking in public," he said. "Watch yourself." And then he walked away from her to speak to yet another strange man.

Lilly felt the blood rush to her cheeks; it was exactly how she had felt when they were first married, when Vince had given them their only bridal party, a large, crowded reception in his apartment, making the best of the situation by introducing Harry with thinly veiled contempt as his "protégé-in-law." She had wanted to cling to Harry that night, too. Only then it was out of a contentment that she belonged with him. But he had disengaged her arm, just like tonight, telling her that she should mingle, get to know people.

"I'll take this side of the room, Lilly," he had said. "You take the other."

She had done what he suggested that night and would be glad to do so now but there was no one to move to. Harry's attitude was worse now, she thought; he seemed unusually nervous and anxious to get away from her and she was struck by his pathetic need to ingratiate himself with these new people. Lilly had the distinct impression that he saw himself as stuck with her, like an insecure boy trapped by the prom wallflower.

Again Lilly leaned against the wall in the hall, alone, sipping at the vodka. The ice hit against her front teeth, causing some of the liquid to spill out and run down her chin. She wiped at it with her hand and looked quickly over to where Harry was standing. He had seen. Ashamed and angrier still, she finished off the drink and asked for another, painfully aware that she was going to have to work her side of the room alone this time, too—whether she liked it or not.

Fortunately, the guests were being encouraged to go out onto the terrace for dinner and she followed along gratefully.

Unsure of where she was to sit or of what she expected to do, she dropped into the first available seat before she noticed the place card: *His Excellency the Ambassador of France.* She almost overturned the gold caterer's chair as she jumped up. A waiter asked her who she was and consulted a seating chart on which there were eight velvet circles bearing the names of the guests.

"Mrs. Shawcross," he repeated, studying the table arrangements. "I think you are over there. Yes. The table with blue flowers."

Pleased to have herself called by name, Lilly smiled widely and thanked him twice, found her place card and sank into the chair it designated, relieved to be out of the way at last.

On her left was a man who announced immediately that he was an interior designer, the one who had done both the house and the table decorations. Lilly, in turn, identified herself.

"Who is your husband?" he asked.

"Harry. Over there." She pointed out Harry sitting between two bouffant-coifed women, talking with unusually animated gestures and apparently enjoying himself. Washington was making Harry very sociable indeed.

The decorator sounded disappointed that Harry's face was not one of the famous ones. "What does he do?"

"He's in film."

"Movies?"

She was happy to hear the sound of her voice. "Not really," she elaborated. "He makes documentaries. He did some of the President's campaign spots. For television."

"Oh? Television? Does he like it?"

"Very much."

A waiter removed her vodka and she reached to take it back. Pointing and grabbing. Harry would not approve.

"Well, that's nice," the man said and turned to the lady on his other side; obviously they were old friends.

Lilly looked to the man seated to her right; his back was to her and she would have to wait for him to notice her. Awkwardly she waved toward her empty wineglass for a waiter to fill it and then sat there, sipping at it, wishing it were something stronger.

At nearby tables, talk was rising now to a roar; the band was playing the President's campaign song—Lilly knew it well, Harry had used it in his spots—and she started to hum, at last beginning to feel the warmth of the wine and glad to have it soothe her. Everything would be all right, she told herself. Yes, it would all come up roses just as the song said. She moved her foot to the music as she emptied her glass and then brazenly tapped the tuxedoed back of her unknown dinner partner, who turned quickly enough and looked at her for recognition, even stared a second or so to be positive that he could not place her before his eyebrows shot up in anticipation of what she had interrupted him to say.

"Hi! I'm Harry Shawcross's wife."

"I'm Artie Hamilton. Be with you in a moment."

He wrinkled his nose, his mouth more a pucker than a smile, and returned to his previous conversation. Lilly shrugged and switched her empty wineglass for his full one.

There was dancing during dinner, couples getting up to shuffle around the flagstone area that was left open in the center of the tables. Harry, too, she noticed, first with one partner, then with another. Lilly took another glass of wine and began to smile as she watched Harry. Mr. Astaire, she commanded silently, come and dance with your wife!

The food was served in courses and there were constant rowdy toasts in between, loud and boisterous references to things and people she could not connect. Catcalls followed each speech and then, much to her surprise, Harry was on his feet, telling what appeared to be a very funny anecdote about one of the ladies present, a seemingly hilarious account of how she had left all her underwear drying in a St. Louis hotel bathroom during the campaign and how she had had to board the candidate's train without any. Everyone laughed and drank to that, some adding similar stories as the rest booed or cheered good-naturedly. Lilly sat through the entire dinner wearing her most simple grin. It was the longest meal she could ever remember.

After dessert, the others began to drift down toward the pool, laughing and shouting as they went. Lilly took a firm hold of Artie Hamilton's arm, ignoring the surprise on his face, and rapidly bombarded him with questions and compliments. Her only thought was that she had to hold on to him until she could find someone else. Desperate, she clutched at his limp hand and asked about his tailor, where he lived, what did he do?

"I'm an old family friend." He spoke as though to an idiot, as though his connection to the presidential family was not only common knowledge but a calling sufficient in itself.

"How wonderful." She was gushing and didn't care. "Every

family should have an old friend. Even the Kennedys. How old are you, anyhow?"

Splashing sounds distracted them before he could answer. It was one of the women Lilly had admired earlier, but drenched now, bobbing in the pool, her dark hair dripping around her delighted face; she was happily shouting abuses to the two men who had tossed her into the water. Several other people were thrown in after her and a couple of others followed of their own accord, like a chain reaction. Harry was pushed from behind by a sopping-wet girl who then threw herself back into the water after him and climbed onto his shoulders, forcing him under.

"If she holds him down long enough, she'll be my new best friend," Lilly said, observing the frantic merriment with a tinge of envy.

Artie Hamilton gave her another crinkle-nosed smile, removed his glasses, handed them to her along with his watch and ran toward the pool, doubling himself up in midair and cannonballing into the water. He made a very big splash, drenching a small group of people standing nearby. The hostess, close to where Lilly stood, was bouncing on her toes and clapping her hands; she seemed clearly pleased with the exuberant turn of events. Speaking in Lilly's direction, but not precisely to her, she said, "Isn't Artie terrific?"

"Absolutely," Lilly mumbled.

"So is Harry. He's so helpful. There's nothing we can't count on Harry for."

"He gets right into the swim of things," Lilly agreed, intending to be funny but hearing her words as angry and harsh.

The hostess only stared past her and Lilly was amazed that disapproval could be transmitted by a face that did not for one minute lose its expression of suspended perkiness.

"Excuse me," the young woman said hurriedly, "but it looks like someone is leaving early."

Lilly fervently wished it were she.

Harry was furious with her. He had expected her to dazzle on that first night out and she had rather hoped she might. It confused her that these new people were so indifferent to newcomers, as if they had allotted all the roles long before she arrived and had no need to add to their number. Just to see Harry standing that night in their living room in his damp and rumpled dinner clothes was a reminder of her failure. She had been just about the only dry person to leave the party and it seemed a damning distinction.

Lilly was very much aware of a sense of inner cringing; she had felt it all night but it did not occur to her to hold the alienating people to account for any part of her alienation. Instead, she had only that vague feeling of some unfairness—that and a sharp fear of all the other uncomfortable evenings which undoubtedly lay ahead. For herself she would prefer not to think of this night ever again.

But Harry would not let the matter drop. "For God's sake, did you have to hang on to me like a backwoods dunce?"

"I was nowhere near you. Besides, I was charm itself. Your new pals just aren't in the market for additional friends." Clearly, this was not what he wished to hear, but Lilly simply was not up to arguing her merits like some door-to-door salesperson.

"Look," she said hotly, "I'm not a tasty little dish to be served up to a pack of pseudo-gourmands already too full of themselves to try anything new." Lilly laughed at the analogy but it was no laughing matter to Harry. He was stalking up the stairs and she had to call after him. "I have not yet mastered the art of loving people who are so obviously involved with themselves." Her voice was rising. "Nor do I have any immediate plans to cultivate a bunch of snobs whose particular merits have not exactly been established in headlines."

The anger in her came swift and hard and she was shouting, pounding with her hands on the banister railing. "The privilege of kissing their sacred asses isn't worth the struggle so far as I can see!"

She heard the door to the bedroom slam shut, but still she continued in her own defense. "One such aficionado per family, Harry. That's all the law allows."

Lilly sat down on the bottom step and warned herself that she ought to be reasonable, that the town and the people were important to Harry, almost frighteningly urgent, and he was, after all, the only thing she had. She reminded herself sternly that the easy rider was not allowed to complain. Then she got up and poured a little brandy into a glass and paced around the living room, as if she were about to make an important choice. It was one thing to shrug the evening off. What did it matter to her that these people scurried around massaging each other's sense of self-importance? But somehow she was going to have to work herself into the scheme of things or she might be out of the scheme altogether. Besides, she might even get to like Washington, given half a chance. It was painful to admit, but it would be rather pleasant to be part of it all, to belong. Well, she was going to have to make more of an effort, that was for sure. First of all, she ought to patch things up with Harry. Tonight, right now. She would have to bring him around somehow. She finished off the brandy and slowly climbed the stairs.

In bed, she turned to him. "Are you awake? Listen to me a minute, can you?"

Harry made no response.

"I was thinking downstairs," she continued, "that maybe we ought to give a party of our own. Dinner or cocktails, whatever you think sounds O.K."

Harry rolled over; he was considering the offer.

"You'd just bitch it up." But there was a plea to his voice.

"No. No. I won't. You'll see. It will be the most fantastic party ever. What do you think?"

"What do I think! You see, Lilly? Do you hear yourself? You're saying 'we' and it's your job. Giving a party is what you're supposed to do. It's something I should be able to leave to you."

"But you can. I can do it." She could feel his uncertainty and it made her argumentative. "Christ, they're just people, Harry. I can handle it. I won't bother you with a single detail."

Instead of verbal acquiescence, he moved next to her in the dark and she tried not to stiffen, even took some deep breaths to relax. She knew he would make love to her now. He never touched her otherwise.


From the arrival of the first guest, Lilly felt a mounting sense of rage. Each one of them came into her home looking past her with an attitude of being there only to see the others. It struck Lilly that they dealt with strangers as if they had gloves on, pretending all the time—pretending nice and decent things, she supposed, but pretending, always pretending. She looked about the room studying first one face and then the next. They were all adding to themselves, politely and coolly shopping the room for accessories to their own existence.

Lilly removed a drink from the tray of a passing waiter and walked into her crowded living room, seeing herself as from a distance—there she was among bright and attractive children, all of them playing dress-up, acting out the gestures of grown people when, actually, every single one of them, including herself, was too young, too inexperienced, here too soon. She thought they probably all ought to be elsewhere, learning about themselves, about life—not tagging along after a boy President.

She observed Harry for a moment. He seemed more a stranger tonight than ever, but there he was, the slickest of the slick kids, talking to a group of men and putting himself out as she had never known him to do, laughing, even listening for a change. Charm. Harry's hidden charm. Just seeing him made her angrier than she had ever thought herself capable.

She took a fresh drink and joined a group of four women sitting together on the long couch, lined up like elegant patients in a waiting room.

They fell into categories, these women. Some were strident and sure of themselves, the kind who stick close to their own type as if to ward off intruders, as if they were not quite confident enough to function alone. They approved only of each other, moving, speaking and thinking as a unit, an identical and impenetrable unit. They were the ones she both feared and wanted to be a part of. The rest, like those on the couch, seemed to be more like Lilly, present in history and inseparable from events because of the men they had married. She disliked their docile, accepting faces on sight; she saw for them the same fate that undoubtedly was in store for her, all of them involved in life as part of a package —the female side of a couple, hopelessly or happily living out somebody else's destiny.

She held out her now empty glass to a waiter and pulled up a bench from in front of the fireplace to sit with these women; their conversation halted as she approached and their eyes turned expectantly in her direction. Did they expect something from her? It was impossible to tell. Masks were a part of the Washington uniform, she thought, probably issued at some disbursing office on the moment of arrival and labeled FOR USE IN CROWDS. Lilly shook her head unconsciously and waved her hand for the women to continue talking.

"We were just discussing schools." The voice was somewhat apologetic.

"I guess Harry and I'll have to start thinking along those lines pretty soon," Lilly said.

"Oh?"

126

"Maggie is awfully little but they begin so soon now," she added.

"You may be already too late to apply."

Lilly was not certain which woman had spoken; they seemed so similar.

"Where do you suggest?" She asked the question of no one in particular.

"It depends on what you want . . ."

"It always does, doesn't it?" Lilly snapped.

She had not meant to be abrupt, but it annoyed her that something as simple as putting a child into school should take on such exaggerated social significance. She said as much and waited for a response, but they were staring at her, rather embarrassed for her, as if she had made the most unmaternal kind of statement. Lilly reminded herself of her promise to be good, but there really wasn't anything she wanted to learn from these women, certainly nothing she dared to ask. For a moment she wondered what they would do if she leaned toward them and whispered, "Look, tell me, what are you afraid of?" For a moment she had to actually fight her hysterical impulse to question them.

She caught sight of Harry; he was watching her, judging. She scooted her seat nearer to the women, pretending to enjoy them, wanting—almost desperately—to bargain with them to like her and be her friends. Had she bartered this way someplace long ago? and lost? Well, this was very silly of her and she heard herself laughing; the women seemed to think she was laughing at them. Well, wasn't she? At them and at herself? Angry again, she pushed the bench back and got up, sensing the group's relief as she walked away.

"Can I get you something?" she asked.

Neither man looked at her; one merely shook his head, the other handed her an empty glass.

"Scotch, please. With water. If you don't mind."

Lilly realized that she did mind, one hell of a goddamned lot, but she placed the empty glass into a nearby waiter's hand, relayed the order and pointed out the guest he was to serve, then walked toward a different group, three men, three women—one of the men was speaking of Cuba. When he finished, another of the men took his precise words, rearranged them slightly and repeated what she had just heard. All six heads bobbed in agreement. Lilly felt certain that when he finished, the third man would take his turn and she did not care to hear it again. As she moved away, though, she decided it might be a good idea to learn the words to Cuba, for her own recital, just in case she got the chance.

Tired now, she was ready for everyone to go. It was not fun to be the hostess; she had worked so hard to make things nice. And for what? They might all have been in a public restaurant and she was having to push herself to stay alert. She sat on the floor beside an animated young man who did not halt in his lecture about the Peace Corps. He appeared so certain, so arrogantly sure that everyone agreed with him that Lilly wondered if no one in the Kennedy crowd ever argued; it was so boring not to. But she listened politely; she did not like the young man who was speaking and tried to figure out why. Was it because women judge other men by the behavior of their own husbands? The thought made her slightly nauseated and she turned her gaze toward Harry. Without even trying, he made her feel guilty and stupid and incompetent. He could do this, she knew, because he really believed all women were like that. Not just her but all of them. Lilly fought an impulse to shout a warning to the other women, but they seemed so removed, so glued into the proper positions that she knew they would not hear. To hear would be to act. And how could any of them take action even if they wished to? Lilly picked up another drink from a waiter's tray, determined to make herself as congenial as possible.

"I am sure the Peace Corps is a very worthwhile venture," she said, "but I can't help wondering just where we Americans leave off in imparting technical skills before we start trying to change other people's beliefs?"

She was as surprised at her words as the others; she hadn't realized she was going to say them and the young man who was talking seemed especially affronted by the challenge. Apparently he was as unaccustomed to being questioned by a woman as Lilly was to be questioning a man.

"It is not the business of the Peace Corps to homogenize," he said, "only to share our expertise." He turned aside to dismiss her.

It was strangely important to Lilly that she make her point. "But by doing that, don't we place some kind of obligation for people to assimilate, to be Americanized? Inside plumbing and all that?" She was faltering but determined to finish. "I mean, how do you teach the Burmese to urinate in a latrine and not press upon them our ideas about God? I mean, isn't it inevitable that we missionary?"

"Nonsense." His lips were pursed.

"We agree only in that it's nonsense," she said, embarrassed by his disdain. "I just don't think we have any right to urge our world on anybody else. Help, yes. But my question is where to draw the line between teaching and intruding."

There was a heavy silence before the young man spoke. "All people are basically the same. They want to live the way we do."

"Bullshit." She smiled. "Go tell that to those Buddhists who are setting fire to themselves every day." Lilly sensed she had gone too far and she didn't really object to the Peace Corps—only to the wise-assed bore who was extolling its merits. Well, it was pleasant to unleash her anger on him and she was about to speak again, but out of the corner of her eye she caught a signal from one of the Negro waiters who was standing on the hall landing.

"Excuse me," she said, getting up, a little clumsy from the alcohol. "The help has got to be paid." She went to settle the bill, overtipping as she always did.

She returned from the kitchen and went straight to another group, four men but only three women; her presence evened the number. This time she did not make much of an effort to pick up the drift of their talk; she'd had too much to drink to concentrate. Instead, she quietly studied the women. Each one stood silently; it was obviously not their time to participate. Lilly could not believe that none of them had anything to contribute. Was it that they were never given the chance? Or were they, as she herself seemed, only mirrors? Vain reflections of their husbands' accomplishments? Would they all shatter like glass when dropped?

She beckoned a waiter for another drink, thinking to herself that the real trouble with being a woman was that she has to keep on trying to adapt.

Then someone was directing a question to her, a man; he was speaking to her with exaggerated politeness and she shook her head to clear it, asking if he would mind repeating what he had just said.

"Your husband? What does he think about advisers being sent to Vietnam?"

"Harry's over there"—she pointed, a little drunkenly—"but if you'd like *my* opinion, I'd be delighted to give it."

There was another stunned silence and Lilly realized that maybe the best thing about these people was their unlimited capacity for shock. Just now, one of them was trying to cover her gaffe, trying to fill the void for her.

"Well," the male voice was saying, "my wife certainly agrees that sending in advisers is the right thing to do." He placed his arm around his silent wife.

"Yes," Lilly answered thickly, "and I'm sure she'd say so herself if she were only here."

With a smile more gracious than she believed possible, Lilly bowed and backed away from the group. She did not belong here! She was out of step in her own house and damn it all, she was hiccupping. Quite loudly.

Upstairs, without bothering to turn out the lights or to remove her clothes, she drew back the covers and got into bed. She was disappointed, and furious with herself, but she simply could not cope with any more tonight. Her eyes closed and the room started to circle around her until she slid her left foot to the floor to stop the spinning. It would be nice if she could steady her thoughts so easily.

# 11

LILLY knew the party had been a dismal failure. It wasn't necessary that Harry remind her so often in the weeks that followed, telling her that everything she touched was a disaster and that she would never have any friends. "No one likes you and I can't say as I blame them," he'd said. She listened to him and felt quiet and sick inside, as if her brain had ceased to function. Nor did she feel well physically. Food was repellent and the mere thought of alcohol was impossible. She was glad of the excuse to stay home. In fact, she felt dizzy just seeing invitations to social functions arrive in the mail. For weeks it seemed that Harry was always putting on his dinner clothes to go out without her; he had told her that she was probably anemic and that the least she could do was to look to her own well-being. Any fool could do that, he had said. More to silence him than from any sense of real concern, Lilly had nodded in agreement, saying he was probably right and that she would ask around for the name of a good physician. She had fallen into a deep, safe sleep even before Harry left the house.

"Of course, I'm not an obstetrician, Mrs. Shawcross," the doctor was saying, "but I suspect that you are pregnant. Not quite two months would be my guess."

Lilly stared at him; he was smiling, the bearer of glad tidings; the son of a bitch was giving her the good word. Numbed, Lilly took the slip of paper on which he had written the name of a gynecologist and went home to bed, saying nothing about the doctor to Harry, and found every possible excuse to avoid making an appointment with the obstetrician. It was two weeks before she could summon the courage to do it, and then she had to wait for over an hour in the stuffy outer office before she was directed to the examination room.

The nurse told her to remove her clothing and to put on a white gown; the doctor would be with her "in a jiffy," she said.

Lilly lay back on the fake-leather table, waiting; she could not bring herself to put her feet into the stirrups until she had to. Her right forearm was flung over her closed eyes and she was thinking of her first pregnancy, of Maggie. The bearing of Maggie had been a frightening ordeal that she could not possibly go through another time. She drew the arm from across her face and reached protectively for her abdomen, as if to apologize to the tiny fetus inside. How could she have been so careless as to have let this happen?

It had only been three years since Maggie. Well, she loved the little girl, now, didn't she? Loved her more every day. The trouble with having Maggie was that Lilly had not been ready to cease being a child herself. Well, that was a long time ago but she did not feel any better about it now, perhaps less so. By having Maggie, by giving birth to another life, Lilly had been terrified of losing her own. While her daughter had been growing inside her, so also had the conviction that she would die. She had had trouble sleeping then; at night the fears were everywhere. She had tried to tell Harry how it was.

"The one thing any woman can do is have a baby," he'd said. "Can't you even manage that?"

She had thought him cruel and said so.

"Lilly, a baby will keep you busy. Just what the doctor ordered."

He had tried to be cheerful, she had to give him that, but it was she who had had to carry Maggie, alone, creeping into the bathroom in the early morning to throw up, eating crackers to settle her stomach only to reject them moments later. Never had she felt more alone than she did with another living being inside her. As she grew heavier, so had her nightmares that she would die on the delivery table.

She had tried to stop these morbid thoughts, but they kept springing at her, gnawing on her, even in the taxi that night going to the strange New York hospital where Maggie was born. She kept remembering old bits of movies where the doctor, still in his white robe, came into the waiting room to tell the husband that it would be possible to save only one life, the mother or the child. Lilly had turned to Harry in the cab and clutched at his sleeve. "Listen, if there is any question of its being me or the baby, you'll pick me, Harry. You will, won't you?" She had held tightly to her overnight case as if it were a life preserver, leaning forward and waiting for Harry to say that of course he'd choose her and that she would be just fine.

"If you'd done what you should have done and read the manuals, you'd know those choices don't come up anymore."

It was like Harry to give a lecture when a simple bit of assurance would have done.

At the hospital, she had been turned over to a nurse who put her in a wheelchair and took her away, the overhead lights in the long green corridor whipping past as they moved. Lilly had looked hungrily at each door, the water fountain, the direction signs on the walls, convinced that she would never live to see them again.

Clara had told her often of the twenty-three hours of labor at Lilly's own birth, and she had recalled those stories with horror as she looked at the utensils spread on the table in the hospital preparation room. A muscular black woman in a green wrapper had silently helped her onto the table, and Lilly was unreasonably conscious of her Southern accent, unreasonably terrified that the woman might retaliate now for some ancestral cruelty to the Negro race. Lilly had not dared speak throughout the long, horrible ordeal of enemas and razors, but later she had screamed, so much screaming. Pain became a total commitment until at last a needle had stung her arm.

"Bear down, Mrs. Shawcross," the voice had commanded. "Bear down."

"Mrs. Shawcross, you are not helping. Push!"

"You are going to harm your child if you don't cooperate, Mrs. Shawcross. Do you want that?"

From some great distance Lilly was trying to tell them that she wanted to live and she was dying. She had felt her mouth moving, opening and closing, but there was no sound. Only the screaming, those long howls, over and over, coming from her. Lilly had wanted her own mother that night, not to become someone else's.

Her thoughts were interrupted by the doctor and after the examination she dressed again in her clothes and was seated on a narrow little chair directly in front of the doctor's desk. She scooted the chair closer, wanting to reach over and grab the man by his starched white lapels.

"I don't think I'm up to having another baby, Doctor."

133

"Nonsense, Mrs. Shawcross. You seem perfectly healthy. And not yet thirty, are we?" He put on his glasses to search the records for her age.

"You see . . ." She was stumbling over her words; it was not easy to tell this strange man that she might not be mentally able to go through another pregnancy. "It's . . . well, it's that I'm so depressed lately and I'm not very happy at home and I was thinking that another baby really ought to have more . . ."

"Every women wonders that at some time or other. It's very normal. Having a baby is a perfectly natural thing to do. I don't generally believe in tranquilizers for my mothers, but I can prescribe something mild. Just to ease you over the next several weeks. You'll be fine when the queasiness passes."

"I don't want to be tranquil and I don't want to be pregnant."

Lilly was angry. She rushed headlong into a description of her fears, her sense of personal inadequacy; her voice trailed off, ending with a choked and guilty plea that perhaps he might possibly arrange things so that the pregnancy could be terminated.

"There is no medical indication that bearing a second child is hazardous to your health."

He was looking at her sternly, as though she were a criminal. It was the moment for tears but Lilly could not seem to make them come; she had no control over that process either. Instead there was fury.

"I don't want another baby. It's all I can do to manage the one I have."

Now the tears were coming. Thank God! She put her hands on either side of her head.

"I've been thinking of getting a divorce," she said.

"Well, now, we often find that a baby brightens up the household. Brings mother and dad closer. Easier on sister, too. They learn to share."

Lilly crossed her arms on the desk and bent her head to them.

"Listen to me, please," she said, speaking in a low, thin voice. "I'm trapped and I'm afraid. I'm about out of my mind just thinking of doing it all again. And you don't understand." She looked up at the doctor. "Nothing can help my marriage. It's wrong. For me and the baby."

She was sobbing openly now, and Dr. Umphry was making no effort to hide his impatience.

"Just what is it you have in mind?"

Lilly knew he understood. The bastard knew, but he was waiting for her to beg.

"I want an abortion."

"On what grounds?"

"On the grounds that I want one."

With a desperate kind of helplessness, she gestured with both hands, pressing them over her stomach.

"And is that sufficient reason to halt a life?" The doctor was shaking his head in professional disbelief.

"Yes!" She was shouting at him, trying to make him see how it was. "It's reason enough. I have to work things out for me. I don't want anyone else."

"That's very selfish of us, Mrs. Shawcross. I think you'll be the first to agree when you calm down."

"But I don't want to calm down. Don't you see? I just can't do it."

"And how does your husband feel?"

"He doesn't know."

"Well, now"—Dr. Umphry was smiling, pleased; she had provided him with a new tack—"I suggest you talk it over with Mr. Shawcross. Often we are concerned with what our husbands will think. When we tell them, we find that they are as pleased as you will be when you are less upset."

"I don't care whether he is pleased or not. And, for Christ' sake, stop saying 'we.' I'm the one who is pregnant, Dr. Umphry. Not you. Not Harry. Me. Lilly Shawcross. And I don't want another baby. Not now." She was shouting again, her hand a fist hitting at the desk. "I want to be left alone. I need some time." Her voice was running down, she felt so empty.

"I have a number of other patients to see and this is very indulgent of you." He was straightening his desk papers, waiting, she knew, for her to collect herself, beg his pardon for the intrusion, and get the hell on with the business of procreating. Patiently now, he began describing the tragic young wives who came to him, unable to conceive a child, unhappy and unfulfilled, and who was she to turn aside this wonderful event that fate had selected her to experience—?

The scream was so loud and so unexpectedly chilling that even Lilly turned to see from where it had come.

Then the doctor was giving her a small blue pill, forcing a pleated white paper cup of water to her mouth. Clearly he was shocked by her hysteria and Lilly wondered if it were possible that in all his years of practice no other woman had ever objected to the tyranny of nature? Could she possibly be the first?

"Doctor, I cannot and will not have this baby. You have to help me."

She grabbed at his chalky hands with their neat flat nails, holding on to them with desperation and causing him to spill the water. He was retreating from her now, backing off to his tall leather chair, leaning back in it with his priestlike hands touching at the fingertips. He seemed to be focusing his eyes at some far spot on the ceiling.

"Mrs. Shawcross." He spoke in measured tones. "If you would care to see two qualified psychiatrists, and if they should, after careful and lengthy examination, consider you mentally unable to perform this perfectly natural function . . . *and* . . . should Mr. Shawcross concur in your wishes and sign the necessary legal forms . . . along with the other doctors . . . then and only then can we discuss the aborting of this pregnancy."

"You mean"—her voice was small—"you mean it doesn't matter what I want?"

"That is a very self-centered way of putting it. There are laws. Laws to protect society. Now, where would we all be if everyone had your attitude?"

"Better off."

Lilly picked up her purse. There was no point in talking further. He was telling her that two quacks must determine her insane, and that if Harry agreed that she was crazy, then they might take her seriously. She would have to be certifiably nuts before they would consider her request as that of a responsible adult. Lilly began to laugh; she could not stop the laughter. Impatient, Dr. Umphry came around the desk, standing over her and helping her into her coat.

"You check with the receptionist. She'll give you the first available appointment. That should be in about two weeks. We'll see how we feel then. These things pass, you know. We'll all be grateful someday."

"I'm sure we will," Lilly said.

She did not look back at him, nor did she stop at the front desk where the crisp white nurse kept the records of all the women who filed in and out of the office, like cattle, she thought. In the self-service elevator, the Muzak was playing a song Lilly did not recognize; she pushed the lobby button and leaned against the cool metal wall. She would have the baby. She had known from the beginning that she would have to.

# 12

CAUTIOUSLY Lilly lifted her folded arms from over her face, opening her eyes slowly, carefully, as though she were afraid she might find herself somehow trapped back there in the past. But she was in her own living room, on her own couch, and there was George in his chair, just where she'd left him when she had drifted off into her thoughts. Never was she so glad to see him; Good ole George, she thought, and thank God for him. Lilly looked over and smiled, feeling that some giant hand had swooped her up and taken her away. It was probably the Scotch; she glanced at the half-empty bottle, just where she'd left it on the coffee table. Her mouth tasted of caterpillars and she had to go to the bathroom. She sat up quickly and lifted the short hair from her damp neck, fanning at her flushed face with her free hand.

"I think I'm at the age where you don't fan yourself publicly," she said.

Her voice made George jump; he had been off somewhere, too, lost in his own reveries.

"Who needs hallucinatory drugs when they have a memory like mine, some ninety-proof Scotch and good ole Dr. Sabberstein?" Lilly stretched and yawned as she spoke.

"You may have had enough of all three of us for one day, Lil."

He was giving her an out and she liked him for it.

"Don't go, George. I'm glad you're here. I need you."

Lilly saw that no matter how genuine the sentiment, it sounded only polite when she said that sort of thing to George. She got up and went to him, kissing his broad forehead.

"If a lady is allowed one good friend, she couldn't do better than you," she said; then, to fill the awkward pause, she rubbed her stomach. "How about some food? The patient can now sit up and take a little weak tea. Name your ethnic passion and we'll send out for it. My treat. Chink? Kosher? Tex-Mex? What about a giant pizza only slightly limp from traveling?"

"Lilly!"

George hated racial slurs, even in verbal menus; he despised unfairness and cruelty in any form but he especially deplored it in her.

"Don't boost me on the pedestal today, George. I'm not up to it."

They both grimaced at the unintentional joke. Then Lilly laughed.

"Surprise me," she said. "You order while I go upstairs and slip into something more suitable to my penance. Whatever you want. The sky's the limit."

"The perfect hostess."

There was a slight edge to his words, but Lilly saw him reaching for the telephone as she left the room.

They sat on the floor, each of them at opposite ends of the coffee table covered with opened white cardboard cartons; they used chopsticks, eating without plates. George was drinking beer and placing the empties neatly in front of the fire screen. Lilly sipped her Scotch.

"You know," he said, "while you were upstairs a little while ago, I was thinking about how you've grown and changed since those early days."

"Change isn't always growth." She was clicking her chopsticks at him for emphasis. "You see, that's what bothers me," she went on. "I kept on changing all right, for forty years, but I've only been trying things out—none of it stuck, it's not permanent. There's a difference between trying it all and growing into a solid person."

"Sweet and sour self-pity. How Oriental of you."

"Why is it," she asked in mock exasperation, "that when I truly feel something, no one believes me. I'm not taken seriously."

"Maybe you don't believe it yourself."

"But I do, George. I really don't think I'm solid."

He shrugged, knowing it made her uneasy not to be challenged.

"I mean it. I don't think all those skins I've grown and shed have left me anything but tired."

"For a person who is plenty astute and intuitive about

others, you sure can be blind about yourself. You're just fishing for me to tell you who and what you are, waiting for me to outline you.

"You see"—he was pointing his chopsticks at her now—"laziness like that numbs the brain. You refuse to think about what you are. Oh, yeah, you're good at seeing your faults and pointing them out before someone beats you to it. Pretty handy at pointing out the virtues, too, I might add. But you won't look hard at yourself. Experience ain't self-knowledge, kid. You have to translate what you do into some real understanding of why you do it. It's the taking what you are, seeing it clear, and coming to terms with it that counts. The good and the bad. We're all made up of contradictions, Lil. You just won't accept it."

He drained another brown bottle and added it to the line-up before continuing. "Tell me when it was that you stopped being Harry's docile wife and became a brazen lady? Can you pinpoint it? You know what caused it?"

"Anger. Anger caused it. And insecurity. I'm sure of that."

Lilly leaned back against the side of the couch and thought a moment before she spoke. "I guess the real metamorphosis began the year after I had Teddy—'63 or '64. God! Nearly ten years now."

She sat straight again, her thumbnail caught between her front teeth, her eyes squinted in recall.

"Yes. I had had Teddy. When he was born my excuse for being a social recluse was gone. Christ, I hadn't been home from the hospital three weeks when Harry was nagging at me. A couple of times he even insisted I go to parties with him, saying how awkward it was to explain my absence. I tried to beg off but there was no arguing with him; when the occasion called for wives, I had to go. In those days, I always seemed to be doing things because I had to do them. God, I was mad, about to pop with it. I got so mad that I began to wonder what the hell, why not throw caution to the winds, what did I have to lose anyhow? I kind of liked the freedom that not caring gives you. You know?

"Anyhow, I ended up one night at some dinner or other and while I was sitting there, smiling and trying to be nice and knowing nobody cared whether I was there or not, I got this feeling in my chest, like drums rolling, and I thought, Shit, I'm sick and tired of being ignored and feeling clumsy and stupid. So I turned to this utter fool who was seated on my right and stuck my finger right into his ruffled-front dress shirt." Lilly started dramatizing the incident for George:

"Who did you say you were?"

"I said I'm Uncle Sam's Larynx."

The man began to shift in his chair and Lilly guessed that he was uncomfortable when she didn't catch his little joke "I mean," he said, "I'm at the Voice of America. I work at the Voice of America."

It was nice to have someone else anxious to explain.

"Oh?" was all she said and with no apologetic smile, either; she was enjoying the edge his poor joke gave her.

"Harry and I have a project together." He looked at her intently before he continued. "Surely Harry's told you about the film we're making?"

"Is he better with films than women?"

He laughed at her crudeness, even leaned closer. "I can't speak for Harry," he said, "but my own technique is better with ladies."

"Perhaps your expertise will rub off on him."

"Why not avoid the expense of the middleman?"

She thought this not very bureaucratic of him. Playfully she asked, "Do you think taking up with Harry's colleagues would give me a keener understanding of his art?"

"It would certainly enlighten you about mine. We could start with lunch."

"I've always preferred eating to making love."

He did not flinch. It would not have surprised Lilly if his tongue had rolled out onto the table.

"We could do both," he answered, dropping his hand onto her knee and squeezing it.

For only a moment she was disturbed by her own vulgarity and his response to it; then pleased, pleasantly complimented that he was not only listening to what she was saying but showing a definite physical interest. At the time, she wondered why men seem to have the peculiar notion that women are flattered to be handled. She did not, however, remove his hand, nor did she lower her insolent gaze. She decided that night that promiscuity was a much maligned form of social behavior.

She then turned from the man abruptly to the gentleman on her left, reaching out to arrest his hand as it moved toward a glass of wine, picked it up like a limp kitten, she did, and dropped it onto her thigh beneath the tablecloth. Smiling straight into his surprised face, she announced herself: "I'm Harry's Hostile Wife."

"How do you do? I'm Chick Saunders."

"If you had the choice, would you take me to lunch or to bed?"

He was startled and made no effort to hide it, cautiously glancing about the table and drawing his features into the expression of someone about to laugh off an uncomfortable situation.

"I stay pretty busy at the office," he said.

"Eating or screwing?"

"Say, you're Harry Shawcross's wife!" He glanced quickly down at her place card. "Harry says you've been ill."

"If pregnancy is a sickness. Yes."

Lilly was amazed at how easy it was to be sociable when you did not care, and lunged again with her new directness, asking what precisely it was that kept him so busy in the office.

"I'm Under Secretary, down at Commerce."

She was meant to know that, clearly, but he let it pass.

"What do you do when you're not having babies?" he added.

"Try to keep from having them. I've been toying with the idea of a nervous breakdown, but I can't seem to get the hang of it."

He threw back his head and laughed, tightening his grip on her thigh.

Lilly was unaccountably annoyed; civilized, people ignored her; outrageous, and she was all of a sudden charming. Was it possible that not to give a damn was the secret to Washington success? The secret to everything? She felt as if there were a slight opening in her brain, and she could see now, with enormous distinctness, that she had too long placed a fictitious value on anyone who snubbed her. And she was excited; her face flushed with the new options. She thought of Harry and smiled. He had been so glad to outdistance her these last years; it would annoy him if she were to catch up. The thought of inconveniencing Harry sent a surge of genuine pleasure through her and good humor bubbled upward. It was nice to feel alive, so in control.

She smiled again but in a new way, showing most of her teeth, then threw her head back in too loud a laugh; she felt marvelous, capable of anything. It seemed ridiculous that she had not tried overt sexuality before. Oh, something in her warned that nice ladies did not behave that way—then she remembered how easily nice ladies were lost in the shuffle.

As if what she was doing were the most natural thing in the

world, Lilly took the hand on her knee and joined it with the other hand still in her lap. For a delicious moment she saw both men's fingers eagerly intertwine before they realized they were only clutching the other. She reared back for a better view of their embarrassment, then whispered to them both, "Careful, gentlemen. You political types are permitted to get caught with your hand in anything except another man's!"

She laughed too loud again and heads turned in her direction, but there was no fear of her joke being found out. It was not, Lilly knew, the kind of amusing story her companions were likely to tell on themselves.

She got up from the table that night feeling marvelously in command; the sense of power lasted all the way home, and even later, when she was in bed and Harry reached over to put his arms around her for the first time in over a year. She pushed a pillow very matter-of-factly between them, announcing that she wished to be let alone.

"I have a terrible pain, Harry."

"Where is it this time?" His voice oozed exasperation.

"On its own side of the bed where it belongs."

Lilly was remembering it all so clearly, as if it had just happened. She told George how different she felt after that night. Oh, it hadn't been easy, she said, the new Lilly and the old one had been at such odds; fortunately, it had all happened quickly and once she started letting go, the timid things about her had just tumbled over, one after the other. Once she got the hang of her new personality, she felt as if someone else were occupying her body, a different person, someone who knew how to use it. It wasn't as if she was really doing anything wrong—she wasn't sleeping around—but she was thinking about it. When she realized the direction in which she was headed, the guilt and misgivings flooded over her and she was confused and tempted to revert to her old self, but she brought herself to an abrupt halt whenever that happened and looked carefully at the choices open to her, coldly and deliberately selecting the one that seemed most daring. Frequently at dinner parties she would behave outrageously just for the sake of outrage.

"Would you care to dance?" she might be asked.

"Only if your intentions are dishonorable."

She had danced quite a lot in those days, she told George. The best part was Harry; her surface promiscuity had infuriated him but in some incredible way it seemed to make her more desirable to him. She hated him for that.

"You're very cozy with everybody but me," he said one night, reaching for her.

"And?" She pushed him away.

"And you're forcing me to turn to other women. There happen to be some in this town who find me damned attractive."

"No accounting for taste, is there?"

"Well, there are plenty of them."

"Help yourself."

"You're being very unfair, Lilly." He was pouting again, the way he had when they were first married.

"Life is unfair, my friend."

She opened her purse and tossed him a wad of bills. "Take the grocery money, Harry. Go out and get yourself a mistress. But don't you ever put your hands on me again as long as you live."

"I won't stand for this, Lilly!" he shouted. "You just consider yourself warned."

He stared at her then, coldly, his lip curled. "Just look at yourself," he said. "You're getting so strident and aggressive, you're almost like a man."

"Sorry I can't return the compliment."


At breakfast some weeks later she announced to Harry that he should clear his belongings from the spare room he used as a study.

"For what reason?"

"For Mrs. Gulliver." She loved the name and had been looking forward to springing it on him.

"Mrs. Who?"

"Gulliver. As in Jonathan Swift." She drank her coffee, smiling at him over the rim of the cup.

"Lilly. Your behavior is really too much. God knows I've been patient, but I believe you should see a doctor. You know what kind of doctor I mean. I think you need help."

"It's on the way, Harry. Her name is Minerva Gulliver." She let that sink in. "She's a nurse for the children; a bottle washer for me."

Harry's expression made her laugh. "For you, she will be an expense. A live-in expense. She will cost you eighty-five dollars a week. And your study. What sort of studying did you do in there, anyhow?" She was heady at the effect she was creating.

"Just precisely where do you think that kind of money will come from?"

"From the check my father sends each month."

"And where will we get the money to run the house?" He was reasoning as if with a moron.

"From the breadwinner. I think that's you." She bit into a piece of toast.

"That's preposterous. Your allowance is for living expenses."

"Then we'll cut down on somebody's living. Spread the wealth. My wealth, as it happens."

"Just how do you propose we do that?"

"I'm not proposing, Harry. I insist. For years now, you've complained that I can't do anything. I don't cook well. I can't clean or wash or care for the children to suit you. And you're right. Mrs. Gulliver is going to be all the things I'm not. I think the two of you will be very happy." She had never felt so gay.

"I'm not giving you money for this sort of indulgence."

"I'm not asking you to give it to me. It's mine and I'm going to spend it on me. I have no intention of endorsing my checks over to you anymore. In ways you never asked about, I earned that money. Every single cent of it. I think of it as back salary and I intend to use it when and how I please."

Lilly thought that maybe she sounded like Joan Crawford; she never liked Joan Crawford but she would have to do for now. She deposited her cup and saucer in the sink.

"I only want what's mine, Harry, and I intend to get it one way or another."

She started out of the room. Red-faced and furious, Harry stood to block her. "And is that *all* you want?" Rage was choking him.

"As a matter of fact, it isn't."

His jaw went slack.

"I want this house in my name."

"You want what!"

"For a man who makes a career of putting words in the mouths of fatuous politicians, your own command of the language is certainly limited."

He lifted his arm as if to strike her and she stood very still, rather hoping he might; it would reinforce the loathing she felt for him.

"This house was bought with money from my mother's trust fund and I want it in my name. It occurs to me that we share nothing around here except my personal income. It is your town, Harry, your job, your life, your friends. Every-thing has been what you wanted. Now I want *my* house in *my* name."

She smiled sweetly, then inserted the deepest knife. "We can continue sharing it. Married couples should share, don't you think? All that will change is the deed."

Harry's stricken face touched her and she felt herself close to softening; this was too much for him. Maybe for her.

"You can't force me to change the title," he said.

"No. But I can hire someone who can. Is that what you want? A court case? The publicity should make interesting conversation in the steam room at the Metropolitan Club. Give them something to talk about besides themselves for a change."

"You bitch. You selfish, ungrateful bitch." He spit out the words.

But still she did not let up; the pent-up years of hostility would not let her stop. "Do you remember our honeymoon, Harry? Those two nights you so generously devoted to my pleasure? You told me then you could make me into the perfect woman. You would teach me to be the kind of wife you'd always wanted. Remember? Perfection for perfection?"

He did not move, did not make a sound.

"Well, here I am. Just what you deserve—a bitch perhaps. But ungrateful? No. I am very grateful that you have finally brought out the real me."

Every part of her started to tremble. She had best retreat now, get back into her corner and collect herself.

He followed her out of the room, shouting, and with none of his careful new composure. "Just who the hell have you been talking to? Who's put these goddamned notions in your head?"

He grabbed the sleeve of her robe, forcing her to face him. "Answer me. I want to know who you've gotten this from."

"A friend. The only friend I've ever had. You don't really know her yet but you will. I don't think you'll get along too well."

That she was referring only to herself was lost on Harry.

"She's never to step foot in my house. Do you understand that?" He sounded like a child, a bully. And he was hurting her arm. She shook free.

"*My* house, Harry. *Mine.*"

Lilly ran up the stairs to the bathroom and locked the door, her hands shaking as she turned on the water to cover her sobs. She hadn't really wanted it that way. She did not know what she wanted but she did not want this. Sitting on the edge of the tub she blew her nose on some tissue; the outburst was clearing her head, and she stood and looked defiantly into the vanity mirror. That's how things go, she told herself. A person has to look out for herself. There just isn't any other way. Still, she couldn't stop crying.

Lilly looked up at George, a little embarrassed; there was moisture on her lower lashes and she dabbed at them with her index finger, turning her head away so he wouldn't see.

"That's some story, lady."

"Those were some days."

"Well, we all get hard-nosed at one time or another."

George did not appear convinced. He would not say so, of course, but she knew, she could tell and it bothered her that he might think she had behaved badly toward Harry.

"What else could I have done?"

"I'm not criticizing."

"Then what would you call it?"

"It's not my place to call it anything. I'm just thinking about what you've told me. Just wondering why you don't come right out and admit that you're a survivor. Is there something about surviving you find uncomplimentary? Cruel?"

"Cruel? No. Maybe a little ruthless," she conceded.

"You just can't let up on yourself, can you? You gave Harry what the bastard deserved and you still don't like yourself for it, do you?"

Lilly said nothing.

"Some of us are fighters," George continued. "It's the only way we can find ourselves. Look, perfect you're not, and I'd be lying if I told you I don't feel kind of sorry for Harry after that story."

He held his hand up to quiet her. "Don't worry, my sympathy for him never lasts. But why not? Because of him, you proved you have that ruthless kind of courage, a sixth sense for pulling your fat out of the fire and making things work for you. Hell, don't knock it."

"It's too late to stop, even if I wanted to."

"Trouble with you is that you've also got the habit of fighting. I guess it's what kept you going. But now, because there are no Harrys, no obvious bad guys, you think everything is empty. There comes a time when you don't have to fight. Only, you don't like it that way. Christ, Lil, you put me in mind of a feisty kid who has it all together. Only there's no one trying to take it away from you, so you think that means nothing you have is valuable. You've got your life spread around you for the rest of us poor bastards to see and envy. And there you sit punishing yourself and feeling sorry for yourself. For what? For being tough? For blowing a few lousy chances along the way?"

He opened another bottle of beer. "You're up to where you ought to be, you know? Never mind how you got here. Everything is in order—and you've come by it at high personal expense. I know that. Other people know that. You're the one who won't admit to paying dues on what you've got. Christ, woman, what heavenly pardon or approval do you need to like yourself?"

He looked at her as if for the first time. "Sometimes you give me a big fat pain in the ass," he said.

He stood up, smiling a little to soften the tirade but not enough to make it a retraction. "Right now the pain is more localized. In the vicinity of the bladder, I'd say. Excuse me" —he bowed—"but I'm just an imperfect son of a bitch who's content with surviving long enough to have a good satisfying pee."

"Be sure you wash your hands." She felt she ought to say something.

He walked a few steps back to face her. "Always the smart-mouth, huh? Well, let me tell you something, smart-mouth. Little Jewish boys in South Philly weren't hung up by those fancy rules."

Lilly was startled to see how irritated he was, but the sternness of his face broke with a crooked grin. "We were also taught not to pee on our hands."

Lilly sat motionless as he left the room, cross-legged, still on the floor. She told herself that George was probably right about her; he generally was. Then why was she so defensive around him lately? What was it about him that put her on her guard? She laughed nervously, fluffing her hair with her hands, and then reached for a cigarette. Certainly, there was something strange going on between them and she wondered again if maybe George had heard about Peter. The thought made her shiver and for a small moment she considered the possibility that George might be jealous. It was too bad she didn't have sense enough to love George; it would be so convenient and not at all unpleasant. Yes, goddammit, why didn't she love George and not Peter? Why had it never been George instead of all the others? Because there was no grand passion, that's why, and she knew it, so why bring it up now?

George wasn't exciting. And worse, there was no agonizing punishment in her relationship with him. That is what he had said, wasn't it? She needed to punish herself? Just for a moment Lilly felt she understood something very important, but when she tried to analyze it, it disappeared. She rubbed her hands over her face, feeling strangely threatened but by what she could not think. She poured herself a drink and forced another dry laugh. There really was nobody in the world like George. She was glad of that sometimes.

He came back into the room and lowered his hugeness to the floor. Tactfully, and from long experience with each other, they would not continue their earlier argument. She guessed that he had planned to change the subject, probably had thought it over in the bathroom. This made her grin and he did not miss the expression.

"That the smile that launched the harlot?" Only a laugh labeled the joke.

"Come on. I was never that."

"You fooled a lot of people."

"But never myself. I was a washout as the fallen woman."

"There were a number of scalps, as I recall."

"Washroom gossip."

The subject could still make her stomach churn and Lilly began folding down the lids of the food containers, busy and prim to hide her feelings. The room was so quiet, the sounds of cleaning up seemed excessively loud. Lilly carried the tray of leftover food to the kitchen and was hardly seated again on the couch when George began to speak, using an unusually gruff tone. "The best and worst thing you did was take up with Smithy. God, were you two a mating in hell."

Bitterness in George was strong when it came, and seeing it now reminded her of how well and yet how little they understood each other.

"You hated him, didn't you?" she asked.

There was no need for him to answer.

"Why, George? Why did you despise him? Actually he was a splendid man."

"He was wrong. A meddlesome old fool. When he died, it was the end of those power-crazy columnists who thought they were part of some kind of kitchen cabinet. And thank God! Do you realize the damage to the country that he and his ilk caused?"

"He was a conservative, George. There's still a large constituency for men like Smithy." She looked at him, argumentative. "Weren't you a little jealous? Professionally speaking?"

She was needling him and he knew it. He shrugged off the jab.

"Just a little bit? Weren't you, George?"

"That bastard held more power than any journalist in this town will ever—or should ever—hold again. He had a blind side to him, an arrogance that . . ." His face reddened with remembered anger. "Yes, I hated that chickenshit prig. Hated him for what he didn't do more than for the things he did. He could have been a force for constructive change. For too many years he pulled the kind of punches that clouded the issues. Goddamn right, I hated him. I still do."

"That's not a very tolerant, let alone liberal, attitude," she said.

It was a silly argument; discussing the dead troubled Lilly, no matter who they were. She wanted to drop the subject.

"Oh, hell, George. Give Smithy credit; he could stir the passions. He was never dull."

"No. He was never that. Is that your criterion for a legend? Never to be dull?"

She had always been defensive about Smithy, had not really figured him out until it was too late. But she had cared deeply about him; he was the most complicated person she ever knew. Even his name was a contradiction. *Smithy.* It was what you called a good ole down-home boy, and he was not always good, she knew, and never, ever, was he down-home. George might have been reading her thoughts. "Even the bastard's name was misleading. Just the way he wrote."

"Would you have preferred Nero?"

"He thought he was Jesus Christ."

"From you that sounds a compliment."

"Then scratch the entry. He doesn't deserve the rehash. Not worth it."

That was not true, not in the least. Arthur Smith Stuyvesant. Each name inherited from some historical figure in his ancestry, the tag of Smithy acquired at Harvard years before Lilly was born. He seldom spoke of his lineage, for it had not been necessary; others saw to the legend. If there was anything Smithy knew, it was how to remain aloof and let someone else spread the myth.

The only son of one of the country's most accomplished families, he had never married but his sisters had thoughtfully selected husbands with wealth and power to expand the circle of influence for all of them. For almost half a century, Smithy had capitalized on those connections, making numerous ones of his own, employing them effectively to make his presence and opinions felt. One of America's most revered columnists, that was how his obituaries had read. A man of impeccable taste, acid wit and civilized demeanor.

Well, it was true. All of it was his, Lilly remembered, and he had used it how and when it served his purposes, which, she had to agree, were not always from the most admirable motivations. But he believed what he wrote. Whether anyone else agreed was beside the point and that was what had made Smithy awesome to other journalists. Certainly, it was what Lilly had liked best about him.

In some ways she saw him as precisely what Washington deserved, a power of its own creation. Six Presidents had deferred to him; politicians and officials from every facet of government had sought his counsel, groveled before his by-line if not his wisdom. Even when he was wrong—which he sometimes was, especially toward the end—they had come around for more. As much as anyone in the realm of politics could be, Smithy was durable; like a marble monument, he had survived at the vortex of power where lesser men had not. The regular members of the press feared him even as they lionized him; they made him invincible by their obsequious attention to his every pronouncement, only to turn around and rage at his indestructibility.

Arthur Smith Stuyvesant was not one to be trifled with. Lilly had seen that immediately. Of all the self-aggrandizing and proselytizing buffoons she had encountered in Washington, he had been the only person to penetrate her indifference, to capture her wandering imagination. By the time he and Lilly were friends, he was well over sixty, the undisputed elder statesman of syndicated columnists, complete with an impressive portfolio, a mammoth ego, and a distinct ability to strike concern in the hearts of anyone who opposed him. Oh, when he began his professional decline and got too old, they had turned on him with ridicule and talked of his senility, but when she had first known him, they would not have dared.

If he actually belonged to either political party, he kept his own counsel. He was a conservative, he had told her, not a bigot, but a protector of the status quo based upon a genuine need to curb events that might endanger the quality of life he so strongly believed in.

The most extraordinary thing about him was his timing. Smithy could write a column that was outrageously right-wing, only to turn around and come out heavily for a progressive cause. As no one before him or since, Smithy had been

150

able to move from side to side, being friend or enemy as his conscience dictated. No one ever owned him, and that, as much as anything, caused him to be both hated and revered in a town where dominance was essential; he could not be controlled. Lilly still thought him superior to the contemporary claque of pressmen who allowed themselves to be locked into liberal or reactionary ideals as though it were not in them to think independently. Smithy had known what he was doing at all times—a strength and conviction not often found in the kind of men magnetized by power.

It was his superiority and elegant disdain that had drawn her to him in the first place, for Smithy understood, above all else, that power and politics were really only games and ought to be taken as such. In the handful of years she knew him, the only trite phrase he ever uttered was "And this too shall pass." To Smithy, every person in government had an ax to grind and was not to be trusted.

"Not one of them," he would say as they sat in the press gallery of the House or Senate to look down at the members below scurrying about like red ants on a floating log, "not one among them has the vaguest notion that he is not personally steering the ship of state."

His cynicism was complete. "My child," he would tell her, "to look for the honest politician is as unthinkable as questing the innocent burglar."

It was years before Lilly knew that many of Smithy's wise and witty sayings were directly plagiarized from Mencken or Mark Twain, and when she understood, it had only added to her appreciation of him as the rogue he was.

They had met during those early months when she had begun to behave with her reckless new independence; without him she might possibly have been victimized by the self-destruction she was so intent upon embracing. He had seen it in her, that abandon which urged her to rub Washington's nose in its hypocrisies, to punish people for refusing to accept her. He was the only one who understood that she was hurt and frightened and that she did not realize what she was doing, let alone why she was doing it. Much later he would tell her one of the things that had had a lasting impact on her: "Your instincts, my dear, are keen. They are your most vital weapons. Use them when you feel them. The whys and wherefores will always catch up. You must remember that."

Her pleasure at finding herself seated next to him at dinner one night had been immense. The hostess was brave, she thought; she and Smithy were a pitting rather than a matching, or at least that had most likely been the woman's malicious intent. Well, someone had made a gigantic mistake, for she and Smithy had immediately sensed a kindred spirit in the other.

The table conversation had been turned in such a way that when Lilly first sat down, she and Smithy had only managed to nod, each then forced by social protocol to speak in an opposite direction. When their time to talk together had come, she had not bothered with introductions, nor had Lilly pretended it was necessary; Smithy's reputation preceded him like a marching band. He had faced her comfortably, waiting to be scandalized, and she had not been displeased to see that her own brazen reputation had also been advanced. They had grinned at one another conspiratorially.

"Well, my dear?" This was how he began, his half-glasses perched characteristically on his sizable Anglo-Saxon nose; it was his habit to look over the top of them, narrowing his clear blue eyes menacingly.

Lilly smiled at him, not unaware of a certain dampness in her palms, as he made his famous sound, a throat-clearing noise, something akin to an harrumph, a signal that he was ready to be entertained.

"Play fair," she teased. "I don't need glasses yet and I never acquired the knack of harrumphing."

He did not blink, only glowered again over his spectacles, moving them up for a closer look, lowering them to frown, then to smile. "I shall endeavor to keep my pomposities to a minimum. I will harrumph as seldom as possible. But the glasses I must have in order to see."

"And what is it that you look for?" she asked; his precise use of each word was irresistible and she could not help emulating him, matching his tone with an archness on her part that she had not suspected.

His answer was equally direct. "That is an impertinent question, one I no longer answer. And you? What is it that you look for?"

"That is a question I no longer ask."

He offered her something which was not quite a smile. "Did you ever?" He seemed sincere, cutting into a serving of filet of beef as if to occupy himself only until she responded.

"Maybe. A long time ago."

"And what did you learn?"

"Not much, I'm afraid." It irritated her to sound so young.

"Then"—he smiled, sipping his wine—"it would appear that you have nothing to *unlearn?*"

Lilly had the strange feeling that she had heard herself described in just such words.

"Does innocence make me foolish or wise?" she asked.

"Neither, I suspect. It simply leaves your mind uncluttered with the aspirations of the tiresomely zealous. It is better to learn what you need when you are mature enough to understand it."

"I don't think I'm there yet."

"Your suspicions may be well founded." He made it somehow a compliment.

"Does that shock you?" she asked.

"I am never shocked."

"Bored?" Her anxious tone caught his attention.

"Always, my dear. I am always bored these days. Unless I am alone."

"Then why are you here?" His famous arrogance was annoying.

"Perhaps to frighten."

"Should I be?" she said.

"Are you?"

"No. But I am certainly not bored either."

He bowed, taking some wine, his eyes challenging her. "So now where does that leave us?"

"Nowhere, I guess. But it seems a lonely place to be."

"Ah, but not if you do not care." He was moving his glass of wine back and forth under his nose, savoring its aroma. He looked at her sharply. "Do you care?"

She answered too promptly. "I may have once. I've forgotten; but not now, I don't. I may never."

"Yes," he spoke sternly, "you will care. You will spoil yourself by caring." He began to chuckle. "It's the demise of the deliciously wicked woman," he said. "She learns to care."

"Would that be so bad?" She felt an unaccountable sense of alarm.

"It is the worst possible thing a pretty woman can do." He made it sound terminal.

"Perhaps you can teach me the pitfalls to avoid," she said.

He looked at her quite evenly and harrumphed in spite of his promise, dabbing his white mustache with the large linen cloth from his lap. He looked almost pleased. "My dear young woman, are you trifling with an old man's affections?"

"It's not an actual proposition," she said evenly. "Only it

153

might be nice to sit at your feet and learn how to retain my virginal wickedness."

"That might indeed prove amusing. We shall see."

They did not meet again for several weeks but Lilly thought of him often, a hard subject to avoid, for he was constantly talked about. When his name came up in a conversation, Lilly would rush to defend him; if a story was told in which he was central, she let it be known that she and Smithy Stuyvesant were, well, friends. To make the lie true became an obsession.

Smithy was more than thirty years her senior and it was common knowledge that his interest in women was not great. Because he had never married, there were those inevitable whispered suggestions that he possibly sought the companionship of young boys, but Lilly considered this nothing more than the usual vicious gossip aimed at an indestructibly powerful man. Rather, Lilly thought him simply lacking any kind of sex drive at all; it made him more attractive to her, less a danger. Since their initial meeting, she had had more than one dream of him, dreams of herself curled in his lap as he patted her head and read to her from a large leather book. Even in her sleep she was safe and happy in his approval.

When she saw him next, it was at a large diplomatic reception, he in the center of a small group of military men, their gold braid and ribbons enhancing the impeccableness of Smithy's simple dark suit. She walked straight over to him.

"Are you ready for me yet?" she asked, interrupting his conversation.

"My dear Lilly. How pleasant to see you."

Politely he kissed both her cheeks and included her in the circle of officers, calling her Mrs. Shawcross.

"May I present the Chairman of the Joint Chiefs of Staff." He went around the circle with the proper niceties. The military bored Lilly and she was irritated by the way they were nodding, eager to dismiss the introduction and resume their talk.

Smithy explained. "We have been discussing military intelligence, my dear."

"I didn't know there was any," she said.

"Now, Lilly." He smiled. "Where would we be without our mighty army."

"Where our mighty army would be without your support. At peace."

Only Smithy laughed, pleased by her understanding of the extent of his power.

"And what would you have our soldiers do?" he continued, enjoying himself.

"Parade," she said. "I love parades."

She addressed one of the generals. "You all are so good at marching around," she said, "and it's much tidier than killing."

"Now then." Smithy harrumphed; she had known he would. "Does that mean you are already starting to care?"

Lilly smiled, happy that he remembered their first conversation.

"About the Vietnam war? Yes, I guess maybe I do. You had better take charge of me before it becomes a habit."

"I think perhaps I should." He took her arm. "Gentlemen, kindly excuse us. As you can see, the lady needs civilian briefing."

They walked to the fireplace, both of them tall enough to comfortably prop an elbow on the mantel. He spoke without harshness. "That was dreadful."

"You couldn't have done better yourself," she said.

"I admire arrogance, however misplaced."

"I'm waiting for you to place it."

"Are we back to that?"

"I never left."

"And what will you give me in return?"

"Blind devotion."

"Do you think I need that?"

"As much as I need to give it."

"You are either outrageously flattering or extremely insightful."

"Or caring?" She brought the subject back to where she wanted it.

"Never that, my dear. Never, never that."

But he was amused by her, she could tell. From a nearby group, Smithy summoned Harry; he came immediately.

"My dear young man, I should like to borrow your wife."

"She's yours." Harry was pleased; he beamed at Lilly.

"You are too generous," Smithy said, dismissing him curtly and turning to Lilly to ask if she had a wrap; she shook her head.

Bowing again toward Harry, Smithy steered her through the watchful crowd and toward the door. Lilly had been to too many movies not to recognize a dramatic exit when she saw one.

By limousine they went to his exquisite house in George-town, sitting outside in old wicker rockers under the grape arbor to drink tequila from hand-blown glasses; he showed her how to lick the salt from the palm of her hand and then to suck on half of a lime. He spoke of many things that night, things new and fascinating to Lilly, and with the tedious exception of a rather protracted dissertation on the sacking of Carthage, she found his company hypnotizing as he rambled amiably from Chinese cuisine to eighteenth-century literature and then, quite unexpectedly, waded into an issue of current significance. She had become almost comfortable in his presence when, abruptly, as he would do most things, he stood up to say good-night. Lilly felt a keen disappointment, rather as if he were a disapproving parent already tired by her.

He took her hands. "I am an old man who has been charmed by an extraordinary young woman."

She would learn that he seldom spoke of himself as old unless he was drunk, bested, bored or extremely fatigued.

"Tomorrow I am to lunch with the Russian ambassador. Would you care to join us?"

So relieved that he wanted to see her again, Lilly began to chatter foolishly. "Shame on you," she responded. "You write about how the rest of the world is meant to be terrified of the godless Communists and now I see you break bread with them."

"Ah, my dear. Not bread. Caviar. I should happily sell my soul for it and be the better for the exchange. But you must understand that the ambassador is a man of great charm and wit. In addition to the splendors of his table, he is a most perceptive and highly educated gentleman. We have the perfect friendship, the kind of respectful alliance that seems, unhappily, only to result in the matching of sharply disparate ideas."

He was leading her to the side gate which opened onto the street.

"Tomorrow, then?"

She nodded her head, trying to subdue her enthusiasm.

"Do you like caviar?" he asked.

Lilly shrugged.

"You will learn. It is one of the things about which I shall encourage you to care."

He helped her into the waiting car, barked instructions to his driver and then disappeared into the house. No, his museum, Lilly thought, a museum of books and paintings and sculptures, all wonderful and awesome mementos collected over a lifetime spent in foreign worlds; the house was the perfect shrine for him.

In the rear of the car Lilly sank into the plush upholstery and watched the darkened streets of Georgetown glide by; for once, she was actually looking forward to going home to Harry. He would be waiting for her, she knew, pleased and anxious to hear about the evening. Unconsciously she made a *tsk*ing sound with her mouth; the bastard would have sent her off with Fidel Castro if there'd been something in it for him. It occurred to Lilly that she most likely would have gone.

# 13

WITH Arthur Smith Stuyvesant as her great friend, she could do no wrong, or at least no wrong that anyone dared point out in her presence. It was a strong taste of refracted power, Lilly's first, and she liked it. Harry was especially impressed; he saw the new liaison as useful and it was. Through Smithy, Harry was bringing into his company a sizable number of new accounts. Often now he might be away for long periods of time, putting together commercial documentaries for various foreign governments or for private foundations, which, when persuaded by Smithy, had suddenly decided it good public relations to acquaint television audiences with a highly romanticized view of the organizations. Once Harry remained in South America for several months to package a series of spots that extolled the benefits of offshore oil drilling. Such propaganda was highly remunerative, and while Lilly privately dismissed Harry as a prostitute huckster, he was at least out of her way. When someone inquired as to his whereabouts, she would reply glibly, saying that he was off in some banana republic probably counting his money.

Harry was away the evening of one of Smithy's late dinners, the kind he liked to give on the terrace on those early September nights when the weather, like most everything else, would conform to his wishes.

Smithy's parties were for the people he most enjoyed—important people, but generally the group was interspersed with a few new faces along with the usual assortment of lesser luminaries, for Smithy understood that the powerful enjoyed themselves best when they were surrounded by appreciative listeners.

At her particular table there were three influential politicians, a scattering of wives and at least one young man on the rise to balance off the man who had accomplished very little and probably never would. Her heart went out to the latter; his pride at being included was so obvious; yet he had no idea that his willingness to please was indispensable to the success of a Washington evening.

Lilly had to her left an aging Midwestern congressman, one whose seniority placed him on an important House committee that allocated funds for military spending. Spoiled by being courted and pandered to by special-interest groups, he was an unbearably demanding and arrogant man; Lilly decided to ignore him and turned, instead, to the young man on her left. Smithy had spoken of him earlier. "He's bright, although something of an upstart. The town is spilling with them since Kennedy took office. Ambitious and filled with altruistic ideas about social equality. But he's shrewd and I suppose he will become a trifle less radical the moment he acquires some power of his own." Smithy had sighed at the inevitability of his pronouncement. "His name is Kevin Day, from some dreary little place in Ohio. I should guess that he will make a name for himself at the Justice Department and then run for public office. That seems to be the pattern."

What surprised Lilly about Kevin Day was his openness, a directness not rampant in political types of any age; she figured him to be in his early thirties, and while she did not find him handsome in the conventional way, his face was so undevious as to be attractive. "Honest" was the word that came to mind; she'd almost forgotten what unspoiled people were like. He was also indifferent to his surroundings; as if he preferred to be elsewhere, occupied by other matters. She sensed he might be difficult to shock.

"How are things in the Justice Department? Is Little Brother watching?"

He ignored her reference to the President's younger brother and sat comfortably silent.

From a need to be congenial more than from any real interest, Lilly urged him to talk of his childhood and it proved an inspired topic, for he immediately began to tell her of his boyish preoccupation with World War II and how he had led his class in the collection of old newspapers and tin cans; of his father, the neighborhood air-raid warden, of his adolescent suspicions that the German cleaning woman had been a Nazi agent. He even described the war trophies sent him by some cousins: grenades, a swastika flag, several helmets. He thought they were probably still somewhere back home in the family attic.

He spoke very fast, talking as he devoured a plate of small scallops with no idea of what he was eating.

"Wars are better as memories than as current events, you know?" he said.

"You'd best not let Smithy hear that," she cautioned. "He's behind this one in Vietnam enormously. Sees it as his own fight."

"Yes," he agreed, gulping white wine and grimacing at the taste. "And rightly so."

"Oh?" She sat closer to the edge of her chair; Lilly recognized blasphemy when she heard it.

"Sure. Even in Cleveland, Stuyvesant's fiery warnings to halt the Red incursion have been felt."

"Are you insinuating that we should not be helping out in Southeast Asia?" She was baiting him but he didn't seem bothered by it.

"We've got less business there than we did in Cuba," he said.

"You're in the wrong administration and at the wrong dinner table if you believe that."

"I know."

Lilly was intrigued. "Then why are you here tonight?"

"My wife, over there at the other table, wanted to see how it goes."

"And how does it?"

"Food's great." His smile rearranged his serious features. "And you're not half bad yourself. Nothing like your reputation."

"What were you expecting?"

"Well, I doubt I'll get invited here again and I'd sort of hoped you'd make it an event for me. Something I could spellbind them with back home." He was teasing her and she liked it.

"What should I do?"

"You could jump out of a cake." He thought a moment, then added, "Hit somebody in the face with a custard pie. Whatever's your specialty these days."

"Would it help if I danced with a lampshade on my head?"

"Then I couldn't see your face."

"Would you mind?"

"Probably as much as you." He was besting her at her own routine.

"Truce!" She laughed, trying but failing to outlast his stare. "We'll talk about whatever interests you. Name your subject."

"Tell me about yourself," he said.

"All right. Ask me the most personal and intimate thing you can imagine."

"I want you to tell me"—he leaned closer and drew his arm about her conspiratorially as he spoke—"just which old war movie was your favorite."

He was meaning to taunt her now, however lightly, and he could have no idea that the reverse was true. Lilly was delighted with the subject and began to parade a treasured assortment of memories from childhood matinées. He interrupted only to quiz her about obscure stars or some outlandish plots.

"You know how I knew they were having sex in those old movies?" he asked.

"How?"

"Well, remember *From Here to Eternity?* Burt Lancaster and Deborah Kerr are lying on the beach one night in bathing suits. Right?"

"Yes." She was agreeing animatedly, bobbing her head.

"O.K. Now, what was the close of the scene? The clue that let you know they had gone all the way."

She giggled at the adolescent expression, then answered quickly, "The clouds passed over the moon."

"Exactly! And what made you think they liked it?"

"The sea! The pounding of the waves. And afterward the tide went out so peacefully."

They were laughing now, each totally absorbed in the other.

"You know," he said, "I never saw the ocean till I was twenty and went out West. I took a girl to the beach and tried to reenact the whole Burt Lancaster deal. Know what happened?"

"You got sand in your—"

"Precisely," he broke in.

Kevin began talking about foreign pictures, and he spoke with reverence. Lilly never cared much for European movies, but she was rather impressed with his understanding of the symbolism of Fellini, Truffaut, Buñuel, even Bergman.

"You learned all that in Cleveland!"

"We're not as unlettered as you think."

He continued on the subject throughout dinner, wolfing his food and talking between mouthfuls; Lilly pushed her plate aside and sat there, her arms folded on the table, encouraging him at every pause, and was surprised when the chairs around them scraped against the brick terrace; the other guests had finished and were getting up from the table. The time had gone so quickly. He stood to help her up and she took his hand, tugging at him to sit back down.

"You can't just leave me hanging this way," she said. "You have a moral responsibility to finish my cinematic education. Without the subtleties."

"What is it you want me to do?" His tone cut straight through her nonsense.

"Not to walk away."

"You mean right now?"

"Not exactly."

"Then suppose you tell me what you have in mind."

"I don't know."

"And I don't, either. That can make for trouble." His eyes were very serious.

"Are you afraid?" she asked.

"As a matter of fact, I am."

"Me, too."

For a moment she felt her old vulnerable self and it startled her. The others were moving now to the far end of the garden and Kevin began to carefully refold his napkin as if he might use it another time.

"I'm just a country boy, ma'am. I don't know about any of this." He waved his arm to include the entire party. Then he stood again, pulling her up with him this time until she was close to him, facing him, both of them awkward. Lilly's desire for him to touch her made her shiver. He placed his hands on her bare shoulders, causing her to shake all the harder, but they were smiling at each other, just standing there and smiling; they might easily have stepped straight out of one of the old movies they'd just been discussing. She shuddered again and laughed at the same time, wrapping her arms around her waist but not moving away from him. The novelty of physical arousal was unnerving, but she sensed that whatever she was feeling, he was feeling also. The noise of clearing her throat was audible.

"Will you call me?" she asked.

It seemed a plea and he looked at her very hard.

"I am going to try my darndest not to." Then he turned and started off in the direction of the other guests. Lilly waited a few moments before following, watching him as he walked away. His trousers were much too short and she decided it was one of the things about him she liked best.

Kevin's control had been impressive. For five days he did not call. Lilly spent the time lying in bed, not actually sleeping, just lying about and willing the telephone to ring. Whenever it did she forced herself to let it sound several times before answering, her mood ranging from expectant exhilaration to disappointment and annoyance when the caller was not Kevin. Several times each day Lilly picked up the receiver to call him, only to change her mind; he was not playing a game, she knew. He did not want to become involved with her, but if he called—no, *when* he called—it would mean a commitment to whatever was between them. That was how she wanted it.

When he finally phoned, she was ready.

"Saw your picture in the paper this morning." It was all he said.

"Was it the smile that got you?"

"The proper spelling of the name, actually."

She saw that he was to be in charge. "Did you add it to your Christmas list?"

"Sort of," he said, "but December's a long way off."

"I was thinking the same thing." Her heart was pounding.

"Do you have any special feeling for Halloween?" he asked.

"Still too far off."

"We could celebrate early. You got a mask or a mustache?"

It was settled and she was relieved; the giddiness crept into her voice. "How about dark glasses?" she said.

"Terrific. Get into costume and meet me at the Jefferson Memorial." He paused, thinking, then: "Park in the area next to the Tidal Basin. I'll meet you there."

Lilly was caught up in the intrigue. "How will I recognize you?"

"There'll be a white carnation on the dented left fender of an aging black Pontiac. Ohio tags. Twelve-thirty?"

"Are we tricking or treating?"

"We'll decide later. O.K.?"

"Positively."


He was there when she arrived and got immediately into the front seat with her before she turned off the motor.

"Just do as you're told, lady, and you won't get hurt."

He put a brown paper bag in the back.

"And if I don't?"

"I still won't hurt you. Now, drive out on the parkway and over the Fourteenth Street Bridge. I'll tell you where to stop."

She steered the car toward Virginia, crossing the river. He directed her to a highway motel.

163

Lilly was nervous; for a country boy, he was pretty fast with liaisons.

"I had thought we would exchange astrological signs first," she said.

"Too many movies, lady. Pull over there."

He pointed to the parking lot adjacent to the motel's restaurant. She parked the car and switched off the engine, drying her damp hands on her skirt. Kevin grinned, pleased by her obvious unease, and reached around in the back seat for the paper bag. "I thought I'd feed something other than your vanity. We have ham with mustard and turkey with mayonnaise." He held the sandwiches up for her to choose.

"The mayonnaise, please."

There were two Cokes in paper cups; he removed the lids.

"Wherever did you go to find crushed ice?" She asked this for no particular reason except that she was relieved that they were only to have lunch.

Kevin held his cup between his teeth and pushed with the toe of one shoe at the heel of the other, repeating the action until he was in his stocking feet. He tore open a large bag of potato chips, then handed out straws, napkins, a salt and pepper shaker.

"You've thought of everything, I see."

He smiled and removed a handful of toothpicks from his breast pocket, throwing them onto the dashboard.

"Not everything," he said.

They met that way for a week, each time at a different monument. Always he brought lunch and suggested the new place to picnic; once it was the public lot of the Pentagon and she mentioned his peculiar choice.

"Those bastards!" he said, thumbing over his shoulder at the massive military complex. "It's about time they accommodated us civilians!"

From where they were parked it was possible to see the boats of a small marina. The days were still warm, the trees only beginning to turn. They talked of anything, of the leaves, of the Washington skyline and how it would be different when winter came. They spoke, in fact, of everything except the reason they were together, exploring each other conversationally, careful not to touch. Always Lilly dreaded to see him put his feet back into his shoes, for it meant their time was over, and still they discussed nothing personal, as if each was aware of the immediate pleasure between them and, by some unspoken agreement, they were not to use it up too quickly.

Kevin was tying his shoelaces as she started the engine, thinking as she backed out of the lot that this might be more pain and pleasure than she could bear.

"We're running out of historic campsites," she said.

"We could create a new one."

She did not know what to say and, instead, became very quiet, concentrating unduly on the traffic; she had had no precedent for such excitement. Too quickly they were back at his car. He got out and leaned in through the window, handing her an envelope, and, with a sharp salute, he quickly took the few steps to his old car, got into it and drove away.

She read the note: *Only if you want to. Noon tomorrow. The weatherman says rain, anyhow.*

With the note was a key. Room 714, MAYFLOWER HOTEL. Lilly had no recollection of the drive home.

Time never passed so slowly. Lilly was fully aware of the implication of the key; it would alter her life and she was uncertain that she could handle it. Once again, events were slipping out of her hands and she was disturbed by this new powerlessness. Her life was not unbearable the way it was, so why should she rock the boat? So why not? Inner arguments were useless, she knew she would go, she had to. She would go and she would laugh and tell Kevin how she had watched the clock, like Gary Cooper in *High Noon*, and he would understand. That was what made it all right, the knowing that he'd understand. Headlong into trouble, both of them. She guessed he knew that, too.

It was raining, just as predicted, and Lilly held an old yellow slicker over her head as she dashed from the parking garage, crossing the street and ducking into the side entrance to the Mayflower. On the back elevator, she shook herself off, slightly uncomfortable that the elevator operator suspected what she was up to as she got out and wandered the corridor of the seventh floor to find the right room, only to stand before it, trying to summon the courage to use the key, finally pushing it into the lock; it would not turn. Panicked, she stepped back to recheck the numbers. Kevin opened the door himself.

"Hi!" He glanced cautiously up and down the hall and drew her inside.

They did not look directly at each other while Lilly removed her damp coat and pretended not to notice the twin beds which dominated the room. She stood there rubbing her hands together, her teeth slightly chattering, feeling the perfect fool and clutching at her raincoat, ready to leave. Kevin was leaning against the door, smiling at her.

"You're answering my question," he said. "I wasn't sure this wasn't an old routine for you."

She disliked him for that and made it apparent by her expression.

"Come on, Lilly. You must have known I was wondering."

Suddenly he was a stranger she needed to get away from and she had yet to even say a single word.

Kevin took her coat and held it for her to put back on. "The note said only if you want to."

Lilly stood rigidly as he draped the coat over her shoulders and then turned around to look up at him—like a girl. Did she want this? Did he? Kevin only smiled the crooked smile that made a deep comma around one side of his mouth.

"Do you, Kevin?"

"I'm here." His mouth twitched.

She saw that it was not so easy for him, either; it made her feel better.

"But you still have your shoes on," she said.

They laughed together for a moment, both of them staring down at his worn loafers.

"See"—he was pointing to a room service table by the window—"club sandwiches, but no crushed ice . . ."

There were several Cokes, unopened, next to a wax cooler with a bottle of champagne.

"I brought my guitar."

He was like a boy himself, his sandy hair still flattened from the rain.

"We aren't very good at this, are we?" she asked.

"I'm glad."

Lilly could only nod, but the awkwardness was passing; somehow they would be all right. She smiled then, leaning her head to one side.

"Can you play with your shoes on?"

They turned toward the guitar.

"I'm pretty bad, either way." He picked up the instrument. "Think you can stand it?" he said.

"Only with my shoes off."

They laughed more easily this time and Lilly stepped out of her soggy boots.

Kevin tried some chords, stopping several times to tighten the strings while Lilly sat down on the edge of a chair, still ignoring the bed, listening as he played a song she could not place; unable to stay put, she got up and went to pour some of the opened champagne into two tumblers; she handed one to him, and drank hers down quickly. She didn't much like champagne but she could feel it relax her tense muscles.

Kevin took her glass and refilled it, kicking off his shoes as he poured, and Lilly thought they might have been back in the Pentagon parking lot now; the comfortableness was there once more. He picked up the guitar again, holding it in one hand while he pulled the pillows and blankets from one of the beds with the other, nesting them on the floor beneath the window. It was raining hard outside. Kevin sat down and propped himself against the wall, cushioning his back with several pillows; he patted the blanket for her to join him.

He ate his sandwich first and then licked his fingers, wiping them on his pants leg before handling the guitar. Lilly was feeling suddenly drowsy from the third glass of wine and put her head in his lap. He leaned down gently to kiss each of her closed eyes, then touched her face with his hand; she reached for the hand, her lips lightly moving over his fingers. Then he took both her hands and kissed them. Her eyes were open now, looking straight into his as he slowly bent forward to brush his mouth over hers, touching her arms and shoulders slowly, not taking his eyes from hers as he did.

Later she tried to remember everything, her feelings, her thoughts, but they were not to be recaptured; she could only recall the swell of sound in her ears and the jumping of her heart. She had always willed love-making to be quickly over, rushed to be quit of it, but the afternoon had slipped past faster than she was able to impress it on her memory.

She did remember that he had held her afterward, his face pressed into her neck, and that she had stroked his head, knowing a peculiar satisfaction that was unrelated to sex. She had not told him that he had not taken her along to whatever pleasurable heights he had gone. No, she cared about him too much to disappoint him in any way. It had been enough to feel as she did, gentle, protected, loved. Actually, it had been more happiness than she had ever hoped to find.

Because of Harry and because of Kevin's own wife and children, they never saw each other at night but met always in the early afternoon, sometimes in funny little cafés or bars, out-of-the-way places where they were unlikely to be seen. Kevin would call in the morning to tell her the time and the location and she would be waiting for him when he came in, late and disheveled; she could sense his approach even before she saw him.

Generally she chose a back corner, a booth or a table, it didn't matter; she would be pleased and secure to tell the waitress that, yes, there would be two for lunch. Kevin would come past the counter or the bar where men in overalls and lumber jackets were passing their lunch hour; he might nod to them as if they were old friends, as in some way they were, those working-class people with whom he had such kinship. Kevin's gregariousness was contagious and everyone was Lilly's friend when she was with him. Time was the only enemy; it went so quickly.

When he sat down next to her or across from her, her heart would leap to her throat; their fingertips would touch gently and they would place food orders, absently, just to satisfy the waitress; they had not come to eat. Kevin was full of ideas and information—things she came to take for her own; his thoughts were so right and just that she frequently wondered why she had not arrived at them independently. She listened attentively and with concern as he told her what was going on in the Justice Department; he could even make her laugh at the antics of people she did not know. She asked questions which Kevin was painstaking in answering, explaining carefully and at length the significance of the day's events, impressing upon her the necessity of understanding what was going on in the world. Between them there was never an unused minute.

"I think," he would say in mock seriousness, "that you might perhaps be the most magnificent specimen I've ever seen."

"Specimen of what?" She could never resist.

"Of American Womanhood. Sex and apple pie. The whole silo, honey."

Her smile would be so broad it hurt her cheeks. "That's because you're a hick with no frame of reference."

"Who needs a frame of reference for apple pie?" he'd ask.

"You have a knack for keeping me humble, I'll say that much for you."

"A full-time job. Were I independently wealthy, I'd dedicate myself to the task. Service to the country."

Later on he would glance at his watch and she would know that familiar stab of sadness. There was so little time with him and she had so much of it when she was alone, so much time and nothing to do. It was painful for these few hours to be so important to her, and it sometimes annoyed her that their moments together were not the most special parts of his day, the way they were for her.

"I heard from the county chairman this morning," he said one afternoon, watching closely for her reaction. "It's sounding good. In fact, he told me that things are really beginning to shape up. It seems a barefoot boy opposed to war and deprivation is not the terrible scourge he once was. He thinks I'm ready to run in the next election. At least he says it's worth a try."

For months she had been dreading to hear those words. It was a struggle to keep the panic from her face. "Where does your truth and honor leave my sex and apple pie?"

Kevin's strong wish to return to Ohio and run for Congress was her only rival and it brought out a strange jealousy, one based on more complicated things than just the fear of losing him. Lilly not only wanted Kevin, she wanted also to compete, not with him, but for something that was as essential to her as his ambitions were to him.

She steeled herself for his reply.

"Funny things are happening," he said. "Funny *good* things. The country's rushing headlong into something, Lilly. I can't put my finger on it but I think it's healthy. I want to be on deck when the changes come."

"What about me? Will there be some time for me?" Coyness did not become her, but Lilly wanted to hear that everything was going to be all right, needed to hear it often.

"Always, baby. Always time for you."

Lilly could not bring herself to think otherwise.

On special days they met in the apartment of one of Kevin's single friends from the office, a large studio room in an old building over near the Capitol. He had been very pleased with himself for making the arrangements.

"All I have to do is endure some sly jabs in the ribs whenever one of the girls from the secretarial pool walks by. And a lot of highly unsubtle winks. But for these trivial humiliations, we have a place to be alone."

Still, Lilly persisted in clouding her happiness; it was the kind of happiness that made her worry all the time about him, his health, his eating habits, did he drive carefully? was he dressed warmly? Concern for his safety became obsessive and she was demanding more and more of his time, clutching at every second as if to hang on forever. She wondered why love wasn't simple and easy and honest. Why must she risk her whole life for it in order to believe it was real? All her fantasies of Kevin now included marriage, and she was miserable if she missed seeing him for even one day. It was this greediness that she argued endlessly with herself, telling herself that for the first time in her life she had what she really wanted, so why couldn't she leave well enough alone? Why did she have to nag, to chew her lower lip, to push and press all the time?

"I never wanted anything before you, Kevin. Not really. Nothing in my whole life. Only you."

"I'm right here. I'm not going anywhere."

They were lying together in bed. After making love she became her most querulous self; her happiness seemed so especially fragile then, so frighteningly temporary, and she tried to explain her fear of losing him by talking about Clara, even about her father—a story of estrangement hard for Kevin to understand, for he was so close to his own father.

"Aren't you curious about him after all these years?"

Kevin was propped on his elbow facing her, giving her no choice but to look at him.

"How do you know he's still alive?" he asked. There was some disgust in the question.

"Only the good go early," she said bitterly. "Besides, he signs my checks." It sounded cold; she could hear it. "I don't know him, Kevin. I never did. It's too late now."

"You might like him."

"After what he did to my mother?"

"What makes you so sure he did anything to her? Did she say so?"

"Clara never spoke of him at all. It was as if he never existed." She was uncomfortable with her own harshness. "I mean—oh, hell—maybe he didn't do anything to her in any real sense, but he didn't do anything for her, either. Or for me."

Lilly wore a nasty expression; she was not liking the cavalier way in which Kevin was interpreting her story. He stared at her evenly. "I guess I don't know everything."

He lay back against the pillow dismissing the subject but she could not help feeling a need to further justify herself. She sat up and lit a cigarette. He disliked her to smoke and moved slightly closer to his side of the bed.

"Look"—she was unexpectedly angry now, blowing the smoke out hard as she talked—"all I can tell you is that my mother was in a kind of prison. He held her there and I had to stay, too. He didn't want her but he wouldn't let go. Me?

I was easy to turn loose. He couldn't get rid of me fast enough. Those checks buy me off every month."

Kevin was angry too; he hated her to be narrow-minded. She didn't like herself this way, either. At the moment, she didn't much like Kevin.

"Lilly, has it ever occurred to you that your mother wanted to be imprisoned, that it was easier to be the captive than to be responsible for her own life? It sounds to me like you and your mother never gave the old boy a chance."

Lilly's hands trembled as she lit another cigarette from the stub of the one she was smoking. This was certainly not the reassurance she had expected when she introduced the subject of her parents. She should have known better!

"O.K.," he went on, "so your mother was biologically rooted in duty. Her need for freedom was at some kind of cross purposes with her responsibility to you. Is that your father's fault? Is it any man's fault? Were there bars on the doors?"

She did not like his pompous logic. When the chips are down, she thought, men always stick together.

"My father killed my mother, Kevin Day, and you are one hundred percent right: you don't know everything." Her voice was pitched quite high, filled with resentment.

"Be fair, Lil. Couldn't it just be that he was trapped, too? I mean, maybe he was the victim. Maybe he thought you all didn't want him."

"I told you, my mother drank herself to death to get away from him." Her teeth hurt, they were so tightly clenched.

"So your father caused your mother to die and you feel guilty because you did nothing to stop it. You despise him, but what about her? Plenty of women lead lives worse than that but they don't methodically, day by day, destroy themselves and everyone around them."

He was trying to turn her around to face him but she pulled away angrily.

"Lil. Listen to me. Just be sure who you blame and for what. I think you're carrying around an unnecessary burden, a kind of desperate hatred because your mother bound you to her and she was bound to a man who wasn't able to feel or to articulate an affection for either of you. They both sound like pitiful souls to me. But, honey, everyone makes terrible mistakes sometime in their lives. At some point, we're all cowards. It's human nature. It appears to me that anything short of perfection is your natural object of hatred. Suppose you find that Lilly Shawcross is not perfect, either." He pulled

171

at her arm, hurting her. "Look at yourself, Lilly, that's all I'm asking. Hating other people is a waste. Why spend yourself railing at them?"

Lilly scrambled from the bed, grabbing up her clothes awkwardly, fury narrowing her eyes and squeezing out the tears. She had begged for emotional confirmation, not a lecture in filial tolerance.

"You goddamned manure-heeled know-it-all. You stroll out of the cornfed bosom of a happy family that thinks you walk on water and have the audacity to tell me to check out my hate objects. I should have known better than to trust you. You're just like Harry. I'm wrong every time. That's what you think, isn't it. Isn't it?" She was screaming now, her body quivering with cold and emotion. "I hate you, too, Kevin Day. I hate all of you."

She sank to the floor in sobs, wracking sobs she was helpless to control. Kevin came and knelt beside her, gently stroking her shoulder and lifting her head to wipe at her tears with a corner of the bed sheet.

"Look at me, now." He held her chin so that she had no choice. "You are too fine and special to act like this. Hate is for the unjust things. For war and bigotry and disease and hunger."

He forced her chin higher. "It's not an emotion to be turned on ignorant and troubled people who didn't know any better than to hurt and disappoint you. If you give in to that, Lilly, then they beat you. They take you with them, don't you see? You turn into a spiteful destructive person who's no better than they were. Look, baby, blaming somebody else is admitting you don't trust you." He was holding her very tightly. "We're all weak, honey, all of us in our own way. You're the one in charge of Lilly Shawcross, not Clara, or your father, or Harry. Or me."

He was rocking her now as if she were a small and valuable child, his words coming out in hoarse whispers. "You can rise above us all, baby. There are splendid things in you, things that I love very much."

Her face was against his bare chest, her words muffled. "I don't know anything without you, Kevin. Except that I love you so much, I'd die without you."

"And aren't I right here? Listen, one of these days, you'll see that you have so much strength and courage. It comes from inside you. Not from anybody else."

She grabbed at him harder, wrapping herself around him. "Promise you'll never leave me?"

"I promise."

"You mean that? Really?"

"Yes, Lilly. I really mean it."

For the first time, she knew that he did.

"But what about Congress? And your wife?"

"I'll work something out. Just hush now. I'll work something out."

She decided that afternoon to drive home along Constitution Avenue, turning on the radio as she maneuvered in and around the unusually slow and congested traffic. She pushed another button on the radio, looking for a music station.

"Shot . . . President Kennedy . . . Parkland Memorial Hospital . . . shot . . . Dallas Book Repository . . . shot. The President of the United States is dead . . ."

Lilly switched from station to station, horrified as the same glob of words pounded at her stomach like fast fists until she could not breathe. She twisted the dial with her hand; it had to be a joke, a crude sick joke, but all around her, she saw cars stopping in the street, pulling off to the side. They must know. My God, it must be true. Jack Kennedy is dead. Oh, my God, my God, he's really dead. It's not possible. This can't be happening. *Kevin!* Yes, Kevin. She had to go back to Kevin. All of this would stop if only she could get to Kevin.

# 14

IT surprised Lilly that she could still cry over something that happened so long ago. She leaned toward George as she spoke. "Can you believe it's been almost ten years since Jack Kennedy was shot?" Lilly checked her wristwatch, as if the time of day had anything to do with the past.

George did not answer immediately; when he did it sounded vague. "I'm always amazed to look around and find the years have slipped by so fast."

George did not like to discuss the assassination. There was a part of him that continued to resent the way Kennedy had let his aides be instrumental in having George recalled from Vietnam back in the early days of the war when the Sabberstein by-line was among the first to register journalistic dissent about the fighting in Southeast Asia. George had come home from Saigon with a Pulitzer but he had also brought with him a continuing disillusionment with power and its inevitable abuse by those who hold it. Still, he had admired the dead President, though with considerable reservation; Lilly knew that he would find some way to ease around the unpleasant subject.

"How have we arrived at Dallas?" he asked.

"Oh, I was just remembering where I was that day."

"Everyone's precise whereabouts that afternoon is still a national parlor game, isn't it? Every person has a detailed account."

Perhaps George was thinking of where he had been but she knew he would not elaborate. Instead, he asked, almost too politely, where she was that day. It was Lilly's memories they were exploring, he said. George's mind was orderly that way.

"I was with Kevin Day."

"Him, too?"

"Him first."

Kevin had been so important in Lilly's life that she assumed their liaison was common knowledge. George often said that thinking what affected her affected the universe was among Lilly's grandest vanities. Sho would examine that particular arrogance later. For the moment it pleased her that she could speak of Kevin with such detachment.

"Yes," she said, "Kevin was the one to lead me down the primrose path." That was not fair. He had also steered her onto new and higher ground. "Kevin tried to make me think, George. He did a pretty good job of it, too. I wonder where I'd be now if things had been different."

"How different?"

"Well, we never got around to working it out but we had it in our heads that we would stay together always."

Even now her naïveté was embarrassing.

"Kevin Day was a man on the rise, Lil. Those types travel light."

"I don't think we knew that then."

"What happened?"

She wasn't sure George actually cared to hear, but she told him about Kevin anyway, briefly and dispassionately outlining what she remembered, especially the afternoon that Kennedy was shot.

"The tragedy triggered something in Kevin that would have come about sooner or later," she said.

"How so?"

"Oh, he was too practiced at modesty to admit it, even to himself, but he wanted to save the world. Even then. It was ingrained in him. I think I sensed it all along."

She was leaning forward now, putting her forehead between her knees, more tired than she realized; thinking was hard work. She lifted her head and looked back at George. "For three days after Dallas, Kevin disappeared. Vanished. I was frantic. I guess it scared me to see how much I needed him. I was always casting outside myself for help in those days too. Anyhow, I was desperate to find him. No one in the Justice Department had any idea where he was. I even took a chance and called his home. Not there. He was just gone, his wife said. Hell, maybe he was avoiding me, I don't know. But for three long and horrible days I remember that the only things that existed for me were the television and the telephone. I couldn't believe what was happening. Especially why Kevin didn't realize how much I needed him."

She was leaning back on the couch again, the recalled frustrations too real. "When I did hear from him, he was deathly calm. He phoned after the funeral. All he said was that I should meet him in the airport bar."

"And?"

"And I did. He was sitting on a stool, kind of over to the side. The place was jammed and noisy. I remember thinking that this is what public places must have been like during the war. Except there was no whiskey. The old Virginia law, remember? Beer. Everyone was sitting with beer bottles in front of them. Kevin, too."

She paused to get it all straight. "It had turned cold. Funny, I can almost feel the cold. Kevin had no overcoat and it was my first thought when I saw him. He barely looked up when I came over to him. George, it was like he had this speech prepared and if he didn't get straight to it, he'd change his mind or something. I must have understood because I just stood there, waiting. I couldn't think of anything to say anyhow.

"Christ! I just stood there staring at him while he stared at a round cardboard coaster, outlining the Pabst label with his pen, making doodles on the edges. Finally he said that he was going home."

Lilly closed her eyes, seeing the day clearly.

"Why, Kevin?" she had asked.

"Because I have to get started."

"Please. Please don't go away like this—not now." She had put her hand against him and he drew back.

He wouldn't even look at her. "It won't work any other way."

"But what about me?" She had hardly been able to keep from screaming. "What about us? You promised." Then the tears. "Kevin, answer me."

She had shaken him until it suddenly dawned on her that they were in the airport because he was leaving, right then, that very day. And soon. She had started to pull at him with both hands and he turned to her with those tortured eyes. "Because, baby."

Those eyes had made her look down. He was talking then, very fast. "Can't you see that if I don't go now, I'll never forgive myself? That it will eat at me until there's nothing left? Nothing you or I would want."

"I'll always want you."

But he couldn't see that. "You say so now. Maybe you would. I don't think so."

176

He had swiveled his barstool around until they were very close and she had moved to him, her body sagging against his. He had not pushed her back, only ruffled her hair and let her put her head on his shoulder.

"Listen to me hard. You are going to be all right, Lilly. A real person, the kind of woman who would never be able to love a man who didn't try to do the things he had to do. You don't see it now, but you need a man whose strength will someday match your own. You remember what you told me about Clara, about your father, how you hated them for being weak? Well, you'd end up hating me for the same reason. I would hate me."

His voice had pleaded with her to understand and all she had wanted to do was hold on to him for dear life but something kept her from it, some kind of pride. He had gone on talking, convincing them both, or trying to.

"I love you, Lilly. For a lot of reasons you don't even know. One of them is because you believe in me. I've needed that. You thought it was a one-way street, that only you needed me. Wrong. More than anything, I want to stay with you or take you with me. Except the world doesn't see it that way. And if I don't go—now—this very minute, what we have will rot on us. The things you care about in me will be gone. Take away the dream and we won't like me anymore."

"Maybe you won't like you, but I will."

"Would you? Would you really, Lilly?"

He was so very sad.

"Look," he had said, "I know I'm right. It may sound like the cornball-est thing I've ever said but the minute I heard Jack Kennedy was shot down like some dog in the street, something went click in my head and I knew I had to go home and ring every doorbell and shake every hand in Ohio. I want to tell them how the world should be, beg them, kiss their ass, anything for the chance to come back here to Congress and try to do some of the things that have to be done."

He lifted her chin to look at her, the way he always did.

"And when you come back?"

He had laughed a little then, saying that she would be too good for him, but he did not look directly at her when he said that, nor did she look at him. It was that final; they both understood that it was the last time they would ever be together.

"You like yourself, lady. You hear?" Those were his last words and Lilly had just nodded, stood there with tears streaming down her face, and nodded.

She stopped the story abruptly and looked over to George. He was listening intently and Lilly smiled at him, grateful that he was letting her go on this way.

"You know, George," she said, "I could have made it easier on Kevin. I could have helped. At least I could have told him I understood because in some crazy way I did, almost like I'd expected it, but that it took Lee Harvey Oswald to make me realize it.

"There were so many things I thought about later, those wonderful brave things I can come up with afterwards—when it's too late . . . but I just stood there, letting Kevin do it all. You know what he did? He reached in his pocket and pulled out a little gold cross on a gold chain and put it over my head. All I could think was how like Kevin it was to think of God at a time like that, about what a country boy he was, and why had he spent his money on me when he didn't even have an overcoat. Then he looked at his watch and I knew he was going and that I couldn't bear to see him walk away.

"So I turned and ran out of that bar, ran as fast as I could until I was in the car and driving, driving like demons were after me. I cried and then I got mad, mad at life and at Kevin and at God. Especially God, who never does anything anyhow but take away the people you love.

"I pulled off that cross and flung it out the window somewhere on Memorial Bridge. Oh, I went back later but I couldn't find it. I went back a lot of times, as a matter of fact, but it was gone and I was sick that I had lost the only thing I had left of him. I bought another cross just like it but it wasn't the same. Finally I put it away in a box in a bureau drawer and tried not to think about it. After a while I made myself stop thinking about Kevin, too. Until now."

"How'd you manage that?" It was like George to inquire about the mechanics.

"I learned to hate him. I made myself despise him, despise him because he had something to do with his life and I didn't have anything without him. I had to do it that way; it was the only way to stop loving him."

"Ever run into him?"

"I don't go up on the Hill anymore, but it wouldn't matter. Ten years is a long time. When I hear or read about him, it's like he's a stranger. Practice, George. All it took was practice." Her breath was hard to catch and she was making a gulping noise.

"Do you still hate him?"

"I hate all politicians. It's just that Kevin is more honest than most."

"And righter?"

"About me? Then? Yeah . . ."

"You've forgiven him?"

She nodded. "But not myself. If I'd been a better person, he might have stayed. I still think dumb thoughts like that."

"That is pretty dumb."

"So I am."

"Like a fox! Listen, why don't you look at it as a time of learning? Oh, God, I sound pretty corny myself, Lilly, but why don't you accept it as a turning point, something that few people ever have. Hell, you even knew grand passion, straight out of those sobbing movies you love. It is, you know."

"Movies have happier endings. Sometimes."

"So will you."

"Bullshit."

"There's that, Lil, but it's coming from you. My brand is a hell of a lot less dramatic. Or interesting."

"I learned one good lesson." She smiled.

"Yeah?"

"Yeah. The only passion that lasts is the kind that's cut off before it runs out."

"You have some imagination, kid." He was disgusted. "Imagination becomes a vice if you don't exercise it. But you go too far."

"I don't expect you to feel sorry for me."

He did, though. She knew. At the moment there seemed no pressure in the world like the effort to beat off George's compassion. Well, it served her right; it was time to put those thoughts away, maybe for good. Loneliness might be difficult but so was love, even the memory of it.

"God," she said, "I really am a mess."

"That thought has crossed my mind a time or two this very day." But George was smiling. "How a mess, Lilly? In what way?" he asked.

"Kevin. All these other wacky romances."

"You never pick on anyone your own size."

"Do you believe that?" For a moment her concern for his answer was so intense she knew nothing to measure it by. "Do you really think that's what I've done?" she repeated.

"Yes and no and I'm not sure."

"One of those should fit."

"All right," he said. "I'll tell you what I think. But it shouldn't matter. It's what *you* think that counts. For me, I see your romances as a very bizarre form of self-punishment. A constant need to reaffirm some weird guilt. If you ever knew what you were guilty about in the first place, it's been lost in the emotional crises you've created to feed it." He shook his head. "Does that make sense?"

"Does anything?"

"Look." He sat up straighter, excited by his amateur psychiatry. "Let us not fool ourselves about what we've been doing all day. We've been enumerating the bad times, all the weak people, yourself included. Mostly Harry and now Kevin, the bad guys who let you down. Maybe, Lil, maybe they and some of the others were victims of you. Ever think that's what's bothering you lately? *You* are bothering you."

"You don't leave much fighting ground."

"Why do you have to fight?"

"Because what you're saying is a little bit true. But not fair."

"In what way?"

"If what you propose is accurate, do you think that I knew, that I understood that what I was doing was helping those men to punish me?"

"I never said you acted deliberately."

"It sounded like it to me." She wasn't sulking; rather, she was garnering her defenses, an old habit. "The way you put it, there should be a mass men's movement against women like me," she said.

"Why not? Yeah, why the hell not? It's easy enough for women to leap around screeching about disappointments. Society—your fathers and your husbands, sons, lovers—has been rough on you, yes, but don't think for a minute that it isn't tough on men, too. Don't talk about unfairness as if it only applies to broads. It happens to every one of us, both sexes. Hell-fire, Lilly. I pay every day for something I didn't do. I got taken in, too."

He was warming to the subject. "Look at me. I'm a man, in case you haven't noticed. Do I look like an ogre? Do you think I don't want to see you happy—all you women? I go home every night to a wife who didn't have any choice except to marry me and have babies and hang on for dear life. She got into it worse and deeper than you ever were and she can't break away the way you have. She's fifty years old and disappointed and I know that deep down she hates being dependent on me. She knows I want out. Christ, *she* wants out. But she can't *do* anything. And, Lilly, I can't help her. I'm trapped because she's trapped. I can't get inside her and make her have the confidence the world cheated her of. I can't even love her. How do you think I feel about that? Talk about unfairness."

He lit a cigarette. "You don't own the local franchise on guilt and disappointment." He threw the match into the fireplace. "Look, Lilly, it's how the world works. Change the goddamned world if you can, but let's not kid ourselves that we men have victimized women on an emotional level. Professional, yeah. Emotional, no. Our tails are caught in the same fucking mousetrap."

He paused again. "I'm not crazy about myself or my life, either. But I'm not hamstrung by it. And you are damn right, life is unfair. For you and me and all the other poor sons of bitches who were born into a male-female struggle we didn't start."

He refilled his glass at the bar.

"What can we do about life, George?"

"We do what we have to, what we can. What we don't do is think we're the only ones who have questions and doubts and fears. We don't give up on ourselves. Mostly, Lil, we don't sit in a corner and punish ourselves. We stop feeling sorry about the way things were; we look to the good things. We could be untouchables in India, you know."

She looked up to see that he was smiling now.

"Don't go Christian on me, George."

They both laughed, glad to have the tension eased.

"I sound pretty selfish," she said. "Even to myself."

"Not selfish. You just have a low threshold for your own shortcomings. And that's my point. You're ahead of the game but you keep wanting to count yourself out. I think I know what's bothering you, and I appreciate your sensitivity, but try to come to terms with some of it anyway. You can't undo the past, Lil. Rethink it if you have to. Understand what happened but put the understanding to work for you. Separate those loose ends. Make them meet or they'll strangle the life out of you."

"Forty seems late to begin."

"Life begins there. Haven't you heard?"

"Once or twice. It's a cozy slogan when you're stuck with it."

"For some. Not for you," he answered.

"Oh yeah?"

His voice rose. "Yeah, goddammit. Yeah. Yeah. Yeah."

"You think it's so easy for me—that all I have to do is pick up sticks? That's the way you see me, George, don't you?"

Her brain was tired, like the rest of her. She had nothing more to say.

"I can't tell you any more than I've already said, Lil. You've got one hell of a chance left at life. I'm fifty-one years old. It's not my turn anymore, but it's still yours. Somewhere back when, I realized that I had had my turn and that I somehow blew it. I said to myself, George, old boy, time's up. You got your Pulitzer and you couldn't follow your own act. Step aside and give someone else a go. Jesus, Lilly, now you've got me doing it. Self-pity is contagious and destructive. I've got to get out of here."

He stood to leave, a little wobbly as he moved.

"I can't let you go like this," she said.

"Nor can you stop me." He was hiking his pants, stuffing his shirt inside.

"George, please don't go."

"Why not? You can nail up your cross without an audience."

She knew he had to be hurting to be so hurtful.

"Sorry," he said, "I'm a little drunk. I'm going to walk down into Georgetown and ogle a few repressed girls in short skirts."

"Will you come back?"

He nodded.

"You never let me down, do you, George?"

"Hell, honey, let's table that herring, too. I hang around you because when you're not punishing yourself you happen to be the best damn company going. We see things the same—usually—we laugh, we talk, we argue. You do more to make me feel alive than any person I've ever known. But I'm no saint, Lilly. I wish you'd get that in your head."

She knew enough to let him go; it was pride now, he'd shown too much of himself. She made her words sound casual. "Okay, fellow, twice around the block. The gate is always open."

He walked out of the house without looking back, but not letting the door slam behind him.

Lilly felt a new and different heaviness with George gone; it was easier to think when he was helping her. It had been like that since she'd known him. Sometimes she wondered if maybe George made things too easy for her, always saving her ass, the way he had when they first met.

The Diem regime had fallen, American troops and aircraft were deep into that doomed chunk of Asia. Mississippi voter

182

registration had put two white youths in a common grave with a black boy. Harlem and Bedford-Stuyvesant had erupted and Lyndon Johnson seemed determined to continue the holocaust in Vietnam. In Lilly's mind, Harry and LBJ had commingled into the enemy.

She had overheard Harry on the telephone only a few weeks after Kennedy's murder, after Johnson was sworn into office, talking to someone in the White House.

"Tragic business," he had said, speaking to one of Johnson's aides. "It's a terrible time for the country. Thank God for Lyndon. I mean the President . . . that'll take a little getting used to, huh? Look, all I want to say is that you fellows can count on me. The man will have to stand election in a year and this interim period could be crucial."

There had been a pause on Harry's end. Then he said, "Precisely. I was thinking how reassuring it would be to the public to have a few good television spots—LBJ in the Oval Office; down on the ranch—how he holds fast in troubled times. A jump on the real campaign, you know?"

"Right," Harry continued, "sure. Thursday's fine with me. I'll bring along a few ideas I've sketched out. Good. See you then."

Dancing on the coffin; Harry and Lyndon, hands joined, dancing on the coffin.

Lilly had very nearly thrown up—a state of near nausea that had stayed with her over the next several years as she became anti-everything. At first it did not matter what, she just kept falling in love with causes, any causes; causes were safer than people. It had infuriated Harry that she opposed anything he worked for. Which was true, Lilly told herself, true because the things Harry believed in were things she deplored. Mostly she deplored Harry.

It was in the peace movement that she had finally taken refuge, carrying the children along with her at every opportunity, once even letting Mags and Teddy spend a Saturday afternoon picketing the White House. It was shortly after Easter and Teddy had a live white bunny named Rabbit E. Lee on a small poodle leash that kept tangling in Teddy's fat little legs as he dragged the creature behind him, following Mags, who carried a sign that said ANIMALS AND CHILDREN DON'T LIKE WAR. The demonstration had not been particularly effective, except to enrage Harry, who told Lilly that she had no right to use his children in that manner. She had told him to go back down to his office and make some more films about how Johnson would soon nail the coonskin of Vietnam to the cabin wall.

Another time, a particularly bitter quarrel had taken place over whether or not she should take Maggie to a peace rally on a school night.

"The child is only eight years old," Harry had said. "Her function is to be educated. Not to march with a pack of dirty hippies."

"She learns more in the streets than in some anally repressive private school."

"Well, does it ever occur to you that it is publicly and professionally embarrassing to have my wife and daughter picketing the White House when I have to work with the people there?"

"As a matter of fact, it occurs to me almost constantly."

"And what about Maggie?" he had countered.

"Would it be better if you took her down to the Oval Office, Harry? Let her watch Daddy film the President making plans to kill off everybody in Vietnam to save them from Communism? Why, you might even explain to her how financially remunerating that little service to your country is."

She had taken Mags to the rally. It was not a massive gathering, not as Washington peace demonstrations were to become, but there were thousands of people, mostly students and members of the local anti-war factions. Near where she and Maggie were to meet with the others, there were groupings of welfare mothers demanding WAR ON POVERTY NOW, gay liberationists, feminists, some clergymen in white collars and nuns in reformed dress; militant blacks seemed to be everywhere, demanding everything.

Some of the kids played guitars while others, in drab army surplus uniforms, unfurled Viet Cong flags and distributed Marxist literature. Here and there Lilly caught sight of a few liberal politicians; a bearded senator was standing with his small, wiry wife, who had twice been jailed for demonstrating on previous occasions. Some children Maggie's age were darting in and around the older people, several of them becoming separated in the crowd and announced moments later over loudspeakers as "lost children."

Lilly clutched at Maggie's small hand, sensing in her child the same excitement she was aware of in herself, for beyond the carnival-like air there was the almost tangible swelling of action, of hope. The arm-banded monitors began calling for order, sounding a bit righteous even to Lilly. She hated bullhorns ever since.

"Okay now. Everybody form a double line in front of the horse monument."

There was confusion and disorder, for horse monuments accounted for more than half of the Washington landmarks, but the crowd was clumsily queuing up at the statue of Lafayette, spilling over into the street and backing up to the Hay Adams hotel.

Grass and handbills were trampled underfoot as lighted candles were passed among the marchers. In the dark the thousands of ghostly faces began to sing, to chant for peace as, in a mammoth body, they snaked slowly down the long distance to the iron fence that divided the public street from the manicured grounds of the White House.

The metropolitan police, their gas masks hooked to their holsters, linked arms to cordon off the area around the presidential security guards. A few television remote-trucks blocked off one end of Pennsylvania Avenue and the angry sound of automobile horns was audible above the swell of voices.

Somewhere far up front a skirmish broke out and the shouts of discord quickly reached back into the thick crowd where Lilly and Mags were surrounded by other demonstrators. Slowly at first, then rapidly, the melee oozed through the marchers, bringing with it the inevitable panic. Lilly could see ahead: the police were charging into the mass of bodies forty or so feet in front of her—their clubs flashed in the street lights. Candles were being knocked to the ground and screams and groans followed the thud of blunt instruments making bloody contact with human flesh. The struggle spread immediately to where she and Maggie were imprisoned by the others. People surged in and around them, making it impossible for Lilly to move, pressing her and Maggie with their bodies, cursing them and shoving them and then falling to the ground near them. Over the screams of the mob came the sound of chanting voices from way to the rear: FUCK JOHNSON, FUCK JOHNSON, FUCK JOHNSON.

Instantly alert to the danger they were in, Lilly grabbed for Maggie, who was clinging to her legs; she lifted the child up in her arms and tried to break free. FUCK JOHNSON, FUCK JOHNSON. They could turn in no direction. Lilly was terrified. A bearded young man beside her screamed, FUCK YOU, LYNDON JOHNSON, FUCK YOU! Well, somebody had to, Lilly thought, but not me! She had to get Maggie out of this! But they were caught now, completely trapped in the thick of unbelievable havoc. Nor could she hold Maggie's weight much longer. People shoved closer and she felt the breath being squeezed out of her. Her chin took a sharp blow from the elbow of a wild-eyed student as he threw back his arm to hurl a rock at one of the policemen some dozen feet away.

And then she tripped and fell, taking Maggie down with her, and there was the acid smell of tear gas, choking and burning her eyes, closing her throat. People stumbled over them, gagging and gasping for air and falling helplessly over each other, piling themselves over bodies already on the ground. From where she huddled with her arms covering Maggie, Lilly could see only feet, the boots, the hands, the pained faces that fell so near her own. She and Maggie were being crushed to death in full view of the White House! She had to get up but it was impossible. Oh God, she prayed, get Maggie out of this. Just this one time. Do this for me and I'll pay you back, I swear.

Weeping hysterically, she made one more effort to stand, holding on to Mags as she struggled upward. Using her free arm to fight back the crowd, she managed to get to her knees, pushing with her back to block the mob. She dragged Maggie close to her, screaming and cursing those around her, beating at them with her fist. The smell of vomit was everywhere now, sharp and acrid like regurgitated orange juice. Another canister of gas exploded close by, causing a fiercer lunge from the crowd; they were all stampeding animals now and Lilly was falling again, falling back under the boots and the screaming bodies. They would not make it up again. She covered Maggie's small body with her own and wept to the little girl, "Oh, baby, I'm sorry, I'm so sorry . . ."

Two large arms had come around Lilly from the rear, squeezing so tightly over her breasts that pain shot to her head, making her dizzy and blurring her vision. Someone was dragging her backwards now, her limp legs bumping over other bodies still on the ground.

"Maggie! Maggie!" She was shouting to the child left behind; the crowd was closing in, blocking out everything. Lilly bit her lip to keep from fainting; blood filled her mouth as she choked and vomited.

"Shut up. Just shut your mouth."

Then the voice behind her shouted, "Karl! The kid. Get the kid."

One of the arms holding Lilly let go long enough to shove aside a falling mass of human flesh, then retightened its grip.

"Here, Karl. Through here."

The last thing Lilly saw was a tall, reedlike young man wearing broken eyeglasses and carrying Maggie over his shoulder; the child's body swung alongside the cameras that dangled from his neck. Then a head of long hair fell hard against her own and the desperate, hate-filled screams of FUCK JOHNSON, FUCK JOHNSON slowly faded from her ears.

When she woke up, someone was pulling her into the lobby of the Hay Adams. Only half-conscious, she tried to find her feet to help whoever was dragging her, taking a few uncertain steps. The thin young man was in front of her now, carrying Maggie like a baby, cradling her; the child's arms were fastened tightly around his neck, her head rested against the leather camera straps. Lilly felt herself drifting away once more. Blood was streaming from her nose and she unconsciously wiped at it with the back of her hand. Pain exploded in her head and she blacked out a second time.

For what seemed hours, she was vaguely aware of lying on a flowered couch; she could hear voices but was unable to use her own. A sharp smell assaulted her nostrils, making her move her head left and right, the odor of ammonia following her relentlessly, forcing her awake. A wet washcloth was dabbed at a cut near her eye and someone was bending her legs, first one, then the other. Her arms were lifted, folded at the elbows, then placed at her side. The sharp smell was at her nose once more and she opened her eyes to see a hairy hand about to pour iodine onto her brow; she tried to speak but her mouth was too swollen. The big hairy hands were at her again, and as she tried to sit up, the hands held her back. "It's O.K., Mrs. Shawcross. You are all right. Can you understand? You are all right. The little girl is fine. Tell your mama you're O.K., honey."

Maggie's face bent over Lilly's, nodding, tear-stained; the child smiled, her front left tooth was chipped. Lilly's hand moved to touch her; it was Maggie's good tooth, a big one!

The man's hands were putting a glass of brown whiskey to Lilly's lips; the alcohol stung but she drank it all as he pushed a bed pillow under her neck. The liquor was burning in her chest now and she tried to pull herself up on the pillow.

"Easy now." The man leaned closer; he smelled of liquor, too, but his broad face made her lean back; it was a good face, not un-handsome—thick, dark hair, navy neck tie with white dots, a blue oxford-cloth shirt stained with blood. It was unreal that she should notice these things, particularly the man's smile; it was the most genuine smile ever. It broke its pose to speak. "Everyone said you'd get into real trouble one of these days."

The mouth laughed, then made more words. "I guess this is one of those days," he added.

She grabbed tightly at his hand.

"You're all right," he said. "Just some bad cuts and bruises. No breaks." He was looking her over. "Nothing a new pair of stockings won't hide."

"I'm O.K.," she mumbled, turning her head to Maggie. "Hi, baby."

She reached for Mags and they moved toward each other, crying, hugging tightly to reassure themselves that they were safe. Lilly began to shake very hard, the way she did when she had a near miss driving the car, or when she had grabbed Teddy from in front of a fast-moving playground swing when he was just learning to walk—she couldn't stop shaking then, either. Another glass of whiskey was put to her mouth.

"You're just a little het up. 'Mob shock' is what we called it in Vietnam."

The man was calling to the boy who had carried Mags; the boy was smiling, using his bandaged hands to dismantle a shattered camera. "I think we were safer there than we are here," he said.

The boy was examining a broken round lens, a long-distance attachment. Lilly had seen one only once before. Never was she so glad to see one again.

She thought maybe she could sit up now and was determined to try; the danger would be really past if she were sitting up. She ached all over, any movement was agony.

"It'll be worse tomorrow," the man warned.

"Nothing will ever be worse." She spoke thickly.

She sat up and was immediately dizzy. It made her giddy. "Where've you been all my life?" she said to the man who had carried her, who was holding her up now. She had meant to convey a deeper gratitude.

"Glad to be of service. I'm George Sabberstein." He added the alphabet letters of a national wire service but Lilly could not concentrate.

"I've seen you before." She was squinting woozily at him, recognition coming slowly. "Hey, they kicked you out of Vietnam, didn't they? For calling the war unpopular."

He nodded. She held out her glass for more whiskey, looking around. They were in a hotel suite, the parlor part, a long front room with a half-dozen elaborately draped windows overlooking Lafayette Park. The place was a shambles. A group of men were stationed at the windows; the scrawny young man with the cameras was hanging over the ledge with Maggie next to him. Phones rang constantly, stopped only when answered, then rang again. Low buzzing noises came up from the street along with the sound of sirens and shouts and the thud of running feet. Lilly managed to hobble to the window and leaned against the cool of a green damask curtain.

"It's about over," George Sabberstein said. He was pointing toward the police truck; uniformed men in gas masks were herding demonstrators inside them. Circles of kids sat cross-legged in the street lights, their faces partially covered by dirty white surgical masks, the kind you get at the drug counter when you have a sick child. Lilly was again unnerved to be registering such funny observations that had no real significance. Shock! She sat down in a chair and tried to collect herself. Maggie was now over by the television set watching the electronic replay of the violence they had barely escaped. Pride and fear mixed inside Lilly as she studied the child. History in the making, that was what she had wanted Maggie to see, and she had very nearly got her killed in the process. Lilly shuddered involuntarily.

"What's all this?" she asked George Sabberstein. It hurt to lift her arm in the questioning gesture.

"The press box. Some are wire service guys; those two over there are Time-Life. We'll bill their bureau chief tomorrow."

He was pretty jolly amid havoc, Lilly thought, feeling strangely exuberant herself. Some people are more capable of meeting disaster than anticipating it. She said as much aloud.

"Nobody's anticipated the kind of hell there's going to be from now on. This was serious business tonight. Johnson didn't just repress a peace rally, honey, he's started an all-out war on the home front. It's a hell of a way to run a democracy." His jolliness was ebbing.

"What's the casualty count, Joey?" he called.

A heavy-set young man standing near the television shouted back, not turning around. "This channel gives a loose count into the hundreds. No dead. Plenty of action in the emergency rooms, though. The guys downtown don't have any statistics, either. Too soon. My guess is that at least a thousand injured; twice that many in jail. It'll be a late night for the ACLU."

The young man reached a couple of sandwiches from a tray, handing one to Maggie. The thought of food turned

189

Lilly's stomach and she looked quickly away, thinking as she did that, despite his bulk, the man called Joey was little more than a kid himself. Suddenly she felt very old.

"Who was the genius who said never to trust anyone over thirty?" she asked aloud of no one in particular. At thirty-two, Lilly was supposed to have better sense. Or should have.

"Can I use one of those phones if they ever stop ringing?" she said.

George Sabberstein nodded.

She dialed her own number. It rang several times before Harry answered.

"It's me."

"Where the hell are you?" A slight crack in his voice was the single indication of concern.

"The Hay Adams. AP—UPI—something. I don't know. I just wanted to tell you we're all right."

"A wire service?"

Harry was shouting and Lilly moved closer to the receiver, embarrassed lest someone overhear.

"Have you gotten your goddamned picture in the paper?" he asked.

"Waving the Viet Cong flag, Harry. It should be good for business."

The son of a bitch! She hung up and asked for another drink.

It was quieter now; the streets below were almost empty except for a few scattered kids and some armed police stationed at every corner. The newsmen were drifting out, too; those who remained were over by the television. Several more bottles of whiskey were brought in and George went to fix new drinks, filling one with extra ice and handing it to her. "Let the cold rest on that lip."

He asked if she thought she could smoke and she nodded as he took out a couple of unfiltered French cigarettes, lighting them both and handing one to her.

"*Now Voyager,*" she joked. "I've been waiting for a Paul Henreid for years but I'm not up to it tonight." She smiled at her misplaced sense of whimsy and accepted the smelly cigarette. The unfiltered tip stuck to her lip and she would remember this night every time she was in the same room with a burning Gauloise.

"I can't thank you enough for what you did," she said. "If there is any way to repay you, I'll think of it."

"That's not an offer you make lightly to a journalist." But he was laughing again. "No good deed goes unpunished," he added, and Lilly wondered if he was always able to find humor in such unholy situations.

"I've seen you around but we were never properly introduced, Mrs. Shawcross." He exaggerated the formal name, waiting for her to correct him.

"Please. I'm Lilly. I think saving a person's life puts us on a first-name basis."

"Your liberality knows no bounds."

"After tonight, I'm not so sure. Being a liberal is hard on the body."

She licked her index finger and rubbed at a bloodied cut on her right knee.

"Just don't list it as 'occupation' on your medical insurance."

They laughed together this time, as if they'd done so many times before.

"You got a Pulitzer Prize out of Vietnam, didn't you?"

She could vaguely recall Smithy being furious at the award. He had thought Sabberstein a traitor to his country with his anti-war articles and had written an open letter to the Pulitzer Committee to that effect. Lilly had the funny feeling that George was able to read her thoughts.

"A few of your friends thought I shouldn't have gotten out of Saigon alive, let alone with a prize."

He was grinning but he obviously knew that she and Smithy Stuyvesant were friends. She would try to justify Smithy to him some other time, if there were to be one. Tonight, she did not have the energy even if she had the explanation.

"What will be the upshot of all this?" she asked. Her eyes widened toward the windows. Even that hurt; she felt at the cut in her eyebrow.

"Just a cosmetic war wound." He took a cube of ice from his glass and directed her to hold it on the abrasion, then answered her question. "Things will get worse. Or better. Depends on your point of view. Too early to score it yet."

He drained his glass and stared down into it. "The guys in the White House and the Pentagon will try to bluff this one as being a necessary precaution. Law and order. They'll have the drums beating all night about how a bunch of souped-up hippies tried to storm the Oval Office and scalp the President."

"*Fuck* the President was the way I heard it," she said.

"The irony is that he isn't even there."

Lilly looked at him in disbelief. He shook his head. "Camp David."

She felt the tears smart.

"But the administration lost this round whether they

admit it or not," he said. "This bloody crap will go on and on. A lot of heads will be bashed in before some sense is knocked into the right people. It's the long haul now. Johnson will have to come to grips with it or get the hell out.

"He's got less than two years before he has to run again, and it will take more than your husband's fancy camera work to help him belch this one down. My guess is that his stubborn Texas pride will get him in the end. Frankly, unless he can stop nights like this, I don't think he'll run."

Such a thought was alien to Lilly. "But he's been so popular."

"Did that look like a fan club meeting out there?"

"Hardly."

"Then stick around for the rest. You'll need a few pointers on crowd behavior. My card, madam, if I can be of service." He gave her his card and another smile.

The smile was more than gentlemanly; it was an offer of friendship. She could have hugged him.

"Come on, Wonder Woman," he said. "I'll take you and Mary Marvel home."

Lilly looked over at Mags; her devotion to the cause of discipline had always been qualified. Tonight was a harrowing experience and the child would be even more impossible to control.

"Tomorrow, little Miss Marvel's cheekiness will be a pain in Wonder Woman's backside." But Lilly was only slightly concerned; she was proud of Maggie's resilience.

"Impertinence wisely guided becomes audacity," Sabberstein said, then smiled. "Not a bad trait in broads of any age."

Lilly would analyze the compliment later; right now, she would have trouble prying Maggie loose. She called her over.

"Mommy, Stan took my picture. He says I can be the peaceniks' poster girl."

Maggie's cheeks were flushed, and looking at her, Lilly felt a prideful vanity: motherhood rearing its complicated head. Never again would she take this little girl for granted. She could have killed her, lost her before she even knew how important she was. Lilly swallowed the tears back.

"Mags, you'd better save those patriotic words for your father. We're in big trouble when we get home."

"*Fuck Daddy.*"

Maggie's chipped tooth flashed in a devilish grin and Lilly

192

glanced toward George Sabberstein. "I guess she learned a few new words tonight, too," she said.

"Never too young for the right lesson."

Then he swung Maggie up on his shoulders and turned to take Lilly's arm.

"I make it a rule never to trust any woman over seven, myself," he said.

Lilly looked up at him. "Fuck Sabberstein." She grinned at him playfully.

"You have my card."

# 15

LILLY remembered far more of the months that followed that peace demonstration than she wished to recall. As George Sabberstein had predicted, the streets of Washington became a veritable parade ground for marches and other demonstrations that reflected the national discontent with the war. There seemed to be no let-up in sight; Lyndon Johnson was deeply mired not only in foreign battles but in domestic ones as well. Every front was gaping open; black was beautiful and dangerous, kids were anathema to some, heroes to others who, like Lilly, saw leadership as coming from the college campus rather than from Congress. Actually she had been strangely energized by the disastrous demonstration that had very nearly been the death of her and Maggie. She began to organize for the peace movement, telling people on the list of calls given her to make that what had happened that night was only the beginning. Angrily, she had informed Harry that she intended to join any and all groups that were willing to take a public stand against the war.

"That's the last time you pull a stunt like that," he had said.

"Just watch me, Harry. Just you watch."

But Harry was right; that one peace demonstration was her only opportunity to stand up and be counted, for in the space of the next two months, tragedy overshadowed her militancy like a massive mental blackout that darkened everything around her. Vincent Lazlo was killed in a light-plane crash somewhere off the coast of Yugoslavia. She read about it in the *Times;* sitting alone one Saturday morning, she had stumbled over the article quite by chance. "Noted Fashion Designer Dies in Crash." Lilly had to read and reread the item before she could believe it was true; the final realization was devastating, as if part of her youth had been wiped from her slate.

She told Harry that she would go to Indianapolis for Vince's funeral. She made a plane reservation and left for the airport, a new black suit carefully packed in a light piece of hand luggage, but when the loudspeaker called her flight for the final time, Lilly sat there in the noisy terminal staring straight ahead, unable to move. Finally she got up and walked slowly back through the long tunnel-like area that led to the taxi stand, ashamed and sickened by the self-knowledge that she simply could not be present when Vince was returned to the very place he had fought all his life to outdistance. Instead, she checked into a hotel, spending a sleepless night watching television. Late the next day she went home and got into bed and stayed there for several days, speaking to no one, especially not to Harry. More than anything, she could not bear Harry's having this painful evidence of her disgusting cowardice.

Three weeks later the telephone rang and she absently picked it up to hear Smithy Stuyvesant's research assistant sobbing and telling her that Mr. Stuyvesant had had a heart attack in a crude rural fishing village on Spain's Costa Brava. Lilly interrupted the woman, her own heart seeming to stop, and asked tensely which hospital Smithy was in. There was a heavy silence on the other end of the wire and Lilly understood that Smithy was already dead. Gone. Just like that. She did not move from her chair all day. Later, a few people phoned to say they knew of her closeness to Smithy and how hard this must be for her and could they be of any help? Lilly managed only the vaguest kind of response but she waited in that same chair by the phone all afternoon as if for some further message. It was a useless vigil. Smithy, she knew, had long ago arranged for his own death—telling her that a lot of folderol about funerals was barbaric and that for himself there would be none of that; only a simple and private burial in the family plot somewhere in New England. There was nothing she could do now, no way to help either Smithy or herself. She was ashamed, too, ashamed even to admit it to herself, but she was relieved that there was to be no funeral; she could not have stood by and watched Smithy be put into the ground, either. No, he had spared her that. In the weeks that followed, Lilly thought of nothing but Smithy, of how he had always told her that she would learn to care—and she did; she cared for him. In a final elegant gesture he had left her several first editions of rare books, many of them inscribed by the author. They were possessions dear to Smithy and invaluable to collectors; for Lilly they seemed painful reminders of her loss of the man himself and all he represented. She had not believed that posthumous generosity could be so painful. The bequest compounded the guilt she felt from their final encounter.

Ironically, it had been a rare book with which she had stubbornly sought to terminate their friendship only weeks before Smithy left for Spain. They had locked horns that day; smaller incidents had come up to separate them before but nothing like that afternoon. Lilly's hysterical anti-war pronouncements were tiresome to Smithy, for he was of a generation that did not appreciate feminine participation in politics —an area he considered the private preserve of men, older men—but he had been tolerant of her, making her the exception to his rigid rule of never discussing anything of importance with women. Not at any time during her moral renaissance had Lilly been adult enough to accord Smithy the same understanding and acceptance that he extended to her.

His persistence in supporting the war had made him seem to Lilly part and parcel of the enemy: The Establishment— that was how she grouped her adversaries. Especially had Smithy seemed removed from her way of thinking that last day she saw him, imperialistic and somehow out of things— a tired old man. His gray face had frightened her and her fright had made her harsh. They were taking tea in the sunny solarium off his main drawing room, and she was, she knew, sounding militant and perhaps boring, filled as she was with the rhetoric of pacificism, but Smithy had patiently heard her out before giving her the gentle warning not to let her politics come between them and the good thing they shared. He told her that it was foolish to run with the pack and to trample the fine bonds of respect they enjoyed.

Whenever Smithy had suggested she was foolish, Lilly felt foolish, resenting him because she did, but she had persisted in haranguing against the war that afternoon as if converting him to her side would save the world. She had very nearly been shouting at him.

"Lilly, my dear child, your ignorance of history is appalling. Even in my somewhat long and belabored lifetime, it has been *peace* which breaks out every twenty-five years or so. War is inevitable. For man, disorder is the natural order; human beings are too greedy for it to be otherwise. You would be wise to channel your crusading instincts. The only durable peace must come first from within."

"Smithy, kindly do not sit here and lecture me about the inevitability of this blood bath. I am not stupid, you know."

He had smiled; it seemed an effort for him to do so.

"I think you many things. Not all of them good." He had peered meaningfully over his glasses—the gesture annoying her as much as his words. "But," he went on, "I by no means count you among the ignorant. You are overly passionate but not ignorant." He began stirring his tea as though the discussion was at a close, but Lilly would not let the matter rest.

"You believe in this war. I've always known you do."

"Nonsense. I am an old man who believes in very little. Some wars, however, have more justification than others. Now, Hitler annihilating the Jews is of a cloth with the Romans murdering the Christians. I condone none of that. But it is different in Vietnam. You simply do not understand the dangers of Communism." He had paused to add some brandy to his tea, something she had never known him to do. More from fatigue than exasperation, he had continued in a weary voice. "I must take you to one of the iron curtain countries, my dear; one look is worth a thousand tiresome lectures."

"And so we wipe out an entire country rather than have Communism? Is that so different than killing Christians for their beliefs?" Her voice had trembled with fury, and like all her extremes, he had been annoyed by this.

"You are incredibly childlike to demand so black or white an explanation."

"Then just precisely what do you propose?"

"That we see to the finish the things we were perhaps injudicious to have begun. The balance of power—"

She had interrupted rudely. "You mean compound the felony to save our pride, don't you?"

"There must be a stopping point for evil. I need not remind you that we are committed to the cause of freedom everywhere. Only from armed strength can we preserve it. That is one of history's strongest messages, Lilly dear."

She had been bewildered that so intelligent a person as Smithy could say these things, could believe in them so fully.

"No seminars this time, Smithy. Just a simple yes or no. Should we be fighting this war or not?"

He had set the delicate teacup into its saucer and placed it on a carved Oriental credenza, both the cup and the table ancient reminders of civilizations long past. "I insult you to humor you in this manner. But, no, we should not be in this war. But that is not the question."

"Then what is?"

"It becomes complicated, and in your irrational state I should be wasting both of our time by endeavoring to educate you belatedly in the value of national and moral responsibility. It goes far beyond the Vietnamese, my dear."

She had chosen, as always, to pass over the things she neither understood nor had the desire to learn. Another tack was more likely to prove her point. She had grabbed only at what she wanted to hear.

"If you mean it when you say this war is wrong, then why don't you write that in your column?" She had reared back, glowering, not in the least displeased with her challenge.

"Things have gone too far for that. We have—perhaps imprudently—pursued the policy of collective security too long. Perhaps," he had conceded, "perhaps we are guilty of having tried too hard. It remains for history to judge."

"You mean things have gone too far for you, the whole lot of you, to back down, to admit that you are wrong, that all of us are? You'd rather save faces than lives?"

"I am tired now, Lilly. Your querulousness is too much for one afternoon."

She was being dismissed and this was more infuriating than all his didactic riddles. Snatching up her coat and purse, Lilly had stormed toward the door, only to stop abruptly and speak what would be her last words to him, delivering them unkindly but evenly. "I have defended you, fought with people I agree with over you. But never again." The next words would haunt her. "When someone tells me that our only hope for change in the country will come about when the likes of old Smithy Stuyvesant retires or dies or gets run out of town in tar and feathers, I will hold my tongue. I will sit there nice and ladylike without opening my mouth. Just the way you always say is my finest political posture."

She had meant to add more, to be even more devastating, but the tears were starting, those bloody uncontrollable examples of what Smithy called her sex's inferiority, and he was so white and tired, a very old man indeed. Goddamn you, she had thought, standing mutely before him. Goddamn you for not being invincible. Slowly, and with exaggerated dignity, she had walked away from him.

In the days that followed her outburst she had not been able to curb her thoughts of him, mellowing when she recounted his virtues, hardening at his vices. More than anything, she wanted Smithy to be perfect. Expected it. Needed it. Many times after their argument she had wanted to return, even to apologize, but she could not back down. She was right and he was wrong.

Still, it was impossible to get him off her mind. She purchased an old edition of Dante's *Inferno,* and with a pencil she circled the passages that described the various places in hell for those who were damned for not doing anything either truly right or truly wrong, heavily underlining that part about that special place in hell reserved for those who were indifferent in their sins. She marked the pages with a colorful peace symbol and had the book delivered to Smithy, unsigned.

Several days later there was a note in his graceful, bold handwriting on a thick beige card bearing only his family's crest.

My dearest Lilly, you are indeed a willful child, albeit a valuable one. In my prideful tutoring, I seemed to have neglected to instruct you in the proper care of fine manuscripts. The furies that have taken possession of you are of insufficient velocity to justify the abuse of anything so splendid. And it would appear to me that we are friends far too long for me to be relegated to Mr. Dante's Inferno so unceremoniously. I leave tomorrow for a few months in Spain and shall ring you up upon my return. Perhaps you may yet persuade me to take a less stringent look at the world. We shall see.

S.

Lilly read and reread the note until it was dog-eared, eventually learning it by heart, and would lie in the semi-dark of her room repeating Smithy's phrases over and over. But nothing would bring him back. There was no way now to tell him she was sorry or to let him say to her that maybe he was sorry, too. Hopelessness solidified into a kind of depressed numbness, a stupefying numbness which still held her captive when some weeks later she learned of her father's death. Try as she did, she could feel nothing, no guilt, no loss, just more of this huge black nothingness. Somewhere deep inside there had to be some painful reaction. When a person's father died, it was not right to feel nothing. That she felt nothing troubled her more than if she had passions and feelings that could not be explained. She might be able to deal with that but not with this horrid, frightening void.

The notice of her father's death had been served abruptly also, coming in the form of legal documents from her father's solicitor. "It was your father's wish." the accompanying letter informed her, "that you not be consulted as to the disposition of the body. He has been put to rest near his beloved wife."

Lilly had flung the pages to the floor, retrieving them in anger to continue reading.

"It was the intent of the deceased," she read, "that his only child and heir be his sole beneficiary. To that purpose, a fund was long ago established to defray the inheritance taxes due on the estate which is of some size and consequence. With the exception of small bequests to faithful employees and sundry charitable organizations, and a perpetuating fund for the maintenance of the family grave site, all properties are to be held in trust for the issue of the heir, the grandchildren of the deceased, one Margaret Baldwin Shawcross, and one Theodore Bellingrath Shawcross, until such time as they arrive at the legal age of twenty-one. All monies, stocks and residuals, including personal and household effects, are to be tendered to Lillian Baldwin Bellingrath Shawcross according to the stipulations set forth by the State of South Carolina in such claims."

Lilly could not bring herself to finish. Her father was gone now, too, she thought. Dead to the rest of the world, the way he had seemed to Lilly all along. In the ground before she was even told, his grandchildren remembered and provided for by a man she scarcely knew, a man, her father, the invisible grandfather who had never even seen his descendants. Lilly wondered how her father had known the names of her children, wondered what he had felt when he learned that for some unexplainable reason she had stubbornly insisted on naming her only son after him. So many times she had meant to phone him or at least write a note, but how did one communicate with a father for whom there was no comfortable form of address? So she had let it go, pushing it aside and forgetting it until it was too late. It was all too late now. Everything.

Never had she known such despair. There seemed no point in getting up each morning, the days only loomed long and depressing, and for weeks she did not move from her bed; the curtains at the windows stayed tightly drawn, day and night. Lilly lost a great deal of weight. She ate nothing, but she drank a large amount of Scotch every afternoon; she lost track of the amount, and was generally asleep by the time Harry came home from work. When liquor could not dull her brain. she would take one or two little sleeping pills, husbanding them, terrified she might run out and have to face the night undrugged. Sometime during the second week after she learned of her father's death, Lilly slept through three or four straight days without once seeing Mags or Teddy. She ignored Harry altogether until the night he burst into the bedroom and turned on all the lights. At first Lilly did not know where she was, or even who this strange man was, ranting and flailing his arms and shouting abuse at her. She tried to rouse herself but the heaviness inside kept pulling her back into the comfort of dull sleep.

"Don't, Harry." It was all she could get out.

"Don't, my ass. I'm warning you. Shape up around here, or I'll have you put away. I swear to God I will."

He grabbed her up by the shoulder, lifting her from the bed, shaking her until she could almost feel her eyes rolling about in her head. She tried to push him back but he continued lunging at her, hurting her, until, deeply frightened, she picked up things from the bedside table to throw at him, the ashtray, books, a clock. When she ran out of objects, she knelt in the bed and began to hit at Harry with her fists, beating at his face. He locked his hands around her neck, closing them so tightly that she was unable to breathe or scream. Her nails raked across his face and he finally let go of her, smacking her hard on the side of her head several times before he did. She fell back heavily against the headboard, the blow stunning her.

"You son of a bitch," she gasped, the words hurting her throat. "You dumb, stupid son of a bitch. Help me. For God's sake, somebody please help me." She started to cry, then became hysterical, but Harry only picked up the things she had thrown at him and tossed them back onto her bed.

"You don't need help. You need the shit kicked out of you." He turned to leave the room, then came back again to glower at her. "All your fathers are dead, Lilly. Every single one of them. Try to get that through your drunken head." He switched off the lights and slammed the door behind him.

There were angry red marks on her face and she was appalled by them when she looked at herself in the bathroom mirror. Standing there, touching the welts on her neck and shoulders, Lilly felt a tiny click in her head and her thoughts fell into place. Harry had, without intending to do so, finally given her a real reason to get out of bed, a reason to fight. She would mend, she told her reflection. She would make herself strong again, strong enough to deal with Harry. If it took everything she had left in her, she would get the bastard out of her life once and for all.

Harry dealt her Maggie without argument; it was Teddy he demanded. "No son of mine is going to be left with you."

In the end it was the money that made the difference.

"Harry," she said to him the following week, speaking with a control she did not actually have, her voice hiding her inner instability. "I figure I have about two, maybe three hundred thousand dollars in cash and negotiable securities coming to me from my father's estate. I will transfer half of it to your account so that you can set up your own film company. It's what you've always wanted."

"And what do you get in return?"

"Teddy."

He stared at her, and for a moment Lilly wondered if this was what he had had in mind all along.

"I take Teddy and Mags," she went on. "You take the money."

"You mean buy my own son."

"Our son."

"And what would be the arrangements?"

"The house is already mine. You can see both children at your convenience, and you may remove any items of furniture you wish. I would expect the stock in your company purchased by my money to be registered in the names of both children, reverting to me if they should die before I do."

"And who supports them?"

"From what I understand, there are certain monies from holdings that I cannot legally liquidate that will pay me dividends. The children and I can live on that. I'll get a job if it's not enough."

"I'll talk it over with my attorney." He said nothing else.

Lilly's own lawyer, when she finally enlisted one, considered the offer overgenerous. She had thought it a bargain. It always came down to money, she thought. Money had purchased her freedom. In the long battle between her and Harry, she had bought and paid for the final word.

When the last of his belongings were removed from the house, Lilly had thought to find some peace, but Harry's departure had left yet another void to fill, left a new uncertainty about life and her ability to cope with it alone. For so long now she had been living to contradict Harry; without him to defy, there seemed no pattern to her days. When you existed negatively, she thought, you have no idea of how to be positive.

The days were stretching into months, and she hated their

emptiness, her loneliness, and viewed everything and everyone with caution, as if she were enduring some long but necessary convalescence from a near-fatal illness. Every day she made elaborate promises to herself that if only she would get out of bed and go through the motions of living, then she might make it. Try to survive, she said. She had to, didn't she? Wasn't the choice to fail gone now, right down the drain alongside the option to place the blame on Harry, if she did not make it?

Gradually the weeks began to mix more comfortably; her surroundings seemed less a jail than before. It would be just a matter of time, she promised, before she would be able to make a plan. For thirty-three years she had been threatening to make a plan for her life and it was high time she got around to it. At other times, things did not seem to be as difficult as she had feared; in fact, she told herself that this business of answering only to one's own self was not so bad at all. Sometimes she felt so good that she wondered why the *sadness* of being alone was always stressed, why no one ever mentioned the compensations. When she was calm, she saw that Mags and Teddy relaxed also; like little animated creatures from a Disney cartoon, they scurried out of their secret and protective hiding places to rub themselves pleasurably against her. Together, she thought, they could grow braver every day, the three of them. That was how it should have been all along, she reasoned, just the three of them.

Maggie was eight, Teddy not yet five; seldom did either speak of Harry, sensing intuitively that it was not a subject for happy discussion, but often they spent a day or two at their father's apartment, or went with him for dinner in a restaurant, the untasted wonders of which would be related, guardedly, but with no small amount of enthusiasm. Lilly's jealousy over these excursions had to be pressed back, stored inside her somewhere alongside the ever-present guilt she felt for all the times she had neglected these children, those stupid, wasteful years passed with concern only for herself. Constantly, Lilly searched the children for signs of damage, those psychological wounds which might at any moment break open and cause them further harm. She redoubled her efforts to make up to them for the pain of their ruptured world, dismissing the housekeeper and cooking for them herself, dressing them, taking them special places and, most of all, loving them with all the pent-up need to love that she had so long held inside.

In the evenings she and the children had quiet dinners in the kitchen and the three of them would pass an equally peaceful night at comfortable proximity; somehow it was enough for each of them to know that the others were nearby. There were smothering moments, though, times when the responsibility of the children seemed an awesome burden, times when she would look at them playing or sitting across the table from her and wonder how she had come to be in charge of such small and dependent creatures. Would she ever truly be able to take control of all their lives, handle the never-ending demands being made on her questionable maturity? Somehow she would swallow back the panic, covering her misgivings about her inadequacy with a bleak smile, and remind herself that she owed her children something, maybe everything. They hadn't asked to be delivered into her care, and weren't they, after all, really her salvation? The two small anchors of her sanity? Be patient, she would caution, take time now, go slowly, love these children and give them a whole person to love back.

Eventually, Lilly came to feel that Mags and Teddy held some secret combination in their small hands, the combination to things that were important beyond her present understanding. Sensing this, she was overwhelmed by a wonderful contentment, reasoning on those occasions that there was a great deal of difference between solitude and loneliness, but always lurking behind her pleasure was the suspicion that she was not paying heavily enough for her past mistakes, that she was getting off too easily, her debts too graciously canceled. Somewhere, she fretted, somewhere and somehow she would have all the mistakes of her life catch up with her. The piper was bound to demand payment sooner or later.

Her calmness alternated with anxiety; when her mood was pessimistic and she allowed the fright to overtake her, she even thought to phone Harry, to tell him that she couldn't stand alone, that maybe she had not really tried hard enough, and if she did, did he think they might be able to work things out? Such urges came late in the night and she would fight them, perhaps drinking a bit too much, or taking one or two sleeping pills to get her through, hoping to feel differently in the light of day, which, of course, she did, but still, she kept wishing for someone, Harry, Kevin, maybe a strange new person, someone, anyone, who would come into her life and give it direction.

Eventually the reclusive existence began to wear thin and Lilly felt the old desire to be once again at the center, to know people who disposed of power, who moved and shaped events. For so long she had taken those prerogatives for granted, and now it disturbed her to be left out of the decorative and decorated world; she missed that funny call to excitement and it became more and more difficult to ignore it. But how was she to reenter the world? And with whom? It worried Lilly that more and more she was allowing herself to long for her childhood, reasoning that childhood was painful but it was also a time of options; adulthood was having made all the choices, rightly or wrongly, and being stuck with them. More than anything else, she wished for a friend.

# 16

THERE had really been nothing else to do but telephone George Sabberstein. The decision was instant and she picked up the phone immediately and dialed his number. His voice sounded impatient and Lilly nearly hung up before announcing herself. "Have you been rescuing any maidens in distress lately?" she asked.

"The streets are full of them," was the terse reply. "Who is this?"

"I think I'm Lilly Shawcross." The pause was unbearable. "Remember? You gave me your card for emergencies?"

"Oh! The lady with the hard head? The same one who wouldn't return any of my calls a few months back?"

"Invincibly yours."

"How've you been? Street brawls aren't the same without you."

"I've been looking for myself."

"Any luck?"

"I'm around here somewhere, I think!"

He laughed. "You should be more careful with your valuables."

"You sound like an insurance adjuster." She was beating around the bush and thought he probably knew it.

"What can I do for you?" he asked.

Lilly wasn't sure how to put it.

"Well, I thought that maybe Mags and I might repay your gallantry with a drink or dinner."

"Yeah, uh. Sure."

"How does your dance card look?" she asked.

"Like my bank balance."

"Can I make an appointment?"

"I think I can pencil you in. What's your pleasure?"

"Whatever suits you," she said.

"The ball's in your court, honey."

"Tonight?"

"It just so happens"—he paused, making himself sound deliberately executive—"that I am planning to be starved this very evening."

"Eight o'clock?"

"Sounds good."

"Reserve judgment till you've tried my cooking."

"I'm a stoic, not an epicure. You still in Georgetown? Same place?"

"So that's where I'm at! Yes, same address you delivered the battered goods. What was it, four months ago?"

"Six," he said. "But who's counting?"

There was an awkward pause.

"I'll be there at eight," he said.

"George?"

"Yeah?"

"You can leave your white charger home this time."

"Why?" He was laughing.

"It's already on the menu."

"I can eat one." He broke the connection.


It was a lovely evening. Maggie was unusually glad to see George, even surprising Lilly with her vivid recollection of their first meeting. Teddy was less enthusiastic, asking immediately if George was to be his new daddy.

"You've already got one, son."

"Are you going to put a seed in my mother's tummy?"

Lilly took the little boy up to bed and returned to fix a drink for her and George.

"He's into the birds and bees," she said, referring to Teddy.

"More into my motives, I'd say."

"That part of the New Chivalry?"

"Just wishful thinking. We white knights are filthy beasts at heart."

"Have you had much experience with that sort of thing?"

"Having my dirty mind read by kids?"

"No"—she laughed—"putting seeds in ladies' stomachs."

"Once or twice too often." Lilly saw it was not a pleasant topic, but George went on talking. "I've got three children. Big. Too big. It was better when they were Teddy's age."

"You mean it gets worse?"

"I mean"—his head shook knowingly, rather sadly—"that about a thousand years ago I had two little boys and a sugar-and-spice girl. When I wasn't looking, something got to them.

That happens, you know?" It seemed such a personal statement; Lilly wished to spare him further explanations, but she said nothing.

"You turn around one day," he said, "and those trusting little faces are replaced by insolent-eyed strangers, lodgers who go by the old names and sleep in the same beds, but you don't know who they are anymore. Neither does Harriette."

"Harriette?"

"The lady whose tummy grew the seeds. My wife."

"Oh?" Had she thought him unmarried? The whole world was married! "I hadn't realized you were married."

"For twenty-two years."

"It makes my ten sound like a suspended sentence."

"Yeah, I read someplace that the Shawcrosses had abandoned the American Dream." He glanced around as if for corroboration.

"The first on the block."

"If you can't fish, cut bait."

"You turn a quaint phrase."

"Part of the profession. Wire-service guys don't get hired for their poetry. But I mean it; if you can't live with somebody then you should get the hell out. If you can afford it."

"Does that imply domestic bliss out your way?" The conversation was getting too heavy too quickly; Lilly walked to the bar to fix more drinks.

"You want that answered?" he asked.

"Only if you want to."

"It's simple enough. About another thousand years ago I was ready to cop a degree at Penn State, my ticket to graduate school, the Philadelphia lawyer bit. Your usual saga: plump Jewish mom educating her son for the bar. You know anything about Jewish mothers? Or any kind of Jews?"

They were definitely getting too personal, but Lilly answered him anyhow. "I was married to one, only he didn't like to be reminded of it. The original anti-Semitic Semite."

"Not so original. Did he have a mother? Or spring full-grown from an ersatz shiksa?"

"A what?"

"You know, was his mother the kind of Jewish lady who wants her kids to be accepted so much that she brings them up to be more Protestant than Norman Vincent Peale?"

" 'Knows Mother!' as the old joke goes."

"It's called pubescent assimilation. The mother makes the kid ashamed of his heritage. Plucks his Jewish feathers young and he grows up hating what he never even tried being. The mother. What was she like?"

"Hard to say. She had more faces than Eve. Actually I only saw her once. Harry and I were living in New York at the time. Her name is Nora—she lives on the West Coast, hates the East, only comes back every four or five years to have something lifted, her chin, her neck; I think it was her eyes that trip, I blot her out. Dreadful woman! You know, she suggested only an hour after we met that I should consider siliconing my chest. There was this way she had of being constantly magnanimous, the kind of generosity that makes you always have to be grateful. Does that make sense?"

George nodded.

"She took Harry and me to a restaurant one night, an expensive one, and all through the meal she kept on with how much it cost but that nothing was too good for Harry and his sweet little wife. She must have mentioned a dozen times that there was this adorable dress in Bonwit's window that she would have bought but, of course, she would rather treat us to a night on the town. That sort of thing. She brought me a Louis Vuitton purse and didn't have the nerve to come right out and say how much it cost. Just the constant alluding to its chicness—little innuendos about how ridiculously overpriced it was but how worth the sacrifice.

"I once made the terrible mistake of complimenting her on her perfume and she insisted I take the rest of the bottle—'My dear Lilly, you must have this; yes, I am partial to it and heavens knows when I'll get back to Paris at my age, but it will give me more pleasure to see you happy.' Sacrifice. I loathe perfume and I loathed that woman. I mean, she was so awful I could almost feel sorry for Harry. Funny thing is, she had a strange effect on me, gave me an irritating urge to please her, not because I liked her, but in a strange way it was like I was a little kid around her, too polite, nauseatingly deferential—the way I was to my mother's friends.

"She was also the vainest woman I ever saw." Lilly paused to remember. "She spent five hours at the hairdresser's before going into the hospital to have her face tucked up. I was a pretty dumb kid at the time, but I knew a narcissist when I saw one. Being around her made up my mind that the day my appearance becomes that important, I'd perform some drastic home surgery on both wrists.

"Harry and I dropped her off at the hospital that night and we were like two sprung kids, even went to '21' to celebrate."

Lilly smiled at the recollection. "We got pretty drunk. Discussing Harry's mother was about as interesting a conversation as we had had in years. We spent hours at it, laughing and inventing corny stories about her operations and all. Coming out of the restaurant, there was this poor old dwarf on the street corner selling newspapers. Harry pointed to him and said, 'See that little guy? I bet he's made up of all the bits and pieces some plastic surgeon cut out of Nora!' It was a sick joke but the idea broke us up and we walked for blocks falling into each other with laughter. I said to Harry that Nora had been lifted so many times that her navel was where her mouth used to be. Junk like that." Lilly looked sadly off into the distance, then added, "When I think about it, I guess that ridiculous woman gave Harry and me one of the best nights of our entire marriage. It was the same evening that the first seed found its way to the ole tummy." She patted her middle. "It's probably the only time anyone ever got pregnant because of a face lift."

"Not your typical Jewish mother," he said.

"What is?"

"The immediate past Mrs. Sabberstein. There was nothing vain or svelte about my mother. She weighed in at close to two hundred pounds, vowed she never ate a bite. The born martyr. She kept cases of cream soda for my sister and me but there was never one around when we wanted it. She'd act surprised when the icebox was empty; never touched the stuff herself, she said. 'It's for you children.' That's how she saw everything: for us. Everything was ours except what we wanted to do with our lives.

"She meant well. We were all she had and she flung love over us like a wet towel. Muriel, my sister, married a Jersey haberdasher when she was seventeen. She was full of energy and spirit, that girl. When she became Madame Katz, she just solidified, became massive. They live in Brooklyn now and the ironic thing is that Muriel turned into what she had left home to escape. Thoby, her second son, is in law school now. Little George, the oldest, is My Son the Doctor! We never make it far from the tree that grew us, do we?"

"I sure God hope so." Lilly was not at all certain. "Did you marry your mother?" she asked.

"You mean Harriette? God, no. Mom hated her, died happy with ole Harriette to kick around. I think I told you, I was about to graduate and go to law school. That was about the time Harriette and I started hanging around together. She was a literature major, wanted to teach, mold young minds and all that. We managed to mold something else before she got around to getting her degree." George was at the bar, refilling his glass again; he turned to face her as he talked. "We were, to put it indelicately, knocked up in the prime of life. Poor Harriette. We hardly knew each other, but we were married the day after I graduated. My mother never forgave her for trapping her boy. Swell twist, eh?

"She was damn game, Harriette was. She worked for one of the professors in her department for as long as she was able. I was in law school and working nights, and it wasn't much fun for either of us. When Josh was born, it was more than we could manage." He shrugged, turning his attention back to the bar but glancing at her over his shoulder. "The classic story: boy drops out of school; girl tends baby, has a few more. That's all she wrote for the ole dream machine."

"What happened?"

"I wangled a job in the sports department at the *Bulletin*. Hated the hell out of jocks ever since. When their best reporter went to Monaco to cover the Rainier-Kelly wedding, I filled in. Stayed in the job until another international event called away the fellow on the political desk. I guess I did O.K. because they sent me here to Washington. A few lucky breaks on good stories and both wire services were dazzled by my footwork. You know the rest, including the chorus about how I had my ass booted out of Vietnam."

"A Pulitzer Prize counts for something?"

"Not with the butcher, it doesn't. Oh, I'm not complaining. The front office is good to me. Gave me the White House detail. Not a bad substitute for missing out on being the Philadelphia lawyer. My mother was never very enthusiastic about my being the oldest boy on the campaign bus. I'm not so crazy about it anymore myself."

"What would you rather be?"

"I'd like not to be the age I am and still be hanging around the White House pressroom while some kid fifteen years younger than I am lies through his teeth about what goes on in the Oval Office."

"You can write. Why not do it full time?"

"Money. A real writer needs some of that. Or fewer mouths to feed. Fiction or nonfiction, it's all the same. Only the young and unencumbered can afford to take a chance on writing the serious stuff. I'm stuck with reporting, punching the old clock. Look, I don't mean to sound put-upon; it's a boring subject."

Lilly was impressed by George's straightforward attitude. "How about the kids? I mean children; I hate the expression 'kids.'"

"Ah! The precious children. Who knows where to begin with them anymore? Or where to end. Josh is twenty-one; Susan and Mark fall somewhere along the line at yearly intervals. I really don't know what happened to them. They were good Little Leaguers and Brownies one day, and somehow things changed. I scream at Harriette because bringing them up was her job but that's only to make myself feel better. She did what she could, a damn good mother for a lit major who couldn't afford a diaphragm. We spend a lot of time blaming each other, but it doesn't alter the fact that we have raised three zombies who show precious little interest in doing anything besides watching television. Hell, honey, mine don't even get out in the street and protest. Too lazy. They watch it on the tube. Sit there and call the world rotten and never lift a finger except to change channels or stuff their faces.

"Harriette has no control, especially over Susan; wild as a hare, that one is. I hate to admit this, but there are times when I think the pill was invented too soon. It would be a relief to have her follow in our footsteps, but I pity the poor son of a bitch who gets stuck with her.

"Christ, I don't know why I'm telling you this. I got started on it when you brought around your babies. Yes, babies. Too bad there isn't some way to keep them like that. Most kids today would be better off living in endless adolescence than to turn out like ours. Frankly, they don't like me any better than I do them. Pretty heavy stuff, huh? You know I didn't know how much I meant all this till now. I ought to be drunker than I am to run on at the mouth this way." He stood and went back to the bar.

"They never bathe," he said. "I think that gets me the most. I don't believe, between them, they've emptied a whole bottle of shampoo in the last three years. They don't even have the ambition to get stoned. Rude and dirty and lazy. Oh, shit, Lilly. I'm not fooling you, am I? Part of the reason I don't like them is that their very insolent presence reminds me every day that I failed them somewhere along the line and I don't even know how or when."

George Sabberstein was a near stranger but Lilly wanted to walk over to him, to hug him, to say the nice things she felt for him, but she dared not intrude; he already showed signs of disgust with himself for telling her so much, and the horror of his story, Lilly thought, is that it could happen to me, to Mags and Teddy. She shook her head to dispel the terrifying vision, concentrating instead on George, privately thinking him over. No man had ever been so open with her, so clearly vulnerable yet so unconcerned with his image.

"It's just the times," she offered, feeling herself a Pollyanna, but knowing it was the best she could offer.

"Perhaps," he said, becoming suddenly silent.

Lilly felt uncomfortable again. She wanted George Sabberstein as a friend and here she was sitting stupidly by and letting him unfold the ugly part of his life, the very things that he was probably seeking her company to forget.

"Look," she said, a touch too brightly, "unless you like your horse meat well-done, we'd better eat."

He rewarded her with a grateful look, started to say something, then hesitated.

"What, George? Tell me."

"You're a nice lady."

Such a shy offering; she accepted it with the same timidity. "And you are a nice man."

He looked straight at her as he spoke. "The question is, Can a nice man find happiness with a nice lady over a nice dinner?"

"If we aren't any better than the food, then a couple of us are in real trouble," she replied, noticing with relief that his heavy mood was passing, his gloom lifting as if she had somehow helped him over a bad time.

"As my old gentile mother would have put it," Lilly said, "when all else fails, there is still food and drink. The ultimate in Southern comfort."

"We didn't quite get around to your mother, did we? Do we like her?"

"We aren't sure about that. I think the subject will keep."

"But not dinner."

"Definitely not dinner."

Over the ensuing months it occurred to Lilly that she and George had fallen into a fast friendship out of a mutual and desperate need to talk and share their thoughts; he was, in his way, as anxious for companionship as she, and probably as lonely. There were a lot of pals, he told her, mostly guys, the ones who worked at UPI, friendly competitors, other journalists who traveled on the same campaigns vying good-naturedly for leads and stories and swapping the kind of general information that made them look good to their editors, but no nice ladies to rats around with; that was how he put it and that was how he saw her. He could take Lilly as she came, an unfinished person who needed his friendship, a surrogate for the wife he was accustomed to leaving behind.

"You are," he let her know, "O.K. in my book, kid—warts and all." No other demands were made except those Lilly had begun to make on herself. She felt so at ease with George that she tried to explain to him her pushing desire to do something with her life. She was, she said, overwhelmed by her own uselessness.

"I'm just hanging around, you know? I don't *do* anything. I guess I'm the worst kind of cipher, living comfortably on an inheritance, raising two children, and getting green-eyed with envy about the work of my one and only friend." The smile with which she delivered this judgment on herself did not fool George; little did.

"Look. It's me who's selfishly sopping up your spare time," he said. This was partly true; they were together a great deal, almost in the sense of being a couple, however unsexual the liaison. That George was Lilly's only friend did not concern her; she was much too grateful to question herself on the subject. Often they met for lunch and they had dinner together nearly every night. She usually went along with him to cover presidential speeches, ending the evening hanging over his typewriter as he filed his copy, accepting each page as he finished to read and approve it, sometimes to make suggestions. George seldom rejected her additions to his story, saying that four eyes were better than two. Her insights were often keen, and although slanted differently than his, combined, they made his reporting fuller, more colorful. They thought so much alike, arriving at conclusions in their different ways but each adding to the knowledge and perceptions of the other. Being with George was such fun, such a warm kind of completeness, that Lilly repressed her misgivings that he was spending too much time away from his family, making it easy for her not to bother to enlarge her own circle of acquaintances. They could discuss everything together, even laugh guardedly about the platonic nature of their relationship. The absence of sex between them bothered George, she knew, but it bothered her only because it bothered him. Things were enough for Lilly as they were, but occasionally he seemed to question their arrangement.

"Some of the guys think you and I are having a hot and heavy time of it."

"You make it sound like a matter of national concern."

"Well, I guess our togetherness isn't what you could call a

classified secret. An inquisitive free press is just another name for busybodies."

Lilly had long realized that George, in his funny way, was annoyed that his colleagues thought he was enjoying special favors, as he put it; he seldom broached the subject but he was rather old-fashioned and she was aware of his concern for her reputation. Especially did his attitude come to light one night as they were pulling apart lobsters in the back room of a restaurant on K Street, their presence there so accepted that the black waiters in their long white aprons greeted them pleasantly and seated them deferentially. George had two paper bibs tied ceremoniously about his neck in a futile attempt to spare his clothing; he was dipping his napkin in water and rubbing at the butter stain on his tie.

"Why is it that whenever you see me in a necktie you crave lobster?"

"I own stock in your dry cleaner's." Lilly was licking her own greasy fingers, talking as she did. "Wouldn't it be an easier life all around if we could wipe out all the messy spots we leave behind?" She was wetting her napkin now, dabbing at his tie, too.

"You mean, Lady Macbeth, that a little water could cleanse us of all our evil deeds?"

"Not with all the perfume in Arabia, you ass. But yes, I wouldn't mind going back and erasing a few mistakes."

"Like where to begin?" he asked. She knew not to be insulted. George understood what she was getting at; he always did. "You want to wipe out some of your past?" he said. "Like the bomber pilot no longer proud of the target count on the fuselage?"

Lilly smiled. George enjoyed the occasional reference to his years in the Air Force; he was part of the generation who had fought the "good war" and for whom all the things that followed were strangely anticlimactic.

"I thought we were speaking of loves, not wars, to contort a cliché," she said.

George was swishing his fingers in a bowl of water and drying them on a crumpled napkin; he motioned to the waiter for another bottle of wine before he lit a cigarette, waiting for her to go on.

"You know, it doesn't bother me what people think," she said. "It has never bothered me. Never had enough friends to get the habit of worrying about the impression I make on them, but there were plenty of people who saw me as a wanton, back when Harry and I were married, and I guess I talked a great game, let them draw all the wrong conclusions. It didn't faze me; doesn't now. What does bother me is different."

George did not speak, knowing her too well by now to interrupt her train of thought.

"All those notches that were supposed to be on my belt? Those scalps that were supposedly dangling from my rear-view mirror?"

"I remember hearing a rumor or two."

"Well, most of them—actually all of them except one—were part of a legend that didn't take place. Just my way of being noticed."

"You as pure as the driven snow, Lilly? I'm only the latest in a long line of unconsummated affairs?"

"That dog don't hunt, huh?" They laughed at her use of Lyndon Johnson's phrase; quoting the President was not popular. "I know it's hard to believe, but I never went to bed with my old running mates."

"Politics makes empty beds, fellows!"

"You had to say that!"

"Low resistance for bad jokes. Sorry about that one. Go on, I'm chastened."

"Look, put aside the reputation I had when I lived with Harry. I don't care about that. What I care about is that there is, or was, something, well, kind of lacking in my emotional makeup—something that could permit me those drawing-room romances, which is mostly what they were. The trouble was that I was content without the sexual rapture. I still am. That's sick, isn't it?" Lilly's face was drained of color whereas it should have been flushed. George was staring at her, thinking over what she had said. She rushed ahead. "I mean, anyone can sleep around for whatever reasons. People meet, like each other, make love. That's normal, and unless a woman gives out numbers like they do at the bakery, it's all right by me. Whose business is it who does what to whom and all that? I'm saying that that is at least healthy. What concerns me is that I could have had those flirtations *without* falling into bed. It's the worst type of promiscuity."

"Are you trying to tell me that Lilly Shawcross, the flamboyant talk of the Kennedy years, was, beneath it all, a run-of-the-mill cock teaser?"

"I haven't had that precise compliment since high school. But, yes, if it must be so charmingly phrased. And with none of the mitigating circumstances of adolescence. No fear of pregnancy, or social censure, or ridicule or exposure. None of the above. You see, that's the sick part, George. I was playing games to get attention and then refused to deliver the goods. When I finally did take up with somebody, it was for the romance, the animal warmth, never mind the sex. Now, that's abnormal and don't try to argue me out of it."

"Who's arguing?"

"I'm afraid of sex. That's it, isn't it? How in God's name have I gotten to be thirty-four years old, the mother of two children, and still be terrified of sex?"

George was pensive, then he questioned her gently, almost in a whisper: "Hasn't it ever been good for you?"

She could only manage a negative shake of her head.

"Lilly, I know I may be taking this to a more gut level than you've put in for, and if I'm being a lout, throw something at me. But surely there have been times, somebody, somewhere?"

She continued shaking her head.

"I guess I needn't ask about Harry."

"It went from bad to worse. I used to lie there and plan my spring wardrobe."

"Christ, what a waste of natural resources."

"That's the point, George." Lilly stubbed out her cigarette. "Are there any natural resources?"

"Sweetheart, it'll happen." He took her hand. "You are a full, complete and lovely woman. A lot of passion there, Lil. You don't fool old George about things like that." He looked at her hard. "Son of a bitch, what a fucking waste." They both laughed; unintentional or not, the humor was appropriate. "I promise, honey. There is nothing missing inside you. It will happen and you'll be ready. Look at me, Lilly. I know what I'm telling you is true."

"When?" She was about to cry.

"When you respect someone, learn to trust yourself to him. The right person and a little know-how. It's worth waiting for."

Lilly drew up her brows in comic disbelief.

"You know, honey," he said, "if you'd just learn to like yourself a little more, you could let go to someone else who likes you." She glanced up sharply, disturbed by the tacit suggestion in the statement, but George was signaling the waiter again.

"What we need to work on first," he said, looking back to Lilly, "is finding you something to do. Honest toil, something of your own to believe in. The other will happen."

Lilly seized upon the change of subject, delighted to add to it. "How about my giving cooking lessons?" It was an old joke between them.

"We've enough war, famine and pestilence without turning you loose on what's left of the world. There has to be some less lethal outlet for your genius."

"I could sign on in the White House kitchen. Kill a lot of birds with one meal."

"There's a more humane way of getting Johnson out of office! What interests you? What would you really like to do?"

"You've ruled out the culinary possibilities. I've vetoed the hooking profession. When we chalk off cooking and screwing, what's left to us unlettered females?"

"What gives you the most pleasure in the world? Come on —one, two, three. Name them."

She only had to think a moment. "Showing off is top of the list. I like the sound of my own voice and I adore fingering fatuousness in others—ignoring it in myself, of course."

"You've just described all our most eminent politicians. There's more to you than that. Come on now, what are you truly happy doing?"

"Well, I love movies. Perhaps my single passion."

"God knows you go enough. Maybe that's what you ought to do. Combine passion with your exhibitionism. You know, you might just be damn good at it."

"At what?"

"Reviewing movies. You use words well."

"I wouldn't be up to a typewriter. I can only talk about them."

"Then why not do that? Get on the air and talk about movies."

"Over what? Ham radio?" Somewhere inside Lilly was stirring the kind of enthusiasm that made her uneasy; she knew better than to yearn after something that sounded so good— letting herself in for disappointment was the old Lilly; the new one knew better. Still?

"With all this screaming and hollering about equal opportunity for broads and blacks, those television types are pretty pressured to take a chance on you mouthy minorities. Too bad you're not black. It would make things easier. A real twofer: Black, Female and Qualified."

"Just female." Lilly's enthusiasm was passing.

"Kid, you are as qualified to see a movie and give your opinion of it as anybody of any sex or color."

"Sorry you aren't World Commander. Actually, George, it's not my Walter Mitty dream of greatness, being a film critic. The whole world is turning upside down and I should admit to people how much I like Doris Day?"

"I've heard you on your soapbox. Don't traffic with me on that. 'George Sabberstein, movies are one of the clearest and handiest mirrors we have.' I can hear you now, all that shit about films being cultural artifacts. The 'big lie,' that's what you're always bellowing about. Well, why not get paid for it. Listen, honey, under the clever disguise of movie buff, you could say a whole lot more, a lot about why we dream the dreams we do. Why we want to be sought-after, successful. Christ, for that matter, why we fail. The whole smorgasbord of human disappointment. The price of movies has gone up, but the message sure hasn't changed." George was caught up by the idea, urging her along. "By God, Lil, it's a natural. I think we ought to give it a try." He was motioning to the waiter, going through the pantomime of signing the check. "We just might be on to something. What do you say?"

"I say, 'Ready whenever you are, C.B.' I also say, 'How?'"

"Leave it to Mike Todd here. Christ, a star is born. I feel like a stage mother!"

"I prefer Mike Todd."

"Then I'll buy a cigar. A big, long black cigar." He was helping her on with her coat, lifting her slightly off the floor, and hugging her in the middle of the crowded room. "Come on, baby. Cheer up. We's goin' into show biz."

George left early the next morning on Air Force One, accompanying the President on a junket as part of the press pool, the kind of hectic two days he hated—he'd often described it to her, the thanklessness of monitoring the President's actions and then having to dole out the facts to the rest of the reporters.

"The other guys always think you're holding back the good stuff—judging everyone by their own standards. I'm guilty, too, I guess. It's a crummy job. I'd rather be the tellee than the teller. Funny thing, Lil, the gals on the White House detail don't expect you to level with them; they know better than to expect fair play. Sometimes I believe those broads file better stories because they're never let inside the fraternity, not so accustomed to being spoonfed their lines. It makes those old war horses come closer to the truth and there just may be a message in that somewhere. Christ! What bliss to be a woman and not have to be the pool reporter! I'm all for it."

Still, he had gone. She fretted over their conversation while he was away. The possibility of her becoming a film critic had taken a firm grip; right or wrong, the long repressed wish to have a job was now out in the open and she could deal with nothing until she came to terms with it. But she needed George, needed him to energize her. I am not, she accused herself, a self-starter, and she wondered for the hundredth time if all women were like her, waiting around for direction. So often now Lilly wished for a woman friend to whom she could make these admissions—if not to be reassured, then to wallow in the comfort of a similar misery—but there were no women she cared to confide in even if she were to overcome, miraculously, her distrust of other females. Always with Harry she had felt he compared her with and pitted her against others of her own sex, and the memory of her inadequacy left her apprehensive. Women made her uncomfortable, frightened her, and she knew it was useless to wish it were otherwise.

Lilly's relief was enormous when George returned. He phoned in the late morning.

"Your friendly theatrical agent, Sabberstein, here. Home from the wars and up to here in barbecue and the bucolic bliss of the Pedernales." George did not go in much for the protracted exchange of telephone niceties.

"What's your pleasure, treasure?" he said.

"Still the same dreamy little creature you left behind, George. Looking for a mate and a place in the sun. And it's raining. That answer your question?" She was irritable, more than she had been in months.

"Do not impale the bearer of glad tidings on your spearlike tongue."

"What tidings?" She did not miss the upbeat sound to his voice; he had good news—she recognized the playfulness that generally preceded its delivery.

"Put on some sexy outfit that would make even an honest judge think you're courting rape. Perfume, the whole bag of tricks. Meet me at the expense account joint, can't recall the name, but it's the big restaurant next to ABC's office on Connecticut Avenue—across from the Mayflower—you know the one?"

She did.

"All right, then, twelve-thirty."

"What's up besides my curiosity?"

"You'll see. Just keep the sarcasm at a minimum. I'll hold up cue cards. You know how to do. Cross your legs a lot and try not to give it away immediately that you're the smartest piece of ass around." Flippancy did not conceal his urgency.

"George, what's this all about?"

"I promised you a star on the door and a Bigelow on the floor. Today's the day."

"What do I have to do for it?" She wanted the ground rules made clear; she could guess at the rest.

"No casting couch. Not yet, anyhow. Just paint yourself up and try not to be a wise guy. No one-liners, Lil. O.K.?" He was warning her; she understood that much.

"I'll be naked without one-liners."

"That's the ticket, kid. Come as naked as you can." He hung up in his usual brusque manner. George, she thought fondly, missed his calling by not being a collection agent.

She arrived early, took her time parking the car and then walked up and down in front of the shops, pretending interest in the window displays at Elizabeth Arden until a stylish ten minutes after the appointed hour when she crossed the street and went down the restaurant's wide carpeted stairs to present herself to the maître d'. "Mr. Sabberstein's table," she said. "He's expecting me."

"Walk this way, please."

Lilly started to giggle—too many Groucho movies, but she controlled an urge to imitate the man's prissy gait. George stood to greet her, all business, making the introductions with unusual formality. A Mr. Sheepshanks on one side—was it Bob or Bill? *Sheepshanks!* She would break up if she caught George's eye; she looked demurely down. Ed Something or Other was to George's left. Lilly nodded to them both, wondering if she was allowed to drink; she ordered a martini anyway, addressing the waiter directly. "Vodka," she said, "and very dry."

"As I'm sure you know," George said, looking toward her meaningfully, "Bill and Ed are with Channel Eight."

Lilly did not know but pretended the knowledge was universal.

"I've been telling them about you, Lilly. I thought it was time to bring you together."

"Our first nondancing performance?" It slipped out, one of those convenient quips that were supposed to hide her nervousness. George shot her a look of caution and Lilly tried to recoup with a broad smile.

"I'm very pleased to be here," she added. Well, she was certainly not that; this lady-at-the-tea-party bit was not going to be easy.

George continued. "Bill and Ed are starting a new early-hour news program. Going on the air from ten to eleven, beating the other late-night wrap-ups. They're toying with the idea of reviewing movies—something totally new in the Washington market—and seeing as there aren't any established pros in the field to call upon, I thought maybe you might have something to contribute." Lilly marveled at George's ability to sound so offhand.

"An early news show is a brilliant idea," she said.

George rewarded her with a smile and Lilly swallowed some of her drink, rubbing her palms on her skirt. Both men were eager to acknowledge her compliment, almost preening, she noticed.

"We have some real problems, however." This came from Sheepshanks and was delivered in grave tones; he proceeded as if from memory. "You see, the local theater owners do a lot of important advertising, revenue necessary to an independent station." He paused for her to absorb the significance of his words. "We wouldn't want to lose income by offending anyone with the wrong kind of reviews."

"We also don't want to short-sheet our viewers by not offering some type of movie comment." This was offered by the man named Ed; Lilly sipped her drink, mentally filing away his reference to the bed.

"Yes," she said. "I can see your problem."

"We also have some misgivings about a girl in that role. The public may not be ready to accept a female in a position of authority."

Look humble, Lilly told herself, darting a glance at George and seeing him deliberately look the other way.

"I see." She emulated their concern, but her temper was rising; she shifted uncomfortably on the banquette, her bare thighs stuck to the leather.

"Naturally, we are going to talk to a lot of gals. We see the opening as a real break for women. What do you think?" Sheepshanks was speaking to her.

"I think I'll have another drink."

"The idea, Lil. What about the idea?" George's foot was kicking her shins.

"I think," she said, choosing her words carefully, "that any television station clever enough to conceive so unique a news format could handle the advertisers *and* a female reviewer."

Lilly looked down to hide her annoyance; George, however, was entirely pleased with her response. The others straightened in their seats, clearly delighted by the praise and waiting for more.

"I mean, times are changing and a station with your reputation for honesty—" She paused to collect her thoughts, especially the channel's call number. "Well, Channel Eight has a responsibility to the public." Her new drink came and she took two large swallows, warming to the subject. "It would just somehow figure that the theater owners need you just as much as you need them. And the audience undoubtedly deserves full coverage on all levels of everyday life."

Bill and Ed exchanged approving glances as she continued. "As for using a woman, that, of course, takes equal courage. But if the theater owners should object to an occasionally harsh review, then they can always discredit it as having come from a female. What do *we girls* know?" She looked down at her empty glass; the second drink was finished—Lilly, unfortunately, was not. "Oh, let's be straight with each other. I'm a woman."

Overlooking their patronizing grins, she went on, lighting a cigarette first. "I know a little something about films. It's the directors who are important now, the techniques, the script, the complete package." They were listening to her very carefully, weighing and judging each word.

"But I've been able to recognize a piece of shit on the screen since I was twelve and I take the medium more seriously than it takes itself. I would not be particularly ladylike in anything I said about a film—a ticket to which is now costing the general public almost the price of a roast beef." There was a stunned silence and Lilly motioned to the waiter for another drink.

"I guess what I'm saying, gentlemen, is that if you're looking for a token female to give token praise to a sloppy piece of work, I would be more than a token pain in your ass." The third drink was set before her.

"Hollywood has promoted most of the fantasies we live by —especially women; movies have helped persuade us not to act on the same power drive as men. We're almost drowning in that image today." Lilly frowned a little and went on. "And I'm kind of sick of being guilty because I'm not a love goddess or a supermom or a martyr or the girl-next-door. I'm tired of feeling anxious because I'm getting to look a little older than the nymphets on the screen. And the men! I'm really sorry for you poor bastards who think you have to be constantly brave, killing bad guys—looking for women who are eternally flattering *girls*.

"So you see, gentlemen, I see films as important, either for escapism or as honest touchstones to reality. I never saw a movie I couldn't sit through, but I've seldom—especially lately—seen one that has a decent message, or even some good honest fun or, God forbid, both! I'm a bit of a bore on the subject, as you can see."

There was no argument; George merely stared at her, dumbfounded.

"Movies matter to me as I suspect they do to thousands of others. I didn't know before this very minute just how much I'd like to go on your air and talk about these things. I'd do anything for the chance. But I am not about to mislead you as to what I would say or how I would say it . . ." Her voice trailed off. She was looking into first one startled face, then the other.

"I guess what I am, gentlemen, is honest and blunt and very, very sorry that I'm not what you're looking for." All three men disappeared behind the large menus the waiter passed around. Lilly picked up hers and chose the only inexpensive thing on the list. It was the least she could do for good ole Bill and good ole Ed for having wasted their afternoon.

# 17

LILLY looked out the living-room window, guessing it to be about seven; it had been dark for quite a while now. She stretched on the couch, unbending cramped knees that had been curled beneath her for however long she'd been sitting there, lost in thought. Letting her head roll from side to side, she felt the muscles pull; searching one's soul was physically painful too, damn it. She stood up and yawned, feeling unaccountably better than she had felt all day. It was nice to remember the pleasant way her life had changed since that long-ago lunch with Sheepshanks. She would remind George of that when he came back; so much of the credit went to him.

Optimism, the first she'd felt in months, welled inside; she should put some wood in the grate and have a fire burning by the time George got there. Stuffing the logs with newspaper, Lilly thought warmly of George: cheating—that's what he called her excessive use of newspaper in building fires. She smiled again, stacking the full ashtrays and balancing them on top of the empty ice bucket as she went to the kitchen. The clock showed precisely seven. Well, the hour for serious debauchery was now legitimate.

The refrigerator was bare and she was hungry again. They would have to eat out. Where the hell was George? It's time to come home, George, she thought, come share my high spirits—ally, ally, all-in-free. Not quite, but there was definitely light at the end of the tunnel. George hated that phrase, despised it when Nixon and Kissinger allowed it to creep prematurely into the political jargon. God, so many things had changed over the last five years! While she had gone on the air to dissect movies, the war kept on winding its bloody way down. Down to what? Better not get George started on that one either, she cautioned, but she had to laugh, remembering how hard George had worked at knocking Lyndon Johnson off and setting Lilly up.

"Pushing LBJ out of the public eye was nowhere near as difficult as getting Lilly into it," he would say, but her ascent had certainly been faster than Johnson's decline. Probably it would be better not to remind George of Lyndon Johnson, either; the subject wouldn't upset him so much if Johnson had been followed by anyone but Nixon. It was curious that George, like so many of the journalists instrumental in deposing Johnson, now felt such a retrospective affection for the man. Compared to Nixon, they saw LBJ as a paragon of virtue; sometimes they even sounded nostalgic for him. George was always saying that next to Richard Nixon, Genghis Khan looked good.

Rummaging in the pantry, Lilly found two small cans of chili and a large one of corned-beef hash, and sat them on the stove just in case George might not want to go out. She smiled. George said she could lethalize food in tin containers as effectively as runaway botulism.

"You can fuck up a two-car funeral, Lil." Wasn't that how he had described the lunch with Sheepshanks, that lunch that was meant to launch her television career? She had been plenty disappointment by her outburst at the time, too, but she had also been strangely pleased to learn from that encounter just how strongly she was capable of feeling about something that mattered to her. She had been determined not to prostitute herself for the job and would not admit, even to George, that she had been anything but right about her behavior that day. Well, honest, anyhow. Yes, she was certainly honest; she'd learned that much from the experience and was positive of it now. Whatever else she might find lacking in herself lately, her integrity was still intact.

Her depression, however, had been enormous for weeks after she met Bill Sheepshanks. It had taken so little to push her over the edge of despair; Lilly shuddered to recall how easy it had been to give up on herself. No job; no lover. Nothing. Poor, poor Lilly.

Weeks had gone by, she remembered; she never expected to run across Sheepshanks again and she was just going to have to accept the bitter truth that she was never going to do anything constructive with her life. God, she'd been eager to accept defeat, embracing it with the resignation of the weak. One afternoon had been particularly bleak. It was snowing, of all the picturesque backdrops, and Lilly was expecting a return call from Teddy's pediatrician. Foul weather, forlorn woman, sick baby. Too much, even for the silver screen. Had it been a film plot, she would have been the first to poke holes in it. Still, it had been just such a setting when she picked up the phone, ready to give the pharmacist's number to the doctor.

"Hello."

"Is Mrs. Shawcross in?"

At the sound of a strange voice, Lilly subtly altered her accent. "May I say who's calling?"

"Is this the housekeeper?"

"The secretary," Lilly replied efficiently.

"Would you ask Mrs. Shawcross to get in touch with Bill Sheepshanks? If you have a pencil, I'll give you my direct line."

"Bill?" She felt clumsy using his first name. Her voice returned to normal, but she was embarrassed. "This *is* Lilly," she stammered.

"Oh! Well, hello there. It's Bill Sheepshanks here."

"I know." She forced a dry laugh; no need to underscore his stupidity.

"Of course." He returned the fake chuckle. "I was wondering if you were still interested in talking about that spot on the news."

Lilly could hear the roar from the silent receiver. Her breath was slow in coming.

"Sure. If you want to." Leave out the amazement, she warned herself. Show some indifference. Even this guy can smell insecurity.

"We thought we might run a few test tapes on you. No visuals, of course, but you could take a couple of movies you've already seen and wing it. Something we might all be familiar with—you know, a golden oldie. Heh. Heh. Just to get the idea of how it would look."

"Sure. If you want to." Hadn't she just said that?

"We've some studio time on Wednesday. Late. Say around six-thirty?"

"I'll be there."

"Good girl." She let the chauvinistic reference pass; she owed him that much.

Lilly hung up in a state of shock and dialed George, hardly able to get out the good news.

"Oh, baby. Terrific. Goddamn, I'm happy. It must have been your legs."

"Yeah, they were connected to the feet I kept putting in my mouth."

"Lil, you were right. Remember that. It's going to work out. They must have already decided they want you. After all you laid on them, they sure as hell know what they're getting into."

"What shall I play for my first number?" She explained the arrangement.

"How about *The Wizard of Oz?* Even Sheepshanks is bound to have seen that one."

"I was leaning toward *The Man in the Gray Flannel Suit* myself." She was bubbling, drunk on good feeling.

"You won't let up, will you?"

He was happy for her, though, and she knew it; their enthusiasm warranted celebration.

"I'm taking you out to dinner tonight," she said. "I pay."

"Speaking of pay, what is it?"

"I never asked."

"You rich kids have all the fun," he said. She ignored the reference. Never had she been able to disabuse George of the notion that she was above mundane financial concerns.

"I'm honored to be first participant in the rewards of your unexecuted labors," he said. "I've never been comfortable freeloading on the unemployed."

"You'll earn every mouthful. Wait till you hear my routine."

"I thought I had."

"Oh, George, it is going to be all right, isn't it? I'm going to make it."

"I never doubted it."

"Liar."

"Fatalist."

"Oh, George, I do love you so!"

For a moment she thought he'd hung up.

"Don't start lying, kid, you're no good at it." George's laugh was strained. "I'm part of that audience out there that's hankering for truth and candor," he said.

Somehow she had hurt him; she'd figure it out later and make it up to him. Right now she was too excited to think.

"How would I ever get along without you?"

"You don't have to." He was gone before she could say anything more.

It certainly had not been easy; even in retrospect, Lilly saw the fine line she had had to tread to get the job, then to hang on to it. Learning the subtle techniques of television had taken a good many months and the greater part of her energy. Her voice was bad, too slow for the allotted three minutes, too shrill when she was making a point, and much too Southern all around. There were many anxious moments when she had to tape and retape, often three or four tries before the director phoned down from his booth that it was a "keeper."

Changing cameras had been the hardest thing to master; the directions to turn from one camera to another were plainly marked on her script, but Lilly would get so carried away by her own enthusiasm that often she would not see the technical instructions and would talk into the wrong camera. The tape would have to be rewound and she would have to start again. Sheepshanks, she knew, was being unduly patient; his tolerance made her determined to perfect her performance, and the pressure to please made her more nervous and tense. It seemed a comic circle now. But only now.

Lilly had been positively no good with a TelePrompTer; her eyes looked large and blank when she read the big words moving slowly down the apparatus connected to the cameras. She'd had to work strictly from notes, but gradually she got the knack of pacing her words to synchronize with the background visuals—those clips from whatever film she was reviewing and over which she was chromo-keyed, her image made smaller and superimposed over the film she was referring to. Every day she sat herself down in a small office, smoking steadily as she watched her segments played back on the monitor, over and over, making notes for improvement, watching for imperfections that had to be studiously weeded out. A couple of times George joined her for what he called "the water torture tapes," making suggestions with a tactfulness she had not suspected he possessed. Professionals are seldom tolerant of beginners—in any field. Slowly, though, it had all come together, and even she could see the improvement. Sheepshanks had said she was good, damn good.

Once confident of the mechanics and with her voice controlled and conversational, Lilly began to toss into her commentaries the sharp and often harsh parallels between the message of the films and certain events of national significance. She could not resist exposing her own indignation at the repression of women, and the switchboard at the station would light with angry calls. Her mail grew steadily, some of it congratulatory, but most of it irate over her introduction of unpopular opinions into film critiques. At least once each week she found herself sitting before Bill Sheepshanks as he went through the list of adverse calls, handing her the tediously written hate letters, and the dozens of telegrams addressed to the station demanding that "that broad stick to movies."

One religious group monitored her nightly for what they called "Un-American, obscene and unnecessary comments." Her favorite complainer wrote regularly each week, addressing the envelopes in red, white and blue pencil, and demanding that "the Commie-Pinko bitch be fired." The more venomous the message, the more illiterate the missile. A local Zionist group threatened to organize an advertisers' boycott when she reviewed an Israeli film commenting that the movie was dealing with too much propaganda. Actually she had only said that "in the wake of the tragic and sorrowful situation that followed the Six-Day War, it would seem reasonable to expect rational and talented film makers to present a fairer picture of Israeli conditions."

Once, when dissecting a poorly made but commercially popular film in which a young woman's life was tragically ended in a back-alley abortion, Lilly commented that "it seems ironic in an era of moon missiles and immoral land wars that this savagery should be necessary." The Right to Life organization had actually picketed the station, waving glass jars filled with unformed fetuses floating in alcohol.

In a mini-documentary on the deteriorating working conditions in Hollywood and the mass exodus of the country's finest film makers to the more permissive and less costly places in Europe, she had made the seemingly mild observation that the American film industry was suffering not merely from creative stagnation but from greed and lack of innovation, ending her remarks by saying that "institutions rarely die because they perform poorly—witness the survival of the U.S. Postal System." When, in a review of a rerelease of Buñuel's *Belle de Jour*, she had casually suggested it was high time to legalize prostitution, even George said she had gone too far.

Sheepshanks, surrounded by a bevy of accepting subordinates, had urged her to curb her personal views and stick to objective reporting; the threats came later, threats she obstinately ignored. By that time she was equipped with other job offers from competing stations and the perceptible rise in the rating charts during her portion of the broadcast greatly supported her behavior. Lilly was popular with the general public; they either loved or hated her, it did not matter which, because she was watched by a large number of people, statistics of vital importance to the programming department. It had not taken Lilly long to see that the whole point of television was merely to satisfy the sponsors' demand for a large share of the audience.

The theater owners were the worst. Helpful at the beginning, they had bent backwards to accommodate her, but as it became apparent that Lillian Shawcross was not always good for box office, they began complaining, then they threatened and cajoled, daring in some instances to withdraw their advertising dollar from the station unless she softened her attitude. The station, however, realized that if it lost the theater owners' revenue, it could easily be made up by new sponsors who were anxious to buy time on a popular broadcast. Some of the movie houses, especially those located in suburban Virginia and Maryland, took her reviews in stride, maybe howling a bit over a bad critique, but expressing some gratitude for the good ones, which, even they had to admit, were plentiful enough. But not one commercial theater allowed her private screenings. One family-owned chain of District theaters even posted her photograph in their box offices and instructed their cashiers not to admit her to a public showing. The station's lawyers had instituted legal action, and in the end Lilly was permitted to purchase a ticket the same as anyone else.

As she became a more popular attraction, she was allocated additional air time for short specials on films and film techniques and the station also used her frequently on their afternoon talk show, eventually easing the restrictions of her contract to allow her to participate in group discussions on films aired on public broadcasting's education channels. Lilly began to receive a number of assignments from local publications to write articles on movies and their impact on the changing social mores of the sixties; national magazines eventually picked up on her and she began writing for *Cosmopolitan* and *Redbook* on a semi-frequent basis. Then she was even appearing occasionally on daytime talk shows syndicated out of New York, and she was already a familiar panelist on similar shows that emanated from other cities across the country, appearances she programmed to coincide with lectures she was invited to give to women's clubs and organizations where, as a paid speaker, she was permitted the opportunity to acquaint female audiences with the ridiculous image of women in movies. By using old slides of Katharine Hepburn in *Alice Adams,* she sarcastically summed up the plot wherein Miss Hepburn achieves her "grandest ambitions" in the arms of Fred MacMurray; still shots showed Bette Davis, in *June Bride*, "surrendering" her independence at the altar; Margaret Sullavan, in *The Moon's Our Home*, symbolically subjugated by the strait jacket in which Henry Fonda enfolds her; Joan Crawford, the head of a trucking firm, in *They All Kissed the Bride*, falling into a silly swoon at the mere sight of Melvyn Douglas as a labor leader. These films, she would tell her audience, have done as much as anything to make women fearful of asserting their natural need for power.

Lilly could happily discuss endlessly the merits and techniques of Howard Hawks and George Cukor and Frank Capra, the early directors who brought women a sense of their own importance by showing, for example, Jean Arthur's independence in *Mr. Smith Goes to Washington*, Lauren Bacall's equality in *To Have and Have Not*, Hepburn's stridence in *Pat and Mike* and *Adam's Rib*.

"Cukor is my personal favorite," she would announce from the podium, "because he allowed women an intelligent side to their personalities." Her lectures were a mixture of nostalgia and feminine indignation that made Lilly a much-sought-after speaker on the lecture circuit. She ate thousands of chicken parts at hundreds of luncheons, and added to her reputation both as a film critic and as an advocate of the growing movement to free women from their ridiculous and often Hollywood-oriented stereotypes.

There was nothing about movies, new or old, that Lilly was not willing to study and learn. The current Hollywood offerings were a special target; often they were sordid stories of self-defeatism in women who were forced into endless apathy, or plots involving women who used underhanded feminine wiles to disguise their independence in order to partake of romantic love. She was particularly outspoken about the films of Rossellini and Antonioni in which the heroine always met violent death for pursuing her own interests as opposed to those of their American counterparts who depicted women who arrived at a living death, drugged into submission as in the smothering plot of *The Diary of a Mad Housewife*—disillusioned and enslaved by motherhood and housewife drudgery, home and children their jailers. Lilly always ended her diatribe by calling passionately for film heroines who do what they want with their lives and who triumphed in the end.

George summed up her militancy in a tidy phrase. "You're a bore, Lil, a smart-mouthed, moneymaking little bore."

He was right, of course, for that was about the size of it. Lilly was indeed a stellar television attraction and whether George was sarcastic about it or not, she had come a long way on the coattails of the feminist wave. She was vaguely aware of the disparity between her thinking and her behavior—she could argue effectively about the need for women to lead their own lives rather than merely helping a man to lead his—but she did not function so independently in her own emotions. The paradox was that she got a platform for her views only with help from the gentlemen. But only in her work, she thought; there was no helping hand from the men in her personal life. No, that was not quite accurate. Didn't every single broken romance make her throw herself more energetically into her work? Every time a relationship failed, hadn't she picked herself up and concentrated totally on her job? Yes, by God, George had seen to that.

"The best medicine for a broken heart, kid, is hard work." Well, if broken hearts and constant failure with the opposite sex were keys to success, she had every reason to be successful.

Sweet, wonderful George; he'd not only helped her with her career but he was always around to pick up the pieces of her shattered love affairs when, time after time, she was unable to practice the female independence she preached. Christ—she laughed—he's very nearly followed me around with a wheelbarrow. Lilly went over to peer out the kitchen window into the dark, looking for him.

"Where the hell are you, George?" Talking to myself again, she cautioned, the minute George turns his back; but the clock was moving toward eight and she was mildly alarmed—this wasn't like George at all, something must have happened! Ridiculous! Lilly poured herself a stiff drink and went back into the living room to stuff more paper and wood into the dying fire, then fluffed the couch pillows; she wet a cocktail napkin and removed the glass stains from the coffee table before idly straightening the books and magazines on the long side table, picking at random from the framed photographs of Mags and Teddy and rubbing the glass frames against her backside to remove the dust.

Photographs of the children were everywhere; Mags on her tricycle, Teddy on a pony, the two of them on Christmas morning. Looking at their faces now, she was reminded of what a brave little band they were, those two. From that day six years ago, when she and Harry had sat them down and tried to explain that their Mommy and Daddy hated each other's guts, they had held fast, loyal in their own way to both of them. Lilly sighed; she and Harry had produced something fine from the waste of their lives together, at least. She felt another strange pang for Harry and thought again how funny it was, this complicated affection she had come to feel for him lately, this recurring curiosity as to what might have happened if she and Harry had been all along the kind of people they were now. Certainly Harry had changed, even grown, and he was very successful. By God, give the devil his due, Harry had turned out to be a damned good documentary man. What if he'd had that confidence all along? What if they'd tried harder, not been so bloody dumb and selfish? Maybe they would have made it, if they had had then the patience and understanding that always come too late in this life. Lilly frowned. If they'd just talked, for God's sake, opened their mouths and communicated like two intelligent human beings.

Her eye was caught by an enlarged photograph of Maggie with no front teeth; even then the child had that determined look about her, that very same expression she had the day she was told of the divorce, the eyes wide and astonished, filled with seriousness.

"Does divorce mean I can't take guitar lessons?"

"No, sweetheart." Harry had done most of the talking, for Lilly did not trust herself. "It just means that Mommy and I will be happier living in separate houses. It won't change anything for you and Teddy. We love you both and you'll be with each of us a lot. It doesn't have anything to do with you and your brother."

Lilly had been so moved by Harry's words that she considered calling the whole thing off. She hadn't, of course, and Harry had continued his explanations; he'd been into Dr. Spock again and, for once, Lilly was glad. She had never got past the chapter on projectile vomiting herself.

At eight, Maggie had fidgeted throughout the conversation, then inquired once more about her guitar lessons before asking to go outside and play. Teddy, almost four, was interested in none of it and had sat happily unnoticed as he picked apart the cigarette butts in the ashtray. Some years later, when he asked out of the blue, "Why did Daddy quit us?" Lilly had hugged him and said that Daddy had not done that at all. "Mommy and Daddy just like it better with Daddy in his house and Mommy in ours. You want us to be happy, don't you?"

"I guess." The answer had stung Lilly in all its versions. The little boy loved his father, looked up to him with a sense of awe that Lilly did nothing to distort, but somewhere inside, just as it no doubt lurked within Maggie, there was the lingering fear that the good things of life would not last, that people would always quit them. Maggie appeared to handle the insecurity better, but Lilly sensed that Teddy, no matter how clearly or how often she let him know that the divorce was not his fault, concealed inside his private self a fermenting guilt along with a subtle mistrust for handing out his affections.

Lilly had been very determined not to belittle or criticize Harry in front of the children, but they were perceptive little creatures, all of them—they understood that their natural love of the one parent was hurtful to the other. If parents ever thought they fooled children, they were fooling themselves. Seldom did either child speak critically of their father to her and she believed the reverse to be true when they were with Harry, but it had to be there somewhere; they were just good at hiding it. Perhaps there were too many divorces among their friends' parents for the problem to stand out the way it would have when Lilly was young. A sad but reassuring paradox, she thought, but broken homes are so common that maybe some good has come of it.

The divorce had been hard on Harry, too. It was he who was dislodged, the inconvenienced party uprooted from his home and routine, and however much the separation had been better for them both in the long run, it was Harry who probably had the hardest adjustment to make. It hadn't seemed to bother him at the time; in fact, he'd adjusted rather quickly. After all, he at least had some friends and his work. Again there was an uninvited feeling for Harry. Time, she thought, time takes the edge off everything, the good parts and the bad. She thought over the changes in Harry through the years. He was calmer now; actually, neither of them began to quarrel after saying hello anymore, and he seemed especially at peace with himself this morning, something she had never been able to help him find. And all the early problems over who saw the children at which holiday had gradually given way to their current politeness, their almost deferential consideration of the other, as if they had become aging adversaries who had more immediate concerns. Manners. Yes, after all else failed, she thought, Harry and I have manners.

At first they had deliberately picked at each other, even enjoyed it. She had been able, with a word or look, to reduce him to the insecure person she had married, just as he, as recently as this morning, was still able to make her seem lacking, inferior to other women in that same mysterious way he could when they lived together. It was terrible that they could dramatically and with no exchange of words turn each other into the very people they had come to dislike. Lilly wondered if that was the way with every couple who were divorced; they go their separate ways to obscure their emotional hold on each other but in some funny way it's always there.

Lilly lit another cigarette, considering whether or not Harry ever thought about her the way she was thinking about him. She laughed; if she kept this up, she might actually get to like the son of a bitch, but still she couldn't stop remembering Harry's changes after they separated, how he'd moved along, gotten better—even how his dressing habits had manifested his inner evolution. From neatly obscure dark suits, he had worked through the costumes of the times, the deliberately faded jeans and work shirts; the denim suits with short jackets and silver studs, then the bright embroidery —somewhere in between were the funny-looking swallow-tailed clothes of European cut, the velvet blazers, the wide ties. Now he seemed to be sewn into twill trousers and boots; it had been a couple of years since she'd seen him in anything other than a turtlenecked sweater. The hair had grown progressively longer each year, the sideburns inching down and then up again. For a couple of those years there was a beard. Gone now. And the hair was short once more, shaped and professionally styled, she knew, but he looked well, damned well. Lilly wondered if Harry had dreaded turning forty as she did. Or was fifty the age to make men cower? Maybe men were better about age than women—even those who ran off with young girls when the first gray hairs appeared. No, men didn't have to worry about their faces, but getting old was something else. Male or female, another birthday is just that much closer to death. George was fifty-two and he never seemed to mind. And Peter, he was fifty and it didn't worry him. Hell, nothing worried Peter.

Noticing the time again, Lilly switched her concern to George, wondering what could possibly be keeping him. She lay down on the couch sipping her drink and watched, disgustedly, as her fire burned out. Fires were nice and warm and wonderful while they lasted but so cold and final when down to the embers, just like being in love, she thought. Getting up and taking the brass tongs, she shoved and pushed at the gray, smoking wood, trying to force the flames back to life, then grimaced, wondering why she bothered—it was like rekindling warm human feelings once the affection had gone. Impossible. Lilly tried to do that with the men she knew, ever since she'd left Harry, every single goddamned time. Was it because she needed someone to love, anyone, regardless of the cost? Or did she just detest the sense of failure, the sense of her own inadequacy, that a broken romance left her with?

It had been like that for her, starting with the first man she had taken an interest in after the divorce. All right, so she had been bored and felt useless, but did she have to keep doing it over and over, as if a man's rejection was something she expected? Maybe at first, but her excuse then had been that she had nothing else to do with herself except to fall in love, to find somebody to belong to. But what about all the times since? She couldn't pretend anymore that she was only looking for a replacement for Harry. That's what she had fooled herself into thinking then. She had begged for affection, put herself squarely into the position of being hurt, and yes, she had come out of that first romantic encounter with a profound and highly deserved sense of being conned.

It had been 1968, the summer after the divorce. Because she had nothing else to do and because George would be away at the Democratic and Republican conventions, Lilly had decided to rent a house in Westhampton, Long Island, in the season. Lilly frowned, remembering that she had been rather in season herself, well past thirty, lonely, tired of spending her nights in the Hampton Bays amusement park watching Teddy ride the go-carts while she sat on the hard wooden bench next to other parents, the women with scarves tied over their hair curlers, their husbands with printed shirts hanging over huge beer stomachs. Automatically, on those nights, her hand had gone up to wave to Teddy as he rounded the speedway for what seemed the millionth time. Her mind had been elsewhere. Yes, she most certainly had been ready for anything when she met Dwight.

They'd been introduced at a small cocktail party given by the people renting the house next to hers. She had thought him the most handsome man there, which looking back, was not much of a distinction, but Dwight had a very compact and athletic body and a deep tan that showed through the unbuttoned voile shirt he was wearing: several gold chains hung from his neck and dropped along his exposed chest. Divorced, he'd told her as they talked, divorced now and fitting in a month in the Hamptons before going back to work. A television director, he said. Was he good? The best, he assured her, the best there was at everything. The affair had strung out even after the summer ended, until the week before Thanksgiving. Long enough for Lilly to become so involved that he was able to hurt her very much.

During the summer they were together constantly. Dwight liked to have what he called his "toddies," and after the first two or three he would refer to himself as Dwightie, saying it was only fair that his name should end with an "ee" sound, too; Lilly and Maggie and Teddy and Dwightie. They would sit on the beach, he leaning back in a folding chair with a metal reflector under his chin, silent except to ask Lilly to put bronzing lotion on his head; Dwight had very little hair and it was his belief that a tan made his premature balding seem almost attractive and didn't she agree. Of course she did; Lilly agreed with anything he said. Dwight never spoke of age; he was like a woman that way, but she guessed him to be about forty-two or three—a good deal older than Lilly, but he seemed younger—and Lilly told him that she liked his being older, masterful and beautiful and older. When she thought about it, those were about the only things they ever agreed upon.

Despite his vanity, Dwight was sure of himself and out-going; childless and committed to remaining so, he protected his independence and moved easily into social situations. It had not been unpleasant for Lilly to follow along. In fact, she'd been eager to assume the role of perfect mate and did so with no formal request from him. She was quite good at sublimating her desires to his wishes, guessing and second-guessing at what he wanted in a woman and then reshaping herself into precisely the kind of person she assumed he expected. To be fair, Dwight did not demand this of her, but Lilly wanted him to care for her and that was what she had to do. Lying and role-playing became her personality; she would have done anything to keep him. Those small compromises seemed so unimportant at the time, the hiding of her faults, her fears, her romantic dreams, until finally, she had woven about herself a web of lies and fabrications and had no idea who she actually was. So determined not to be with Dwight the kind of cynical, restless person she had been with Harry, Lilly never once criticized anything he said or did. Oh, God, yes, she had been a far cry from the semi-liberated Lillian Shawcross of today. Instead, she had insisted to herself that Dwight was perfect for her and that she was very contented just to be around him.

Dwight had grown up in suburban London and still carried

traces of the distressing accent of that middle-class area, but Lilly chose to hear differently.

"You English always sound so much more educated," she lied. "Have you noticed how you intimidate headwaiters?"

Of course he was a fool; she saw that later. But hadn't she been worse? Deliberately confusing his nonsensical trendiness with original style? Her lonely needs with genuine passion? Yet it was really only Lilly who had spun the web about them and there was no movement in a web. She'd come away with that bit of wisdom, anyhow.

When the summer passed, she would fly to New York to spends weekends with him in his apartment, once staying there alone for several days when he was called to California to work on a television special. It repelled her now to recall the foolish sense of security she had felt among his possessions. She had a key of her own to his apartment—men would always give her keys. Was it something they smelled, her need for keys—those hardware symbols of commitment?

Dwight's favored room was the bath and he spent most of his time there, using the sun lamp and his metal reflector to maintain his tan, doing his push-ups and, she suspected, indulging in a goodly number of other vanities best left uninvestigated. The enormous bathroom was dominated by an oversized, custom-made tub of black marble, his five gold-plated Emmys lined in perfect chronological order around its wide edge. A color television set rested on wall brackets at eye level and two black phones were hung within convenient reach, all instruments seemingly in constant use. How many times had she waited for him while he lounged in that tub of hot water softened by a full bottle of Sardo? Those hours of soaking himself and of talking long distance to the West Coast, lifting an oily foot out of the water to adjust the position of his precious Emmys as he conversed.

Dwight's professional success symbolized by his Emmys was dazzling to Lilly, and with him she met the famous entertainers of the theater, movies, television. With show business people, Lilly's own personality was unimportant. So involved with their latest performance or current analyst, they paid little attention to anything else, and, after all, she was only the current girl with Dwightie, permitted because of him to sit in silent adoration at tables in Italian restaurants, or Chinese or Mexican or Indian; it had not mattered—Lilly was little more than a replaceable spear carrier in yet another male preserve, no better and no worse than the stars of politics.

Everything about Lilly went unheeded. Nor did Dwight seem to find her particularly interesting; he seldom laughed at anything she said, taking himself and his work too seriously to acquire the minor graces of humor and conversation. Lilly felt cheated. She was being the kind of woman he wanted and the least he could do was applaud her efforts. Often he might repeat to others something she said, claiming it for his own, not once giving her credit; in fact, Lilly came to see that he was not actually aware that he was stealing her line, and there were moments when she understood why Zelda Fitzgerald had gone insane, for it was indeed maddening to be unappreciated and then plagiarized.

Still, Lilly was determined to hold on to him, persuading herself that it was better this way than to be alone, to have no one to love, no other life to be a part of. Her desperation to please Dwight, her indulgence of his every whim became obsessive. Especially in bed did all go according to his wishes. It was not that Dwight was strange or had perverted ideas of sexual pleasure. Far from it. He made love as if from habit: tennis on Tuesday; Thursday's, the gym; Lilly on the weekend. And always, always there was his ritual bath. Dwightie, she thought, should have lived in ancient Rome.

It was with him that she perfected the grand drama of pretending sexual ecstasy, a necessary duplicity, for Dwight's ego demanded a physical display of her pleasure. She could easily have won a bathtubful of Emmys and Oscars for her performances. *Awarded to Lillian Shawcross for Outstanding Contributions to the Male Psyche in the Division of Faked Orgasm.* Yes, she had done whatever made him happy.

Her children made it obligatory that Lilly spend some of her weekends in Washington, and Dwight would phone her, usually from his bathtub, and would vow his undying love and constant celibacy. When he was expansive like that, she might even dare to extract from him a few sudsy references to marriage. The real horror was that she probably would have done it. Dwightie and Lilly and Maggie and Teddy and Emmy, all in a row. Hell, all in a divorce court six months later.

Amid the traveling back and forth to New York by plane, the phone calls and the occasional vows of eternal fidelity, word filtered down to Washington that Lilly was not the only person with a key to Dwightie's apartment or a place in his bathroom from which to worship at the feet of the Emmys the man who had won them. She was disbelieving at first;

women's gossip was deplorable to her, especially when maliciously dispensed, but the rumors nagged at her, eating away at whatever thin confidence she had. In her direct manner of speaking, Lilly had asked him jokingly over the phone if "somebody's been sleeping in my bathtub." There had been injured protestations from Dwight but inevitably the interloping Goldilocks was labeled, her name passed on to Lilly by a casual female acquaintance who "thought you ought to know for your own good." Lilly had been furious, felt tricked and humiliated. She screamed her hurt and indignation to George, who did little to console her.

"Face it, Lilly, the bastard's fucked you."

"And poorly."

For several days Lilly tried futilely to reach Dwight by phone. Colorful visions of his infidelity gnawed at her constantly, loss and loneliness ascribing added virtues to the relationship that, of course, had never existed. Only now, so many years later, could she see that she had not loved him, merely the idea. But back then, she had been driven by an uncontrollable jealousy and an obsessive need for confrontation.

She endured yet another sleepless night, intermittently dialing his number and listening to the agonizing drone of unanswered rings. In her mind's eye there came erotic visions that probably approached telepathy: Dwight in his bathtub shaking his head and telling an adoring female to ignore the ringing telephone.

Still awake at five the next morning, Lilly was seized by a stony rage. She got out of bed, dressed quietly and left a note on the refrigerator door for the cleaning woman to get Maggie and Teddy off to school: "Been called unexpectedly to New York and will be back later in the day." She drove in icy calm to the airport, parking easily in the quiet of dawn, and was the first to board Eastern's 6 A.M. shuttle.

She let herself into Dwight's apartment with her key, certain her suspicion would be confirmed, but hoping against hope that she would find him sleeping, alone. The rooms were empty, but everywhere the signs of recent female occupation were apparent—a negligee on the back of the bathroom door, a pair of evening sandals kicked under the coffee table, half-filled wine glasses, cigarette stubs with lipstick—none of it belonging to Lilly. She cursed him, hoping to God that whoever the bastard was with, they had nothing but a dingy stall shower.

Possessed of a fury that transcended humiliation and hurt, Lilly poured herself a glass of Scotch, gulping it as she paced back and forth in the empty apartment. She picked up the strange evening sandals, a shoe in each hand, examining them distastefully—they were at least three sizes too small for Lilly. Impulsively she pitched them, one at a time, out the twelve-story window. Frenzied, she refilled her glass and set out on a thorough search of the rooms, grabbing up items of clothing and tossing them out the window, too: hairbrushes, dusting powder, a slip—that irritated her most, nobody wore slips anymore. How was she to fight an unknown rival with Chinese feet and French underwear?

With the third glass of Scotch, she took entire leave of her senses, becoming someone else altogether, a fool, a strange wild fool. It was nine o'clock in the morning and she was so drunk she could scarcely manage to get down the elevator to the lobby; she weaved her way past the doorman, who was neatly folding and stacking the garments Lilly had thrown out the window.

"Good morning, Foster. Having a rummage sale?"

She did not pause for a reply.

Her head reeled; hard drink and violent jealousy were too much for an empty stomach, but somehow she got over to Lexington Avenue, stopping several times to inquire with slurred words as to the location of the closest art supply store. Nothing shocked New Yorkers, not even during rush hour! From several sets of garbled directions she found a shop on Sixty-third Street. She was staggering under the weight of her purchases and was glad for Foster to relieve her of the packages once back inside the apartment house lobby; he followed her up in the elevator, eyeing her slyly. At the twelfth floor she lifted the bags from him, acknowledging his suspicions. "My dear Foster, you have every right to look at me this way. In a world filled with ignorance, you are in the presence of monumental stupidity." The man was scratching under his brimmed hat as she re-let herself into Dwight's flat.

It did not take long to get everything in order—a wooden spoon from the kitchen and a teacup with some Scotch. The cup made the early-morning drinking seem more decorous.

The big black tub was filling with water as Lilly sat on the edge, watching, sipping daintily from her cup and holding the saucer beneath it. She read the directions on the large boxes of plaster of paris, and when the water was about one-quarter into the tub, she tore open the lids and emptied in the dry powder all at once. Very carefully, she stirred the mixture with the wooden spoon. When she returned from the kitchen with another cup of Scotch, the plaster was almost hardened. The rest was fun.

Lilly backed off to admire her work. Framed by the black ledge of the tub, the white plaster effectively set off her design. Perfectly spaced and pressed neatly into the cement, the engraved Emmy figurines spelled out LIL. Lilly thought that perhaps the most perfectly matched thing in the entire relationship was her short name and those five Emmys. She wondered dreamily how she would have managed this work of art if she were named Henrietta and Dwight were less talented.

One last cup of Scotch and the plaster was firm. Lilly giggled drunkenly; everything, including the cuckolded woman, was nicely plastered. It would take a pickax for Dwight to forget her! With one last appreciative inspection of her handiwork, Lilly dropped her key to the apartment into the commode and flushed it away; the water backed up and overflowed. Dwightie, she reasoned, was finally going to have the ultimate in bathroom experiences.

In the lobby, Lilly saluted a final farewell to Foster.

"Will you be needing a cab, Mrs. Shawcross?"

"The moving finger having writ—moves on. Yes, Foster. A taxi for Zorro!"

He was relieved to hail one, helping her awkwardly inside. "Will there be any message for—"

She held up her hand to stop him. "I left a note!" Then, falling back against the seat, Lilly began to laugh, holding her sides and rocking back and forth, doubled up with hysteria.

"You O.K., lady?" The driver was peering at her through the thick plastic partition.

"Never better. As a reward for your concern, I shall not mug you." Because of the glass partition, she was having to shout to him through the coin drawer.

"Yeah. Well, where to?" He yelled back to be heard.

"The airport."

"Which one?"

"Surprise me," she said, and lapsed once again into convulsive laughter before she put her head down on the seat and passed out.

The bastard drove her to Newark, and it took her last thirty dollars to pay him, but she got out of the cab with some dignity despite her uneven steps and wound her way inside the terminal to the bar and ordered a double Scotch, this time in a glass. Leaving her empty purse on the bar, Lilly deposited her last dime into the pay phone and called George Sabberstein at his office, reversing the charges.

"Where in hell's name are you?"

"Newark." She was seized with hilarity again, hardly able to enunciate through the giggles.

"Are you sick?"

"Never healthier! A little drunk, though." Then suddenly there was no more laughter, only a dreadful fear, and so much pain.

"Come get me, George, please."

"Can you hang on a while longer?" He was calculating the time it would take to shuttle from Washington to La Guardia, then taxi over to Newark.

"Maybe."

"O.K., baby, stay put. I'm on the way." He asked no other questions and left for the airport the moment he hung up.

# 18

REMEMBERING Dwight took the edge off Lilly's earlier good humor and she got up to put some ice and Scotch into a clean glass. She had never told George everything about Dwight; he did not especially like the parts of the story he already knew. She had told him every detail about all the others, though. All but Peter. Damn it all, she was feeling lonely again for Peter and it was likely to get worse if George didn't turn up soon. Lilly thought most about Peter when she was by herself this way. Well, better to think over the good things, like Sheepshanks, like George helping her get a job after her problems with Dwight. That's what had saved her, George and Sheepshanks. She had wanted to work in order to be somebody, the kind of somebody that men like Dwight did not so easily dismiss; she needed a job to make herself more marketable, to make herself a real person. When did it happen that she changed, that she wanted to excel to please Lilly? Whatever the reasons that had made her work so hard, she was grateful for them. It had paid off. George had seen to it that no grass grew under her feet.

The night that he suggested she move from local television to doing syndicated clips for UPI, Lilly had been unresponsive. Damn lucky for her that George persuaded her to take the gamble. When he had the deal pretty well firmed up, he laid it out for her. "This is it, Lil. It's dicey, of course; UPI is new at the television game. Hell, maybe it won't work, but then it just might. These are your choices as I see them. You can stay with Sheepshanks and play it safe or you can give the syndication spot a try. I say you'd be a fool not to give it a go. Being carried on a lot of local stations sure beats growing old on just one channel."

"Why not?" she said, pushing George to make the decision for her.

"Yeah, honey, why not. You've been with Channel Eight almost two years. What have you got to lose except the pleasure of raising ole Sheepshanks' blood pressure every day?"

Actually it had not been necessary to part company with Bill Sheepshanks; a deal was made between him and UPI whereby Lilly would continue to use his facilities, her commentaries taped free of charge in exchange for which he aired Lillian Shawcross as part of his news broadcast without paying the prescribed fee to the wire service. At first, they had only been able to sell her reviews to a handful of the smaller markets across the country—until Detroit picked her up, then Atlanta, Richmond, Trenton, St. Louis. She was still not carried in the New York and Los Angeles outlets she wanted because she liked to imagine how Peter would feel if her face should turn up in a news show. At the very least it would force him to think of her.

When she signed the contract with UPI, she had been sent —rather as a bonus—to cover the Cannes Film Festival and told she could do commentary on the films entered into the competition as well as interview the stars and directors. The results had been good beyond anyone's expectations, and when an anecdote from one of her interviews was quoted in the "People" section of *Time,* George had cabled her in France.

ORDER PLACED FOR BIGGER BRITCHES FOR L SHAWCROSS— STOP—APPRECIATE SHE NOT OUTGROW SAME TOO RAPIDLY— STOP—HUGS AND HEAVY BREATHING—STOP—GEORGE

Lilly had responded gleefully.

CANCEL ALL BUT HEAVY BREATHING—STOP—MOUTH STILL BIGGEST PART OF ANATOMY—STOP—LOVE LIL

Cannes had been an experience for her in more ways than one. The trip had not started well. Not only was Lilly worried about the work that lay ahead but she hated to travel; she looked forward to it in the beginning but no sooner had she fastened her seat belt than the doubts and worries began. She was homesick and wished for George, knowing she wouldn't feel so alone and uncertain if he was with her, nor would the Riviera seem to alienate her—the high *corniche,* the low and the middle, she disliked them all, crowded as they were with people who appeared to be going places and doing things that did not include her. It was beautiful, yes, but with a hedonistic lushness that was disquieting. So much luxury and wealth—the food and the tourists too rich—the natives arrogant and rude and none of it really having to do with Lilly. Never had she known such isolation amid such elaborate gaiety.

The second day in Cannes she was still tired from her flight and was struggling with a French-speaking camera crew supplied by UPI's Paris bureau; they were setting up for an interview on the dining terrace of the Hotel Negresco. Lilly's fluency in French scarcely extended beyond recognizing the difference between a *gigot* and a *jambon* on a menu, and the glaring sun was making her edgy and fearful of being in over her professional depth; she had no idea of what she was actually going to do, let alone how to get on with it. She was supposed to interview a new, young Italian actress, a lady of minimum talent and maximum bosom, and the starlet's English was limited to "yes" and "please," making the whole exercise hopeless; Lilly was going to fail in the job before she even got started. Worse, she was about to cry and ruin her makeup.

"Perhaps I can be of some service." The young man was smiling. It was not necessary that he identify himself; the famous face was enough.

Enormously flustered by now, Lilly could only manage a whispered yes and thank you very much. It was not every day that a well-known actor came along to bail her out of a bad situation.

The boyish face continued to smile as he directed the sound man to remove the dangling neck microphone smothered between the mammoth folds of the Italian starlet's breasts.

"Use a clip," he commanded in excellent French, then turned to the young actress, and in equally perfect Italian spoke some words that apparently put her at ease. He pulled up two chairs and placed one to either side of the lady, directing Lilly to a seat and taking the other for himself. The sound man clipped lapel mikes to the three of them and took a voice level while the actor stood to tilt the table's umbrella out of their way.

"Now then," he said in English, "I think we can begin." He reached for Lilly's carefully typed list of questions and glanced quickly over them, looked up and signaled the cameraman to start the film. In Italian he asked the starlet how she felt about the reception of her latest film. She responded to the question and he turned back to Lilly and translated, very conversationally, precisely what had been said. In English Lilly asked if it was possible that the actress might feel some resentment that her measurements were more carefully scrutinized than her performance. The young man laughed and turned to pose the query in Italian; the actress beamed and launched into animated dialogue that

247

Lilly supposed was quite hilarious because several of the people now grouped about the table seemed highly amused. It was irritating for Lilly to feel that she was perhaps the only person in all Cannes who did not speak either French or Italian.

The interview went on as if the three of them were simply enjoying a pleasant chat over lunch and it was one of her better pieces that week: not-so-famous UPI movie critic surrounded by movie stars, smiling and talking and appearing to be in control when, indeed, the reverse had been the case. Despite her relief that he had made her look good, Lilly could only thank the young actor grudgingly when the interview was finished.

"I didn't realize women did this kind of work," he said.

Lilly was annoyed further. It was one thing for a famous American movie star to do her job for her; it was entirely something else for him to insinuate that it wasn't a woman's profession to begin with. It was impossible to keep the sharpness from her voice. "Considering your reputation with women," she said, "I should think you'd be surprised to find we can do anything except from a horizontal position." She was immediately sorry for her nastiness but he did have a history of taking up with women, any woman, and then leaving them behind as he went on to another. Lilly bent over to gather her papers and her notebook, ready to walk away first before he walked away from her, but he had only laughed and looked at her quizzically. Lilly had no intention of showing that she was flattered by his interest and moved more quickly to depart. Hell, she might be a green reporter but she was no impressionable hick and she would have him understand that.

"Hey"—he touched her sleeve—"don't run off mad. I thought maybe you would like to have dinner tonight." He grinned at her boyishly, then added that, of course, they would eat in an upright position. He gave the impression of a boy tugging at a forelock as he spoke.

Lilly's impulse, despite her earlier irritation, was to say yes and say it quickly, but she waited a moment before speaking. "Well, it's you or a subtitled documentary on Hiroshima." She smiled in spite of herself. "Where?" she said, conceitedly anticipating a "your room or my room" response.

"The best food is up the road—sorry, the *corniche*. In Beaulieu. We could maybe move on up to Monaco afterward." The famous charm. Affected or not, it was appealing.

"About nine? Here. At the bar?" he said.

Lilly said yes, that would be fine, and then started toward the main building of the hotel.

"Hey," she called, "don't you want to know my name?"

"It doesn't matter," he said. The bastard! To him it probably didn't.

"Well, I'm Ursula Andress."

He shrugged. "Whatever you like." He was laughing again and for a moment Lilly had an urge to cross over and hit him with her purse, right in his beautiful arrogant face.

"Nine," he repeated and moved in the direction of the pool. He had managed to walk away from her first, she saw, but she smiled anyhow, wondering just what an impressionable hick was meant to wear for dinner with a famous movie star.

Those had been five of the most pleasant days she could recall, the small sports car, the driving too fast over the mountain roads—like Cary Grant catching a thief. Lilly thought she took very nicely to glamour, considering the novelty of it. She was welcomed and included wherever they went, because of him, she knew, but it was the kind of pleasant attention easy to enjoy, the special treatment for which one might go to any extremes to have forever. Each of their nights had been punctuated by the sound and sight of roulette wheels in the different casinos; on the afternoons when she was not working, there were pots of bouillabaisse in sidewalk cafés over in St. Tropez or sunbathing near the topless girls on the narrow gravel beach at Nice. Not once, Lilly recalled, not one single time did he make any overture toward her that could vaguely be construed as sexual. Even when she wished it, it did not happen. Nor was he the bore that most actors invariably turn out to be, no monologues about his latest picture or current neurosis; in fact, he was quite surprisingly political, talking candidates and issues in all-night *boîtes* before escorting her to the door of her hotel room while Lilly, like a girl after a first date, waited and wished for him to kiss her or to touch her. There was nothing, and it was not easy to correlate his obvious interest in her and his tireless courting of her with this complete sexual detachment. They were friends. Nothing but friends and companions, and while she knew she ought to be highly complimented that he found her company sufficient, she wanted something more, finally admitting to herself that she had something of a crush on him. *A crush on a movie star!* Well, why not? Wouldn't any woman react the same way? It was the only way to rationalize, and Lilly would lie in bed at night and think romantic thoughts before she fell asleep, happy to be meeting him in the morning.

In addition to showing her the best of the Riviera, he arranged for Lilly to have interviews with at least a dozen of the festival's untouchables; because of him, she was filing good stuff out of Cannes and she knew it. Yes, it had been an altogether rewarding encounter, despite her bruised pride, and despite her curiosity being pricked by his carnal disinterest. Funny, too, funny and ironic to finally be in the position of really desiring a man and then to find him determined to be nothing more than her friend.

Still, he had phoned every night after he'd taken her to her room, talking long and low in the most intimate whispers for nearly an hour, allowing sensuous pauses and with many sighs; he would ask questions of her that required prolonged and thoughtful responses. Each time Lilly had become weary of the sound of her own voice before the call was finally terminated, but the next day his nocturnal intimacy would have evaporated and she dared not make reference to it.

On their last evening they had a splendid celebration and drank a good deal of champagne. He talked of maybe meeting her in New York or possibly even flying to Washington, but when he took her back to the hotel, he'd said only his usual, formal good-bye. A little drunk, Lilly considered throwing herself at him, but his distance and composure made that unthinkable.

Inside her room, she found a note from an assistant to Fellini saying the director would be pleased to grant her request for an interview early the next morning. Lilly was elated, and understanding that it was her famous new friend who had set up the appointment, she went straight to the telephone to thank him. Her call was answered by a soft-spoken young man—the voice so sexually modulated that she had at first thought him a woman. Lilly checked her watch. It was four in the morning; she thought perhaps she had the wrong number and asked the voice to verify the connection.

"Yes, this is the right room. But he can't speak with you now. He says that he will ring you back."

Puzzled, Lilly undressed and was getting into bed as the telephone rang; it was he, his voice low and breathless as usual. With instant clarity, Lilly understood the reasons for the phone calls, the reason for everything that had *not* happened between them. It repelled her, even as she was titillated, but she could clearly visualize what was going on at the opposite end of the wire. Bisexuality—her voice, the strange young man's ministrations to her friend; a ménage of four, she thought, him, me, it, and the house phone. Lilly's sleep that night had not been disturbed by further dreams of famous movie stars.

Thinking of him now, Lilly realized that he was perhaps the most honest man ever to cross her path, no lies, no promises; he had, in fact, paid her in full for her companionship. Because of him she had made something of a name for herself in Cannes. Lilly laughed; it was the only thing she made. But it was a fair trade, maybe the only straight deal she'd ever got from a man. The irony made her laugh again. Hell, she thought, he not only paved my way into the movie industry but he brought me as close to an orgy as I'm ever likely to come.

Damn it, it was close to eleven. Lilly refilled her glass and returned to the kitchen to open the tin of corned-beef hash, mashing it into a lightly greased casserole according to the directions; she would leave the dish on the stove, ready to heat it up when George came. She wished he would hurry. There were so many things she had to tell him.

Back in the living room, she sat down on the couch. The couch! The kitchen! God, Lilly thought, if the whole drama of this day were to be staged, the set would include only these two rooms. She glanced around her, rather liking what she saw; it was a happy room and she had never really noticed. Maybe she was a happy person and hadn't noticed that, either. What was happiness, anyhow? The state of not being actively unhappy? Christ! Happiness was episodic at best; she knew that. Well, the good episodes in her life had not precisely fallen one on the heels of the next, that was for sure.

Lilly considered her other romances; they were not all so nice to look back on. How many others of her romantic encounters had ended with her having to painfully piece herself back together? How many firm resolutions had she made never to take another chance with love? Only to put herself squarely back onto the firing line, vulnerable, even eager to chase the dream, over and over. To be part of a loving alliance seemed no less an ambition now than when she was younger. That was the hell of it.

Wasn't that why she had involved herself so readily with Peter? Never stopping to consider the consequences? Just jumped right in. Well, what's wrong with that? At least she was no jaded and cynical woman forswearing love. There was some virtue in that, wasn't there? Sure there was, and maybe, well, just maybe, she might not be such a mess after all. So if she weren't such a mess, then why didn't she hear from Peter? How could he bear to be separated from such an exotic blossom; why didn't he want her? Lilly felt the familiar ebb of confidence. Damn it, if she were really special, she wouldn't be mooning around an empty house, seeing herself as undesirable just because Peter seemed no longer to care about her. The selfish bastard! All this maudlin backsliding was his fault.

They were so good together; she told him that every time she felt comfortable with him, and he would smile down at her, humoring her in that way of his, never actually answering her, just the enigmatic smile. She had loved him right from the start. Sometimes, when they were alone in his apartment in New York, she had tried to cook for him, or clean up his belongings, do the things that would make them seem a family. Once she even ironed his shirts and had done a terrible job of it. Peter had taken the scorched garments from her and wadded them into the closet, telling her that he could hire a laundress and that housework was not what he needed from her. Then what did he need from her? Not one damn thing and that was the trouble. He only wanted to be left alone, the one thing she couldn't do. Wasn't that the only thing he expected of her—for her to be independent of him, make no demands, to do nothing for him? Because if she did and if he accepted, then he would be making some kind of commitment, the one thing she wanted from him, the one thing he could not give to her or to anyone else.

Oh, it was perfect when things between them went well; she would be so happy and would come back to Washington secure that he loved her. Then maybe she would hear from him and then maybe not. If he had become mellow of a weekend and had told her he cared, then the minute she was away from him he would emotionally retrench, steel himself against her memory and manage to forget her. Lilly got so she dreaded to hear the words she wanted most for him to say, for when he said he loved her, she knew that she would pay later for the unguarded moment. The verbal commitment would terrify Peter and he would withdraw into himself, staying away from her, not calling or writing until he felt tough enough once again to deal with her. It had taken a long time for her to see that he was not cruel; he just couldn't handle an involvement. If only he had been cruel, she thought, if only there had been friction between them, even another woman. She could deal with that, she could hate him then and forget him. But Peter felt for her everything he could feel. That was the problem. He felt for her but was simply not able to cope with it. A cripple. George was right about her; she was drawn to cripples.

For over a year now, Lilly had tricked herself into believing that all she needed to do was persevere, make herself part of the pattern. Peter would come around, learn to trust her, talk to her about why he couldn't give himself over to her. Why he also couldn't walk away from her, either. That was what had very nearly driven her crazy, the running hot one day, cold the next. Well, it was Lilly who had tricked herself; Peter was Peter, he never changed. The worst self-trick was to kid yourself that second best could be first-rate if only you worked at it hard enough.

Tears started to form in her eyes and Lilly brought herself up short, telling herself that it was stupid and self-destructive to wish that Peter could be different. He just wasn't a permanent kind of person and that was all there was to it. And what about herself? Did she really think she could ever be a different person? The kind of woman who could be taken or left alone at whim? No, she wanted it all—love, happiness, fame, contentment. And Peter. However miserable he made her, she wanted him.

Lilly walked back into the kitchen; that was the pattern, wasn't it? Settle in one spot until her thoughts forced her to get up and move to another. She sat down in the same kitchen chair she'd spent so much of the day in, leaned back in it and arched her back to exercise her stiff shoulders and neck, extending her legs, pointing her toes and stretching them. The sound of joints popping loudly made her break out laughing.

"Fuck the golden years!" she said and laughed again. Which wasn't so funny, not when you thought about the golden years. What golden years? Brass, they were. Without someone to love, growing old was brass. Christ, she was obsessed by love, almost Stendhalian about it. Why was it so horrendous to do without something one really wanted and was love really so all-fired special when you got right down to it? Or was it like independence—once you had your hands on it you weren't sure what to do with it? Well, being alone wasn't being liberated, either. She had certainly found that out. *Liberation!* The word stuck in her throat, like "comrade" or "sisterhood."

She assumed other women were like this, wanting to be

their own person but still wanting to be a woman in the old sense of the word, a woman who took care of a man, who put him first and who did all the things for him that she had despised doing for Harry. Did other women feel so incomplete without a man? The minute Lilly had felt like relinquishing her independence for Peter, he had become uneasy around her. Damned if she didn't, worse when she did. How many other women were torn in two by this complicated pursuit of themselves and a partner? Better she should be a lesbian, Lilly thought. Hell, lesbians probably narrowed their existence and diminished their accomplishments by woman hunts.

Her stomach growled and she went to put the corned-beef hash into the oven. That done, she refilled her glass and thought over the many books she'd read in a lifetime, wondering why literature, like movies, dealt so harshly with women, why they were always spinsters, suicides, or miserably dedicated to chronicling loneliness. That was not altogether fair, but then she was not in the frame of mind to be altogether fair tonight. She pondered for a moment all the women still alive now whom she admired. Most of them lived alone. Did they choose to be alone? Or had they been unwilling to compromise on the things they needed for themselves? Could anyone live with a man and not compromise? That was what she was prepared to do with Peter—make all the compromises in the world; all her self-determination had vanished when she fell in love with him. It was Peter who could not compromise his independence, not she. What had made her so willing and not him? What, in fact, was so flimsy about her life that she was so quick to alter it for Peter? What was it that she thought she could find with Peter that she could not find alone?

Peter! It did keep coming back to him, didn't it? Well, those were the facts and they were not likely to change. Before Peter, Lilly had convinced herself that she just had not found the right man, that one would eventually come along, one tailor-made for her. Now, she suspected, the bitter truth was that many men were terrified of women—oh, some of them hid the fear, the trendy ones who pretended to like independent females because it was the coming thing. They didn't count. It was the others who were the majority; they acted as if everything was fine—right up to the time when they passed a strong woman by for a clinging girl who hadn't yet grown up enough to be torn apart by the complexities of being her own self and still be part of a man's life. Somewhere there was supposed to be a happy medium. Those screaming women's groups never touched on that subject. No, all that rhetoric about women learning to do without men did not work for Lilly. Someone should invent a magic pill for ladies who do not choose to live without men, one magic pill to be taken as needed. Lilly darkened her drink.

Impulsively she climbed up on her chair, glass in one hand, the other extended in the fashion of a public orator. She was the slightest bit drunk and glad of it.

"Ladies of the world," she began. "Thank you for being with me. Tonight I would like to pose once again the eternal question: Are independent women truly new women? Or, my friends, are we only the old common garden variety of ladies faced now with a unique set of problems? We work, we breed, we raise our young . . . now then, what do we do? How do we age? Cease being individuals in order not to threaten men? Or do we grow stronger and freer and then, at forty, find we are destined to be alone? I ask you, ladies, where is the justice in a liberated woman face-to-face with an empty bed? I rest my case."

Lilly had scarcely gotten down from the chair before she fell. She was indeed drunk and silly and who was she kidding, anyhow? The basic inequities between the sexes would never be righted. Not in her lifetime. It was still a man's world. They can always find a passable partner while women are too long trained to look up for love, too long told they are only as attractive as the men they choose—known by the company they keep! Lilly was hiccupping now; she took nine sips of Scotch and held her breath, waited, then hiccupped loudly. She rose to address the empty room again, punctuating her remarks with hiccups, pacing and waving her arms as she debated. "If a woman takes up with an amiable young man who is kind to her, who waits on her, defers to her wishes and permits her to make decisions—even allows her to guide both their destinies—then she is a ball-breaking weirdo and the man is a sociological freak. Ah, but men can and do select youthful, worshipful women, and they are considered shrewd for making the choice. They become good ole So-and-so who has found himself a sweet young thing.

"Did there ever exist a man whose mother ingrained in him that he must be pure and obedient and that he was to look for a strong girl who was on her way up in this world, a girl who would take care of him for the rest of her life? No, goddammit, no mother ever screwed up her baby boy like that. Sons are trained to be in charge; daughters are the ones meant to pussyfoot around waiting for the right man to come along. That's the trouble; men and women alike, all of us are victims of that kind of shit." Lilly felt dizzy and nauseated. She ran to the sink and threw up, splashed some cold water on her face, then thought of Peter and threw up again.

Peter didn't fit the chauvinistic pattern, never gave lip service to her accomplishments the way most men did. He praised her; he *wanted* her professional ambitions to get in the way of her emotions. He didn't like her to cling and make demands. If she were independent, he was safe with her; they could go their own separate ways and meet for mutual convenience. Only Lilly didn't want to go her separate way. She wanted Peter.

Yes, Peter's life was perfect for him, perfect in almost every way. He taught his classes, wrote an occasional screenplay, had his friends, his books, his music and Lilly, when it suited him—his own tidy world that did not need to be shared on a permanent basis. Yet somewhere along the line some terrible thing had happened that caused him to be contented to be by himself, horrified of being dependent. It wasn't fair that he should be the one man with whom she could live happily and still be herself and then for him to turn out to be the kind of person who didn't need other people. Sometimes she envied him this; mostly she hated him for it. What good was it to find Peter, the first man to understand her, to appreciate and encourage her in her career and, in the end, for him to be the one who could walk away from all that she was?

The son of a bitch, the crippled, wonderful son of a bitch. She missed him so. Maybe when he called again—if he called again—well, maybe she ought to give it one more try. Who was to say that one more go at it wouldn't work?

"Me," she said aloud. "Me. Lilly Shawcross, that's who's to say. He can't do it. He wants to but he can't take the chance." Lilly began to sob. "And I can't take all the chances for both of us anymore. Peter isn't able to do his share. He can never give me what I need. I have to do it without him."

She took down a clean glass from the shelf and poured an inch of Scotch into it, adding milk; it would be easier to get the liquor down with the milk. It certainly would not do to be sober. Sober, nothing made sense. Lilly carried the Scotch back over to the table and took her usual chair. She was behaving like a stupid ass and told herself so; she was a grown woman with a grown woman's responsibilities and obligations and she ought to be able to handle herself in a more reasonable and mature way. Adult and responsible. She had paid a bitter price to learn about being a responsible adult. She had found out about all that from Charles. Lilly sighed—she'd learned that the way she had learned everything she knew. From men. Yes, damn it, everything but how to be happy without one.

Lilly was only thirty-five when Charles came along. Certainly she felt younger, at least her attitude was still that of a stubborn child. She had been doing movie criticisms for UPI for a little better than a year, and then the New York office had suggested she take a leave of absence and go to the University of Chicago for a six-week seminar in film making. It was perhaps the wrong time for her to be off the air, but the experience and the academic credential would more than make up for it, they said. Lilly was uneasy about going, had felt guilty leaving the children with Harry for so long a period, but it was George who had urged her to make the decision, saying that, after all, it was the opportunity of a lifetime and she could be a good mother later, couldn't she? It hurt to count the times she had promised to be a better mother some other time, shuffling Mags and Teddy as she often had to the bottom of her list of priorities. Funny, but it was the trip to Chicago that finally brought Lilly some true understanding of just precisely what it meant to be a mother.

The guilt at leaving had depressed Lilly, and when she was depressed, she wanted most to tuck herself into a secure relationship, perhaps another marriage, one this time that would wrap around her snugly, protect her. The depression had diminished on the flight out to Chicago, but only slightly—she kept closing her eyes only to see Teddy's little face stricken that he was to be left behind. Just the thought of Mags and Teddy made her wish to turn the plane around and go back to where she belonged, but instead she asked the stewardess for a drink, and when it came she gulped it down and waited for the alcohol to lift her spirits.

By the time she landed and began struggling with her luggage at O'Hare Airport, Lilly felt miraculously removed from the Lilly on the plane, strangely freed and excited by what lay ahead. What, after all, was so terrible about six weeks in a strange city with no clock to punch, no calls of "Mommy" to pull at her? She saw herself a fickle creature and tried to resummon her maternalness but all she felt was a wonderful sense of excitement, as if she were being given another chance at girlhood.

His name was Charlie; "good ole Charlie" was how he was introduced. They met at a cocktail party given by a journalist friend of George's whom George had insisted Lilly call when she got to Chicago. Charlie, it appeared, was very popular and she liked to hear him called out to in the crowd. But Charlie was the wrong name for him; she thought him too stable to be a Charlie. So "Charles" was how she referred to him because, of course, no one really falls in love with a Charlie.

They had known each other less than a week when he suggested she bring her things from the small hotel near the university campus and move into his riverside apartment. Lilly had not actually lived with anyone since Harry and she was dubious of the arrangement, but it was nothing like marriage. In fact, it was the most complete combining of freedom and close companionship she had ever known before, or known since.

Charles was the city editor of a liberal newspaper, young for such a position, having turned forty only the summer before—five years Lilly's senior. He was not handsome in any conventional sense, but tall enough and bright enough, a man who laughed easily, who knew things, who was angered by what Lilly thought a good man ought to be angered by. Yes, Charles stood for all the right things; principled, he was, but the best part was his feeling for Lilly. He loved her and had no reservations about telling her so, and telling her often.

No demands were made on her, not really; it was not necessary, for she was on Charles's territory; friends, habits, patterns, everything was already established and Lilly thought it much easier this way, such a pleasant pace. She didn't have to fit in or change herself, for Charles's life was quite to her liking and she could be what she was, hide nothing from him, pretend nothing. He thought her perfect and Lilly liked that most of all.

Charles had a boundless capacity for enjoying himself; he liked to travel, to explore, both literally and figuratively, the world in which he moved, a man blessedly uncomplicated and sane. He was a superb cook, knowledgeable about books and movies—in fact, he was the most dedicated person to creature comforts she had ever been around. Often he told her that nothing was finer than to live one's life at one's own rhythm and it had not taken long to see that he was right.

Several of her classes were late adjourning and she would come home in the dark, bundled in a fur coat, happy to find a fire burning and Charles, a glass of wine in his hand, cooking the dinner and listening to music. He laughed when she told him he'd make some lucky girl the perfect wife. They would have a drink and watch the news, trading stories and the day's events over supper, and then they would either read or continue listening to music while Charles reorganized his library or cataloged his vast record collection, insisting there be a proper place for everything and spending a good deal of time making an effort to make it so. Sleeping with him at night was pleasant enough; he gave her a sense of security beyond anything Lilly had ever known and the frenzied excitement was not something she missed, surprisingly. Charles believed excitement was really only another form of confusion and Lilly came to agree. After being together three weeks, they were as settled and as serene as any long-married couple could ever be.

From the very first, nothing was allowed to enter the relationship that could disturb Lilly; Charles saw to it that nothing upset her, no worries of infidelity, no anxiety that Charles might prefer another, perhaps younger, woman. Instead he often told her how exceptional she was, how warm and yet how capable. Maybe it was because he said it so much, but by the end of the month Lilly thought herself to be just such a person, forgetting completely the other Lilly who could stir up such inner storms of turmoil.

It was not that they lacked spontaneity, not at all. Why, on the spur of the moment one weekend they had thrown some warm clothing into the back of Charles's small car and driven around Lake Michigan for a few days in the Wisconsin woods, an easy excursion devoid of tedious planning, but still they ate properly at the right hours and their conversations were far from frivolous, although they spoke of themselves quite a lot. All their talks ended with a mutual reassurance that they were a lucky couple indeed, compatible and suited in every way. Lilly had seen her new serenity as far and away finer than any passion or excitement could ever be, and she reminded herself every day how fortunate she was to have finally found Charles.

For his part, Charles was fascinated by Lilly's work. She had not realized it before, of course, but Lilly saw then that she had never taken her job seriously. Because of Charles she became, in fact, so convinced of the merit of her profession that she might sometimes view herself a bit too importantly. But it was better to do that than not to think highly of herself, wasn't it? At Charles's suggestion, she decided to try her hand at writing an original screenplay, an as yet unfinished exercise but one, at the time, that had provided wonderful Sundays in front of the fire while she banged away on the portable typewriter, handing Charles each finished page to read aloud and criticize. She trusted his opinions on everything; he was so considerate of her feelings in the way he offered them. They talked of marriage, of course, and Lilly had laughed and told Charles to reserve his proposals until after he'd met her children. He told her he did not know much about children, and she had said what really was there to know and maybe they should even have one of their own. Charles had not seemed especially comfortable with the idea and it did not strike Lilly as being strange that she was so blithely considering having a third child when she already had two others at home. In fact, during that six weeks, it came to seem that Mags and Teddy belonged to someone else and that she was not really responsible for them at all. Oh, she called them every other night and promised them she would be home soon, hinting that she just might have a wonderful surprise for them. It was her only reference to Charles.

When time came to return to Washington, Lilly had been desolate; she was fearful of being away from Charles, for somehow her inner calm seemed to rest with him, a calm Lilly was afraid to lose, afraid because it might not be reclaimable. Charles had taken her to the plane and had been very mature saying his farewell; after all, they would see each other in two weeks, wouldn't they? Lilly had been very careful to make her attitude match his.

It had been a terrible wait, those two weeks. She had been nervous and easily upset, as if she had been too quickly withdrawn from a tranquilizing drug. Charles phoned every night and his steady voice could reassure her and she would say good-bye to him; feeling better, she would sit immediately down at her desk to write him a long letter until she felt sleepy. Other nights she became desperately depressed and felt everything was futile; she cried at those times and just the mere sight of Mags and Teddy could make her feel imprisoned, a single word from either of them a reminder that, without them, she could be free, free and far, far away. She told George Sabberstein that the worst kind of loneliness was being separated from someone you truly loved. George had been exasperated by the entire situation.

"Lilly, don't set yourself up for this. It might not work."

"And why not?"

"Because it's unrealistic."

"For me to be at peace is unrealistic?" She was indignant.

"No, of course not. But it sounds fishy. Well, 'fishy' is not the right word, either. I don't know, kid. Maybe I'm wrong but I don't think it will hang together."

"And why not?"

"Bad geography, for starters."

She had paid George no mind; she never listened to George until she had to. She tried to ignore the children, too; they were so restless, seeming to Lilly that they had turned overnight into demanding and ungrateful weights, dragging her down and holding her back. Especially had they been upset by Charles's first visit to Washington. It had been an awkward time for all of them; the adjustment seemed monumental and Charles was uncomfortable and ill at ease with the children, who persisted in eyeing him suspiciously as if they were stalked animals, as if Charles embodied some threat to their well-being. Lilly was determined that they would get past this nonsense and even took them some weeks later for a long weekend in Chicago, but Teddy had had no playmates and whined about it constantly, while Maggie had complained nonstop of the cold wind and the strange city. Both children sensed an imminent and unwanted change in their lives, and had used their only defense against the unknown: they were perfect pains in the ass.

Charles was quicker than Lilly to see the pitfalls in the arrangement and it was he who commented on the growing odds against a combined life.

"I'm sorry for being so short-tempered, Lilly. Guess I'm just not accustomed to kids' voices and a set routine."

"It does temper a free spirit," she'd said, ashamed to be apologizing.

"I don't think Maggie and Teddy like me very much. Can't blame 'em. I'm not much of a surrogate father. I don't know what to say to them."

"I know. Frankly, they are acting like tyrants. It isn't very fair to tie you down to the very things you've avoided creating for yourself." She wanted him to calm her fears.

"I guess if worst came to worst, we could look into some boarding schools," he said.

And that had, of course, been the beginning of the end. The mere mention of sending Mags and Teddy away made her recoil as though some inner spigot had been shut off. It had not been a harsh suggestion on Charles's part, but it summoned up Lilly's own childhood of feeling unwanted, of Clara and her wish for escape. Lilly could not do that to Mags and Teddy. No matter what, she could not perpetuate that on another generation. The idea of leaving the children with Harry made her equally sick; she could not relinquish them to him or to anyone. She said as much to George.

"It's your ego that's saying that, Lil."

"My ego!"

"Conceit, then. Isn't that what makes you so determined that no one, not even Harry, can properly bring up your children? Teach them the things you want them to believe?"

"You can sit there and chalk this up to maternal arrogance?"

"So listen to yourself."

"Oh, George. Come off it." But she was uneasy that he might be correct.

"A man," he said, "is every bit as capable of rearing children as a woman."

"That's not true, George Sabberstein, and you damn well know it."

"And you damn well know in your heart that you don't want to leave those kids because you love them. Why not admit it, honey, it's not the worst of motivations, you know."

"Kindly stick to the point."

"Then kindly be honest enough to admit that Harry, *even Harry*, can bring up Mags and Teddy. You can't have it both ways."

Lilly had behaved very stubbornly about the whole situation.

Her frustration, combined with the growing unruliness of the children, was altering her attitude toward Charles, making her ambivalent now where she'd once been so certain; she was easily irritated and depressed even when she was alone with Charles. The relationship was subtly changing, and without her knowing precisely when it set in, the comfortableness between them was strained, slipping away, devoured by arguments and disagreements that left everyone exhausted and diminished. She missed Charles when she was at home with the children and she missed the children when she was away with Charles.

One weekend in Washington had been particularly bad. Lilly had told Teddy to wash his face and to comb his hair because they were all going out to dinner.

"I'm not hungry," he said.

"Since when are you ever not hungry?"

"Since Charles. He makes me full."

Lilly had turned to Maggie, telling her to get ready also.

"I'm full, too, Mom."

Lilly and Charles had gone without them but the evening was awful; they had not stayed for dessert.

"Young children need a father," Charles had remarked.

"They need a kick in their behinds," Lilly had said.

"Actually, a bit of both might be in order."

Lilly had sulked over the remark, disliking Charles for making it and the children for deserving it.

"Look, Lilly," Charles had said flatly. "Just pack them up and come on out to Chicago. They'll adjust. Kids do, you know."

"But what about you and me? Will we adjust? We've known each other for such a short time." She was holding her breath for his answer.

"I don't know. I don't know anything anymore. Only that this is getting me down."

"I know. I know. Let's not talk about it now, Charles. O.K.?"

But it wasn't O.K., and it was not going to be O.K., a premise George agreed with wholeheartedly when she related the conversation to him later.

"Listen," he said enthusiastically, "have you thought about the rest of it? You've carried off the incredible task of being a movie critic from Washington. Ever think how hard it would be in Chicago?"

"That's the least of my concerns," she snapped.

"And just what kind of love nest will you have with your identity wrapped up in Charles? It's possible, you know, that without a professional outlet you'd turn into the kind of clinging wife he hasn't bargained for. Picture yourself, kid, a full-time wife and mother again, suffocated by it all."

"George, it's the children who are at issue, not what you consider my vain desires of glory."

"Then what about the kids? It seems to me you have three choices. One, you haul them off to Chicago, expect them to settle in while you try to find another kind of job and hope to God that a ready-made family doesn't send ole Charlie boy packing. Two, you unload the kids on Harry, forget your career and go through the whole marriage bit you've finally extricated yourself from. And, three, you stay here and be a responsible adult."

Anger reddened Lilly's face. "And four, George. There's a fourth alternative."

"Yeah? What?"

"You could go fuck yourself."

It had ended amicably, the thing between her and Charles; there really had been no other way. She had delayed the decision for weeks, at first hoping for a miracle, and then to prepare herself to make the phone call. The phone—she thought —it was always easier over the phone. No one can see or touch over a telephone.

"Charles? Listen to me without saying anything for a minute, will you? I want us to stop seeing each other for a while." She'd had to add "for a while," had to hold on to that slender thread of hope. "I love you. Oh, Charles, I really do love you. But I love Mags and Teddy, too. Getting married would be too much of a gamble for all of us. I belong here for the time being." And then her voice and resolve had broken and she was crying and saying that she only wanted to be with him.

"I know, Lilly. I know." Charles had said nothing more, for there really was nothing to say.

She had wept into George's shoulder that night as she told him about the phone call. She had cried and said she had indeed done the right thing, hadn't she? The right and horrible and miserable thing.

"I don't want to be responsible. I want to be a child again," she said to George. "I want my options back."

"It would only be something else, honey," he said. "When we're grown, there's always something else."

tired of herself Lilly switched off all the lights, something she had never done before—going to bed in a completely dark house. Always she had left one light burning as if for

# 19

LILLY put more Scotch and milk into her glass, half of each this time, and carried the mixture with her into the living room. Changing corners again, she thought, probably wearing a path in the carpet with all this back-and-forth. So what? So the hell what? Lilly fell onto the couch and pulled the afghan over her, a familiar position. She'd slept on the couch this way so many nights when Robbie had been drunk and hostile and she was afraid to sleep in the same bed with him lest some movement wake him and start him into another drunken night of it.

Robbie. She tried never to think of Robbie. Of all the men she had known, he was the one for whom she had no kind thoughts, no good memories. He was such a sad soul; how could she bear him animosity? Why should he still matter? Because she had cared too much, that's why he still mattered —because he had been the one to use her so cruelly.

What was it, three years ago? Closer to four, she thought. She had been so tired in those days; you weren't supposed to be tired like that when you were only thirty-six. Well, she was plenty tired of everything when she met Robbie. George said it was because she had been working too hard, insisting it was only the pressures of her work.

"Selling yourself to half the country three nights a week is not fun and games, Lil. You're wearing yourself out. UPI expects a quart of blood a day, kid, but nobody said you have to kill yourself."

True, ever since she took on the new job with UPI she had been spending long hours in screening rooms and in taping studios, almost never knowing what the weather was like until she went outside. George said it was unnatural to work all day in studios and theaters with no windows—that alone was enough to get anybody down. Lilly didn't argue but she had known better. She was simply restless. Very much on the prowl for some kind of excitement, something to break the solid pattern of her days. Well, she'd found a unique adventure in Robbie. Enough personal turmoil to last any normal fool a lifetime.

It was spring, four years ago. Remembering the season was easy because she had been in New York for a film festival—screenings all day for days, catching a sandwich when she could, if she could. The children were away with Harry on vacation and Lilly had postponed going back to Washington for one more day, dreading the empty house.

She had gone that night with a couple of other film critics to have a decent meal in a popular Upper East Side restaurant, a gathering spot for New York's talented and semi-talented, the place a giant womb packed with the genuinely gifted, the erratically creative and the inevitable hangers-on. Lilly hoped the food was more palatable than the literati.

It was very crowded and noisy; at several of the smaller tables couples played backgammon, and the rattle of dice and the clink of alabaster disks were scarcely audible over the growl of voices. One of the people Lilly was with had run into a friend who invited them to join their large round table; Lilly was tired and hungry and glad to sit down anywhere.

There was no pattern to their group; no one seemed to fit, but Lilly supposed that that was part of the restaurant's boisterous grab-bag charm. Robbie, however, was someone you noticed, pensive and reflective one moment, loud and gregarious the next, not one to be overlooked. She was seated next to him and saw immediately that his round face was quite flushed by alcohol. He had baby-plump hands and a full, pouty mouth.

The conversation at the table turned to the discussion of the films that were shown at the festival and everyone seemed to have an opinion, whether or not they had seen the movie they were talking about. A man, identified as a television journalist, was feigning cinematic knowledge he obviously did not possess while the others interrupted him to vie for verbal control of the table. Lilly thought the struggle amusing but childish and was a little bored by the arch dialogue. Looking back, she realized that evening had marked the beginning of her profound dislike for pseudo-intellectuals. She was scarcely able to endure the bona-fide ones.

By contrast, Robbie was silent. His companion, a lady of perhaps forty-six or so, was dominating the conversation now with an endless monologue about Buñuel versus Truffaut and was well into the symbolism of *Wild Strawberries* when Robbie broke in.

"I just loved *Airport* myself," he said.

Lilly had burst out laughing, the only person at the table to do so.

"Come on, Robbie," the woman said, visibly annoyed. "It's your bedtime." She took her wallet from her purse to pay their bill, but Robbie was calling to a passing waiter for another round of drinks.

"I said it was time to go," the woman repeated.

"I live a long way from here, from all this." He drawled rather than spoke; his accent was easily localized.

"Mississippi?" Lilly ventured.

"Georgia." The pouty mouth could smile.

"You a Carolinian?" His eyes narrowed, trying to place her accent now, the eternal game of transplanted Southerners.

"Guess which," she said.

"North?"

"South." She smiled. "It's television. Tends to make a capon of your voice."

"You in TV? An actress?"

"Film reviews—trailer stuff."

He looked confused. "That's the lighter side of the news. Back of the book." She laughed, explaining: "I come on after the sportscaster."

"You good?"

"Getting there."

"I'm a poet." He pronounced it po-hit. "The best poet you'll ever meet, honey, only don't everybody know that yet."

"I'm sure they will."

"You damn right. Mean old Southern boys make the best kind of poets. We feel things." He patted his paunchy middle for emphasis. Then: "You get home much?"

"No. But I think about it more than I used to."

"What you miss the most?"

"The food." Lilly was surprised by her answer. "And the people. They can be friendly down there without being insulted if you don't fall all over yourself in response. You can be a little weird and it doesn't really matter, you know?"

He nodded. "I'm from upcountry Georgia," he said. "We're so used to freaks, we think it's normal. Hell, in my county, if you don't have a cousin with webbed feet, they think you ain't good enough for your own family."

Lilly laughed again; home for her also meant a log of backwoods intermarrying. Or reproducing, anyhow. Robbie was sitting straight now, talking directly to her, the red eyes showing a keen intelligence she had missed earlier.

"Last time I was home," he said, "I had a real argument with Bubba Dent—we went to high school together—he's in real estate now, tearing everything down for parking lots. Paved over half of Georgia." He signaled the waiter for another drink, ignoring the irate woman next to him. He asked Lilly if she cared for a refill. She did. He held up two fingers, then continued. "I mean we had a *real* set-to. Bubba says he has more lunatics on his mama's side than I can count in my whole family."

"Does he?"

"Well"—he shook his head—"the Dents *are* a strange bunch." The waiter set the new drinks in front of them.

"How many in your family are crazy?" he asked.

"All of us."

"You, too?"

"The worst," she replied. Lilly took a swallow of the drink. Bourbon. She grimaced. Why did all Southerners assume the other drinks bourbon?

"I'll have to cut this with some branch water," she said, her voice sounding very Southern. His accent was contagious; she'd be talking like a hick in another five minutes, the way he talked. But he was not an ignorant country boy, she could see that now.

The lady with Robbie had settled back in her chair again and was talking heatedly with a novelist Lilly recognized from seeing his picture in magazines.

"Is your friend a writer?" Lilly lifted her brows to indicate the woman.

He laughed, not disdainfully, and leaned closer, whispering. "Shit." He drew the word out as if it contained several extra *i*'s. "Hardest work she does is open an alimony check once a month." He drank his entire drink down at once and held up the empty glass to a passing waiter. "She befriends artists and writers," he added.

"And poets?" Lilly said. The question seemed to offend him. "I mean where would art be without its patrons?" she said, trying to make amends.

"Trouble with being 'patronized' is that you always owe. I hate to owe." His mouth was a pout once more.

"Then why do it?"

His face rearranged into a look of impending violence. "Because when you got something in your gut that has to come out, something the world ain't no fucking good without, then you get real mean and selfish. You use anybody and everybody to get at your talent. Honey, you would kill your grandmother for it." He was calmer now. "Lessen she gets you first," he added, grinning.

Lilly turned her gaze to the woman, Robbie's patroness. There was a puffiness about her eyes from too much of whatever she was drinking. The mouth was full and sensuous, a little tight at the corners, but the eyes were smart, dark and piercing. Lilly noticed that she smoked constantly, taking deep, quick little puffs which she exhaled abruptly, using the unfiltered cigarette completely before stubbing it out irritably. No, sister-woman, Lilly thought, I will not go out of my way to end up like you.

It was as if Robbie was reading Lilly's thoughts. "She's all right," he said. "Generous. A little nuts. Mad at everything. But good. Loyal as hell." His fresh drink arrived.

"You see," he said by way of explanation, "she's been hanging around talent so long she thinks she's got some. Lot of people in here get fooled that way." He swung his huge arm to encompass the other tables. "They been sucking up to gifted folks so long, they think it's rubbed off on 'em."

The thought depressed Lilly and she was suddenly aware of her enormous fatigue; it had been a long day and she still hadn't eaten. She looked at her watch.

"You stay in a hotel?" Robbie drew the word "hotel" out further than the others, saying "ho-tail."

She said she was, and he asked which one.

"The Algonquin." She was talking more like him now, falling back into forgotten ways, drawing out the hotel's name just as he did.

"The Al-gone-quin, huh?" he said.

"Sho nuff."

They both laughed and Lilly was sorry to be so tired; she rather liked him, this pudgy poet, but she stood to go, telling him how glad she was to have met him. He rose to help her, returning her politeness and pumping her hand.

"Where'd you say you're from?"

"I didn't. But I live in Washington. Washington, D.C."

"You got a husband?"

"Not recently."

"Any babies?"

"Two big ones."

"Who takes care of them?"

"I do. But they spend a lot of time with their father."

"I mean, who pays their way?"

"Me and Hollywood." She wondered fleetingly why she should still be ashamed of inheriting money, even now when she supported herself with her earnings.

"Y'all live by yourself?" The idea seemed to appall him.

"Very much by ourselves." Without meaning to, she made it sound an invitation, and was annoyed that she had.

"I just might drop in on you one of these days."

Lilly smiled and shrugged. "I'll open Twelve Oaks," she said. "We'll have barbecue on the lawn." They laughed at that final regional joke and said good-night.

At the door, Lilly turned and glanced back toward the table. Robbie was sitting very close to his patron-lady now, his arm slung around her shoulder, smiling and nodding. Befriending the struggling young artist was not without its sly rewards, Lilly thought. Robbie and his friend were very much involved. Which was why she was kind of surprised when he showed up at her hotel at three in the morning.

He had called on the house phone from the lobby. She was in a deep sleep, able to rouse herself only after several rings.

"Uh-uh," she mumbled.

"I got the barbecue."

"What?"

"Some barbecue, honey. It's me, the Tarlton twins."

Awake, at least partially, Lilly tried to clear her head. "Who is this?" The hour illuminated on the traveling clock irritated her.

"I said"—he was slurring his words—"it's me, both the Tarlton twins. One of us has the barbecue. The other has got a fierce temper. I ain't sure what he's liable to do to this fancy lobby if you don't let us come upstairs."

Lilly realized it was Robbie. "Look"—she tried to sound reasonable—"I'm holding out for Ashley or Rhett." Quips, she groaned, even in the middle of the night.

"Well, whichever one of us—we were kind of hoping you'd receive us nice like, so we wouldn't feel a need to kick up a fuss down here and make you be unwelcome next time around."

He was, she saw, accustomed to having his way. Fully awake now, she thought, Oh, what the hell, and mumbled her room number, then got up to put on a robe, almost gagging in the sink as she brushed lightly over her teeth.

Robbie was panting when he arrived, explaining between gasps that the elevator was shut down and he'd had to use the stairs. His bulky frame sagged against the door and she

270

thought he looked like a big, red-necked highway patrolman. He offered a sheepish grin.

"Left the barbecue in the phone booth," he said, and held up instead a bottle of whiskey in a crumpled brown bag. Shades of the old South, Lilly thought as she opened the door wider for him to stumble past; he was very drunk. She shrugged and reached for the glass of whiskey Robbie poured for her, a little toothpaste smudging its rim. What in the world was she doing drinking bourbon in the middle of the night with a drunken poet? Well, she would worry about that tomorrow. Christ, she thought, the *Gone With the Wind* business was as infectious as Robbie's accent. What Southerner could talk long without making reference to the movie? She and Clara had seen it six times; Clara had said that the last two were "only to look at the furniture." Lilly smiled, returning her attention to the huge drunken man sitting opposite her on the other neatly made twin bed, his size giving the effect that he was perched on a footstool.

"How big are you, anyway?" It was a *non sequitur* but he didn't seem to notice.

"Bigger than life, honey. How 'bout you?"

"Too long for hotel beds," she said, sitting down on her own bed.

"We match up pretty good," he said. It was a shy statement.

"Perhaps."

"You always talk in such short sentences?"

"Unless I'm angry."

"You that way much?"

"Enough."

"What makes you maddest?"

"Men who count my words."

"Oh!"

"You don't precisely run on at the mouth your own self." She was talking like him again.

"I save it for my work." He reached inside his pullover sweater and brought out a sheaf of neatly typed pages, handing them to her as if they were a precious gift.

"I thought poets wrote in longhand, quilled pens dipped in the soul's blood," she said.

"Took typing in the tenth grade." He grinned. "That's where the girls were during fourth period." He shifted his weight, causing the edges of the mattress to curl. "Working a typewriter comes more in handy than you girls."

Lilly let that pass.

"I took typing one summer," she said, making conversation. "I guess I was about fifteen—'fur, jug; fur, jug', there was this awful instructor with the darkest dyed hair in town." Lilly laughed at the total recall. "Her name was Elderlene. I swear to God. We called her something else behind her back. She'd take each paper we did our drills on and correct them with a red pencil. What a look she'd give you if just one letter in 'fur' or 'jug' was out of order! We'd have to do it over. She'd tell us that one of these days we'd be glad to have the skill. 'You mark my words! A woman has to know how to be a secretary. You'll thank me someday!' I never got around to it."

"Thanking her?"

"Being a secretary. But the skill is valuable. Even if you're not a poet."

"Must be more fun to go to the picture show and get paid for it."

"Combines passion with pay," she said.

There was a long and not uncomfortable pause, and Lilly was aware that he was the first adult Southern male she had been alone with since that last ride from the cemetery with her father. To end up in the middle of the night with one now seemed ludicrous. Especially one so obviously full of bourbon.

"How old are you?" he asked.

"Thirty-six. You?"

"Same," he said.

Lilly wondered if their mutual ease stemmed from their similar age and backgrounds. She was strangely glad to be with him, but what in the Lord's name was she to do with him?

Again there was the sensation that he could read her mind. "I'm kinda thinking of going home with you," he said.

"I see you brought your luggage." Lilly glanced toward the brown paper bag of liquor.

"I'm a light traveler."

He began to pile the bed pillows behind his head, stretching out, his worn sneakers dangling over the end of the bed; in a few minutes he was snoring. Lilly sat watching him. Robbie would jump in his sleep, shaking his head and mumbling a few words, nothing distinguishable, but he sounded frightened somehow; then with a snorting noise he would stiffen and resettle into his loud slumber. Some poet, Lilly thought as she switched off the light and got into her own bed.

Morning was coming through the drawn curtains when she became aware of another presence in the bed with her. Robbie, still in his clothes, his shoes off, though, and lying next to her, sweaty, reeking of alcohol, holding on to her as if from desperate need. His snoring was awful and Lilly could scarcely move in the small space his body left; his arm was flung across her chest and there was no circulation in her left leg, yet she dared not extricate herself lest she awaken him. Shifting gently, she fell back into sleep.

Awake again, Lilly lifted her stiff neck to see the clock. It was after eleven, half the morning gone. Robbie was next to her but the snoring had stopped and she leaned closer to make sure he wasn't dead. The even breathing reassured her and she lay very still and tried to think. It gave her a strange sense of justice to be wondering how she could get rid of Robbie, a perverse satisfaction to strike a blow for all women who found themselves the ones being got rid of by men. The problem was that she was not positive that she wanted to throw Robbie out.

Lilly eased from under his weight and slid out of bed, reaching for her rumpled robe. She took her glasses from the pile of items on the bureau and went into the bathroom. Maybe she would read his poetry first.

Lilly had never liked poetry—even when it rhymed, it bored her, sounded so pretentious. When a person had something to say, it seemed a bit more straightforward to just come right out and say it—not to belabor the message with a lot of convoluted phrases and coded meter. Robbie's poetry was better than most. Or did she just wish it to be? She realized as she read on that his way with words was a good deal more beautiful on paper than in person. There were no "ain't"s or dropped vowels, and to the best she could figure, he was extolling the horrors of the bulldozer and the cement mixer. *Sonnets from the Portuguese* it was not. Still?

She heard him thumping around in the other room now and wondered exactly how one went about greeting a sober Southern poet with whom one has just passed a chaste and virginal night, like brother and sister. Lilly thought of Faulkner and disqualified the sibling comparison.

She called to him through the closed bathroom door, making a production of running water and clanking jars and bottles so he'd know where she was. "Are you starved?" There was no answer. Had he gone? Opening the door, she walked briskly into the bedroom and headed straight toward her suitcase propped open on the only chair. Robbie was there, sitting rather forlornly on his own bed, looking so enormous that she wondered how one bed had held them both. His head was in his hands; he lifted it to smile.

"I said you must be starved," she repeated.

"What I want is a couple of Cokes, over light."

Lilly reached for the telephone.

"No." It was a command. "Let's go downstairs and find the Round Table. I'll be Robert Lowell and you can be—"

"Dorothy Parker!" she finished. It was a splendid idea, the best she'd ever heard. "It'll only take me a minute to throw something on."

She began dressing, her back to him, not even wondering at her immodesty, certainly not embarrassed. She thought of Faulkner again and grimaced.

"Look," he started. "About last night." He glanced toward the messed bed.

"Nothing happened. You're still intact."

"That's what I mean. I'm sorry about that." He seemed genuinely sorry. For what?

"For what?" she said aloud.

"For letting you down."

She had to laugh. The pig. A pig poet, perhaps the worst kind.

"Are you *that* accustomed to paying for your room and board?" It was not a light remark and she had not meant it to be. The pout was back on his mouth, and his face was crimson. Lilly felt a flash of anger herself. "Robbie, did you come here thinking that I was desperate for your warm body?"

"I, ah . . ." For a moment he looked about to cry. "I have a little problem with that."

Lilly waited.

"You see, well, I've trouble, er, making it, you know? With someone like you."

Lilly said nothing.

"That woman I was with last night? It's O.K. with her because, well, because she doesn't *do* anything. No threat or anything, you know?" His eyes actually teared; Robbie's emotions, Lilly saw, were like a woman's and she didn't like him this way.

"Look," she said, feeling she ought to help him out but unable to choke back a rising sense of disgust. "It's a nice change not to be pawed and mauled. Sorry you didn't pick up on that."

"What I'm trying to tell you is that it's because I respect you. And I like you."

"You like me and you respect me, but can't make love to me?"

He shook his head. "I had a shrink once who explained why

274

I couldn't bring myself to make love to anyone who was like my mother."

Like his mother! Dear God! She had found him with a woman nearly ten years his senior, and he thought Lilly reminded him of his mother! She sat down next to him wondering if he could be serious. Or was this another male trick to blame the woman for his inadequacies? Sparing her the shame of not being desirable?

"Maybe you better run through this once more," she said.

He continued to stare at the carpet.

"Tell me, Robbie. Please."

"It's like this. I have this little ole mother in Georgia. Stubborn as a mule, she is. My father never amounted to much. Drifted off right after I was born. Her family always thought she'd married beneath her. And mother's real proud. Spent her whole life living with their silent recriminations. Never takes a dime. Hell, her family doesn't have much to offer anyway, except 'We told you so.'" He interrupted himself to reach for the glass of stale whiskey left from the night before. His use of the formal word "mother" was something of a jolt, so un-Southern, so out of character. Or was it? Lilly sat very still.

"Mother wanted to be a concert pianist. Used to practice in the parlor day and night, she says. But she married my father. Poor bastard. Then I came along and he left. Smart bastard, anyhow. Mother was above charity; there wasn't much of that in Georgia then or now. So she gave piano lessons. Played the organ at the First Presbyterian over on Tiding Street." He took another swallow of the whiskey.

"It was the piano lessons I hated most. Coming home every afternoon and hearing the sounds of 'Teaching Little Fingers to Play.' Locked in my room and still I couldn't shut it out, the chords, the repeated butchering of Wagner and Beethoven, the tick, tock of the metronome, lesson after lesson. It damned near drove me crazy. It did drive her crazy.

"She didn't say much but I knew. It was always there between us. If I hadn't been born, she would have been somebody. American Beauty roses on a baby grand and all that. What she has is an old upright and a sweet-potato plant. My fault.

"She saved every dime she could from those two-dollar lessons, squirreled it away somewhere in the kitchen, never trusted the banks. It was for me. She did without everything, never a new hat for choir practice or anything. I wore hand-me-down clothes until my high school graduation. We never went anywhere, ate together every single night, her always asking me if I had been the smartest boy in school that day.

"Homework was a ritual she worshiped. She'd never read anything more than a sheet of music but she saw to it that I had read every classic by the time I was fourteen. Each morning she'd follow me to the corner where I'd meet the guys to walk to school—over on Peach Place—calling after me to do good for her today. 'Make an A for me, son, you hear?'

"I was big for my age"—he lifted his shoulders in evidence —"and played pretty good ball. But she hated that. Nagged me every time I went to practice: 'Study, Robert. Study is what will save you. Not ball playing.' The sports field and the schoolroom were the only places I was ever out of her sight. I never had a date till I went to college."

For the first time now, he looked straight at Lilly; she'd never seen such agony. He got up to find his bourbon bottle, emptying it into his glass and pacing up and back in the small room.

"You see"—his voice was still devoid of bitterness—"I was all she had. She'd lost everything because of me and I was to make it up to her. I *owe* her. Always will. Her vindication was to be my success. I was to buy a reprieve from her family, the whole fucking town. Piano Teacher's Son Makes Good. Fine blood will out. All that shit." Still there was the absence of bitterness; Lilly marveled at that.

"She's a strong and determined woman, sugar. Powerful as they come, but hiding it behind a fluttering helplessness that fooled everybody but me. I knew. That woman has a will of iron. She saw me through school, saved every examination paper, every poem published in the college paper—which wasn't often at Georgia Tech. She'd have framed my first bowel movement if she hadn't toilet-trained me so early." He was smiling now, the tension easing.

"I played ball in college, but to tell you the truth, every time some bigger fellow came at me I nearly fainted. You don't be my size and be scared, you know?"

Lilly shook her head; it made sense.

"Well, my mama still writes and phones, tells me to make an A. I got to do that for her, you see. I got to make an A, got to be the best goddamned poet you ever heard tell. She doesn't like me to be a poet. It really pisses her off, calls it 'sissy stuff.' I used to wonder if maybe I was, you know, a sissy? Well, I ain't." His lower lip jutted out stubbornly. "But I'm gonna show her she can be proud. Even of poetry."

Lilly wondered why children have to go through this, wondered how she could comfort him.

He turned to face her but spoke as if to some faraway audience. "I'm gonna make my mother glad she had me. Just watch. One day she'll finally get around to saying it: 'Robert, you're a good boy!' That will be enough, that one line of praise out of that tight little mouth. Hellfire"—he was grinning now—"I'm gonna make her a legend in her own time. The town mama."

Lilly shuddered, not missing the intensity of Robbie's words, however hidden they were behind the disarming grin. Was this how she might have ended up? Maybe she was fortunate to have been turned loose from the parental possessiveness when she was so young.

"You'll never know," he said, "how many times I wished my mother had just taken to the sherry bottle like everybody else. It skipped a generation. The bad seed." Robbie toasted his glass in her direction, finishing it off with a single swallow. "So that's the story. I can fuck around with some women. What I can't do, Miz Scarlett, is to git it up for the likes of you." Now he was showing the self-pity she had thought him above.

Lilly was stunned, yet flattered, that this veritable stranger was telling her of his fears. Should she consider herself warned, put on notice, even before she had made up her mind whether to become involved with him? Good Lord, just listening to him was an involvement, wasn't it?

"Do I really remind you of your mother?" she asked.

"No. Not exactly. But I know about women like you."

"Women like me?" Lilly was annoyed again; he had some nerve to intrude on her this way and then be insulting.

"I read the magazines, sugar." He smiled as if that were explanation enough. "You have a fancy job and raise children. It takes courage to do all that. To live without a man, you have to be pretty tough."

"Tough!" Lilly was incredulous. "Listen, my friend. It's *dealing* with men that's tough. That's where the courage comes in." She knew she was not being honest, but what kind of honesty did she owe him?

"Don't get huffy," he said, still smiling. "I like toughness. Attracted to it plenty. I just can't fuck around with it."

For a fleeting instant Lilly saw the challenge in his eyes, perhaps even a flash of cruelty. Whatever it was, it vanished immediately; he was the boy again, grinning at her sheepishly.

"I don't see myself as tough, thank you. Or brave. Or strong. Actually I'm just a ninety-pound weakling, give or take twenty pounds."

"Sugar, if you don't know about yourself, then you listen to me. You got guts. Shows all over you. Look what you done with your life."

Lilly ignored the deliberate poor grammar but she was uncomfortable under his steady gaze.

"Not too many women your age can take care of herself working on TV."

Despite his corniness and the conflicting emotions he could stir in her, Lilly was pleased to have him think of her as brave. A nice feeling came over her, mixing easily with the sympathy she had for this strange and complex man. What harm could there be in looking a little weak if he needed her that way? Cosmetically adapt? Lilly shook her head angrily and stood to finish dressing. She had promised never to cosmetically alter her personality for a man again, but it was a funny thing about that promise—it made such sense until she was faced with the actual choice.

"Look, believe me," she said. "I'm a card-carrying coward. Besides, you haven't even tried to make love to me."

"Would you like to?"

"It sure would prove or disprove your argument." Lilly grinned, suddenly aware that going to bed with Robbie would not be the worst possible thing to have happen.

"You see," he said, "that's what I mean about guts. After all I've said, you're willing to try. Sugar, that's courage or stupidity, one or the other."

Lilly did not care to explore her motivations at the moment, but she could feel the anger return, the slow rage of a frustrating situation getting to her. Shit, she thought, a woman is damned if she can't stand on her own two feet and damned further when she can. Angrily she turned back to face Robbie, wishing to make a few things clear about herself. Yes, goddammit, why shouldn't she put someone on guard too this time around? This time around. Was she that involved? Lilly turned back and began throwing things into her suitcase, too much a coward to say, "Hey, you, look at perfect me, I have a little problem you ought to know about also." Then what would she say? "Listen, Robbie, I, sir, do not have orgasms." The expression, even unspoken, lodged in Lilly's throat. Hell, she couldn't even get the words up. Lilly laughed, exasperated with herself but also amused by her prudishness. She and

278

Robbie were some coupling. Perhaps they ought to check into a sex clinic, get a special rate or something.

"I hear there's a couple of doctors who give sex therapy in St. Louis. We ought to go as a team."

Robbie looked up sharply and for a moment Lilly thought he might question her need of such doctors, rather wishing he would; it might help to tell her problems to someone other than George Sabberstein. Robbie asked nothing. Rather, he stood up and moved toward the door.

"Let's eat first," he said. "Maybe downstairs at the ole Round Table I'll grow brave and you'll soften up."

Just for a second, Lilly felt every instinct urge her to grab her suitcase and get the hell away from this weirdly charming stranger. But it was only a second. Instead, she picked up her shoes and her purse and followed him to the door, stepping into her shoes as she walked. Robbie leaned down to kiss her cheek in a brotherly fashion and Lilly did not think of Faulkner this time. What she thought was what she always thought when she met a man who interested her: either she would alter herself or she would make him over, change him, overhaul him, turn him into precisely what she wanted. Somewhere within, she had a peculiar inkling that one of them would give in, and that it would probably be she.

They had a wonderful wine-filled lunch. He made her laugh at his stories from his past and he listened to her, encouraging her to talk, reaching out sometimes to touch her face and tell her she was so very beautiful. Just to be with him made Lilly aware of her loneliness.

As though it had long been arranged, he went back to Washington with her that afternoon. A poet can work anywhere, he said, and for Robbie, working was to talk, literally to talk out everything he felt. He would tell her that mankind was doomed—"All of us are doomed, sugar"—and he would drink and ramble on about life and nature, extolling the absence of the Almighty, and then condemn the entire human race, saying over and over that Auden was, of course, right: "It's people who are the spoilers, of the land, of talent, of the superior works of nature and genius." Himself and the good earth, that's how Robbie saw everything, but he only talked about it. Never once would Lilly know him to put his words on paper.

Later, when he'd been in Washington for almost two months, he began to suggest that Lilly's own work was frivolous—perhaps fun, but frivolous, no lasting impact like the written word. "Thin" was how he put it—thin soup, sugar, he would say—and she had argued vehemently at first, until, slowly, she came to believe that maybe what she did was frivolous and lacking in inspiration. Some days it seemed too ridiculous for her to get up and go through the motions of working.

The children had disliked Robbie on sight. Teddy had been openly hostile; Mags, old enough to spot a bore, had contrived to avoid Robbie whenever possible, while Teddy took to skulking about, banging and slamming around the house, his schoolwork deteriorating. Lilly tried to give the boy extra attention but he was insatiable. Whenever Robbie told Lilly to fix him a drink or to raise or lower the heat, Teddy would mutter that Robbie ought to do it himself and then the child would run to do Lilly's chores for her, returning to glare at Robbie and press himself close to Lilly, waiting for her approval. It was not easy to praise a little boy for having the consideration a grown man lacked, not in front of the grown man, anyhow. Lilly tended to make light of these clumsy moments, but there were not enough hours in the day to please both Teddy and Robbie, and pleasing Robbie was more important, for she insisted on seeing herself as the guardian of his genius, telling herself that if she were a calming and steadying influence, Robbie might actually become a good poet and then be happy. If he was happy, then Lilly would be happy. It was so simple if you thought of it that way. She had explained this to George and he had said, "Yeah, Lil, the guy's poetic seeds are flowering all over the place."

George, too, had had an instant and unreasonable distrust of Robbie. Well, Lilly expected that and, anyway, how could she possibly tell George how good it felt for her to have someone around the house who needed her and depended upon her? Certainly, she knew better than to expose Robbie's sexual dilemma to George, knowing he would howl with derision, and besides, the problem was not so bad as announced; those things were improving between her and Robbie. If only he wouldn't drink so much, she thought they might actually be able to make love. No, George would understand none of this; Lilly could scarcely follow it herself.

The five of them—George, the children, herself and Robbie—had been having dinner one night in the dining room; Robbie liked the formality of the dining room. George was silent but observant; the children were pushing food around their plates, resentfully. Robbie was suddenly very drunk; his drunkenness always surprised Lilly—he would be fine one moment, totally out of control the next. That evening he had knocked over his wineglass several times and Lilly had righted the goblet each time, dabbing at the cloth with her napkin and trying to make no fuss over his behavior while George watched her closely, sitting in judgment. Robbie, however, was oblivious to anything other than his own words, rambling on about the rape of nature, the insensitivity of the masses to everything creative, especially his creativeness.

"It's cheap, contemporary journalism that people want." Robbie was addressing the table in general. "Cheap-shot journalists and songwriters. Clever little TV comments, huh, sugar? That's what sells, right?"

Lilly had shrugged the remark aside and glanced nervously toward George, who seemed about to answer when, all of a sudden, Robbie fell drunkenly from his chair. Lilly jumped from her seat and helped him up. She led him upstairs Robbie following her clumsily like a mischievous boy, stumbling on each stair as she said soothing things to him, leading him carefully each step of the way. She'd done it many times before—why was it so particularly tiresome that night? She settled Robbie into bed and removed his shoes, then went into the bathroom and broke off a corner of a Dexedrine tablet, washing it down with some tap water. The Dexedrine would give her the energy she didn't seem able to muster on her own lately. Her eyes looked back at her in the mirror, dark and sunken, but she forced a smile, telling herself that Robbie was a real tiger, a tiger she had by the tail and didn't know how to let go of even if she wanted to. She gave a great sigh, reopened the medicine cabinet and bit off yet another little piece of Dexedrine, then closed the medicine cabinet without looking at herself in the mirror. In the bedroom, she checked to make sure Robbie was sleeping. The big galumph, she thought, and smiled to herself. He was a lot to handle but there was a certain sweetness in him, especially when he was asleep—a certain sweetness that a woman needed in her life.

Back downstairs, she saw that the children had left the table, vanished to their rooms. Lilly was hoping George had gone, too; she was so tired—all the time tired lately—and she was not up to a confrontation. Probably she should not have taken the Dexedrine; she needed to sleep tonight. There was a lot of work to do tomorrow, work she kept putting off. Well, she would need the Dexedrine to cope with Robbie. When he passed out this early, he always woke in the night, filled with fear and remorse, and would need her.

In the kitchen George was stacking plates in the sink. Lilly hated doing dishes and the house was always in a mess these days. She sighed again and George turned at the sound.

"How much longer are you going to do this to yourself, Lilly? To the kids? You're exhausting yourself. And for what? This?" He swung his arms to include the clutter. "For that fool upstairs?"

Lilly turned to stone at the reference to Robbie.

"He'll find himself, George," she said. "Robbie is a highly creative and imaginative person. He'll find himself."

"Find him, lose you." It was all George said, but it struck a chord in Lilly.

"What do you mean by that crack?" She was angered; she was either angry or tired all the time.

"I mean that that overgrown parasite could not possibly have enough talent to justify what you are doing to yourself to nourish it. No one has, Lilly. No one."

"So he does go on a bit about the brutality of life, but he's just more sensitive to it than others."

"He is sensitive to nothing but himself. He's a destroyer, Lil. A selfish, self-centered man who is scared shitless he doesn't have what it takes to succeed. He ridicules everything around him in order to add to his own overblown sense of importance."

"Dr. Freud, I presume?" She started to scrape the dishes, furiously.

"Freud would have a field day with your motives."

"He's dead, you know," she snapped.

"And so will you be if you don't kick that blubbering asshole out on his sodden behind."

Lilly was so weary, so exhausted from juggling her life, falling behind on motherhood, on herself, on George; there was just not enough of her to do everything and George would not let up.

"And your work, babe. It's pretty crappy lately, you know?"

She knew. She just didn't want to hear it now.

"You're like Teddy," she said. "Not enough Mommy to go around." The counterattack, she was good at counterattacking.

"Maybe. Maybe not. But Teddy and Maggie and I put together do not need the mothering Robbie does. He's draining you. Lilly, listen to me. He's taking away all your juice. And for what? Some junk about bulldozers deflowering the virginal trees and forests? Shit.

"I wouldn't open my mouth if I thought you were having

ome high Tennessee Williams thrills from all this, but that uy is not sober long enough to make sense, let alone make ove."

Lilly felt his words were knives being forced into her tired, agging body. George was saying things she already knew, but earing them now made them horrendous. If she did not peak or think of all that was wrong between her and Robbie, hen she could somehow manage to pretend the problems idn't exist, but George was always butting into her life like his, giving her troubles solid form. Lilly shut her eyes tightly; he was being forced to deal with Robbie and George and erself and she wasn't ready. She was tired and frightened and he didn't have the strength right now. Couldn't George see hat she needed Robbie because he needed her? And, oh God, ouldn't he see she didn't want to be left alone again? Not yet, lease God, not yet. Lilly leaned over the sink and cried— ong wailing cries that seemed to take with them all the trength she had. George came and put his arms around her.

"Sweetie." He turned her around. "Look at me. And listen. Do you remember Fitzgerald's *Tender Is the Night?*"

She could scarcely stop crying to answer. "I only saw the movie."

"Close enough. Remember how sick and confused poor Nicole was? And Dr. Diver comes to the rescue. He helped her get strong, too. Took care of her and lived her way until he lost all his strength to her. Gave it all away because he loved her. Nothing was his anymore, nothing he trusted." George shook her gently for emphasis. "Who was strong and who was weak then?" He was reasoning with her as if she were a child.

"Baby, listen to me. You're trying to play Dick Diver to Robbie and he'll never thank you for it. Already he resents you. Feels superior because he's got you apologizing for your work, how you live, your kids. Christ, Lilly, you're fumbling around him like some simple-minded teenager. You're being used up, honey. And getting nothing worthwhile in exchange."

Lilly tried to push back from George but she did not have the strength. *No strength left.* That's what George was saying, wasn't it? Goddamn him, he was right, but why couldn't he leave her be? Why was he always making her face herself? She brushed at the moisture in her nose and tried to control the tears.

"Nice point, George," she said.

He reached around Lilly and tore off a paper towel from the rack over the sink, holding it for her as she blew her nose.

Lilly thanked him and put her head back against George's shoulder, feeling calmer.

"I don't have much left. I think I'm out of gas," she whispered. She blew her nose again. "What do I do, George?"

"Get Robbie out." It sounded so reasonable.

"I can't just turn him out; he's got nowhere to go."

"Don't you know about people like him, Lil? There's always somebody to take them in. He'll be going strong when you and I are dead and gone."

"He gets so violent when he's threatened."

"The spoiled baby who has to be the center of the world," George said. "That guy must have had some mother!"

Lilly was startled by George's insight; everyone was so much better at sizing up situations than she. Was that what Robbie was doing? Breaking her down the way he could not break his mother down? Punishing her because of his mother? Had Lilly wanted him to do that? Her head was reeling; she backed away from George and tried to stop the dizziness.

"I can't tell you the number of nights when Robbie can't sleep," she said, whispering still lest Robbie overhear and become furious. "George," she went on, her voice low, "there are nights when I have to take pills to stay awake just to keep an eye on him. I get terrified he might do something to himself."

Lilly went to sit in the closest chair.

"You know," she continued, "he tells me that great poetry comes from pain and suffering. Sometimes"—Lilly made her voice even lower—"sometimes I have this awful feeling that he might—oh, it sounds so dumb—but I get the idea that he could really harm me. He's told me that people are just as well off dead as alive, that it doesn't really matter much one way or the other."

"He's a bully, honey. Only because you allow it. And he won't harm himself. That kind never harm themselves. Takes too much courage." George laughed; it was a bitter sound. "No. He'll just drink himself into believing he has every right to blame someone else for his life. Look at it this way—if he thinks poetry and suffering go hand and hand, then give him the anguish his artistic soul demands."

George pulled a chair over to face hers, taking her hands in his. "Why, Wonder Woman, kicking him out might provide the grand tragedy that will get him off his ass. It could be your great contribution to literature."

Lilly shook her hands free of George's. He was being facetious and she did not like it. She felt very protective of

284

Robbie, loyal, even, and her eyes glanced toward the back stairs apprehensively.

George became serious again, almost terse. "Think of yourself, then, Lil. You can't rehabilitate a man with Robbie's problems just because you want him to be what you need. And you can't let him drag you down with him."

She gave George another grave look, then lit a cigarette.

"All right," he said, "I admit that Robbie can be pretty charming when he's sober. But he can also be very sly. There's no balance to the scale. Look, I'm not saying any of this very tactfully, but, God, you've got to know what I'm driving at. You do see, Lilly, don't you?"

Her voice was filled with sorrow. "What do I do?" she said. "I can't hurt him. He never meant me any harm. I don't think he even knows what he does to me. God, I couldn't bear it if I thought Robbie was cruel."

"There's some cruelty in all of us, Lil. Sometimes we just can't help it."

Lilly thought again of Robbie, rubbing at her eyes with her hands as she did. Poor, sleeping, sweet Robbie; he couldn't help himself.

"Honey," George said, "why don't I go round him up right this minute."

"No! I don't know what I'm going to do but I know I'll never forgive myself if I don't do it on my own."

George put on his raincoat and walked to the door. "I'll never understand how you can be such a smart broad about so many things and be such a fool when it comes to men."

Lilly laughed for the first time that night. "Me either, pal."

She waved George good-bye as he went out and dragged herself up the stairs; her body was exhausted but her brain danced from the effects of the Dexedrine. Quickly she slipped into bed. Robbie was bulk in the dark, and snoring loudly, the rasping sounds jangling her nerves, raking over her, but she lay there, not daring to move, staring at the ceiling. She wanted to be numb, to anesthetize herself, do something—anything—to stop the tormenting questions in her head. She got out of bed and took a sleeping pill, rationalizing that to mix drugs was dangerous but to be awake was more hazardous still. Back in bed, she waited for sleep to take her over.

Drowsiness crept up slowly, bringing escape: she was almost free, almost gone. Yet dimly she was aware of movement in the bed. Confused, she tried to think where she was. Her body was in a bed, her bed, but her mind was not with her anymore; it had detached itself and moved away, drugged and gone. She was better off without her mind; she could sink into a deep peace now except that she was being pulled back, someone was pulling at her, holding her and touching her when she wanted to sleep, to put the night behind her. He head was sluggish, packed with cotton; only her body coul feel—feel hands moving over her breasts, Robbie's hands. Sh did not want Robbie's hands on her but her brain had gon away and she was powerless: no control, split into separat sections—the brain hovering somewhere overhead watchin; her body as it responded to hands rubbing along her thighs responding as if it had a will of its own.

A mouth was against the lower part of her now, kissing he stomach, tracing her contours with a practiced tongue, goin; lower and lower. She ought to be repelled or frightened; only her strange, willful body was eager, demanding to be touche even more—trusting the tongue which burrowed inside, flick ing for a moment over vulnerable private places and ther stopping, cruelly, forcing her body to arch itself so that thos wonderful places might be caressed again. Above Lilly wa: her shadowy brain, observing her wantonness with shock, trying to transmit to her that it was Robbie who was doing this to her, Robbie who had said so many times that he could not please her body—her body which wanted to feel this way, wanted Robbie never to stop but to go on and on and on There was nothing but her body now, floating lifelessly, then soaring until there was this urgency, this driving need for some part of her to give way, to crack apart like a solid block of ice, breaking now—first into halves, then into tiny, small pieces that started to flow and rush—an unbearable pleasure that she wished would last forever. Her hands, as if of their own accord, went down to the head between her thighs, pressing against it, helping, moving faster and faster, until, from some great distance, Lilly heard the sound of intense cries and, finally, the joy of a sob. Why in the world would she be crying? Crying now when she had never felt so wonderful, so wonderfully good, so full and empty at the same time.

Her brain took control again, maliciously informing her she had every reason to cry, warning her that it was too late, too late for this to be happening to her. She turned on her side and pressed her face into the pillow to cover her sobs, waiting for Robbie to comfort her, to tell her he was sorry that he had not given her this pleasure before, to promise her it would be all right between them now. But he would say nothing now, she realized; he was far over to his side of the bed, bulk in the dark once more.

He knew, though; he knew what he had just given her and still he could draw away like this! He knew how much she had wanted him to love her this way, needed him to make her feel the way no man had ever been able to make her feel before. The selfish son of a bitch knew—he could have given her this all along and yet he had kept it from her, deliberately withheld the one thing she had been so desperate to believe herself capable of experiencing. Instead, he had told her she was hopeless, that they were both hopeless sexual misfits, had let her believe she was responsible for all those nights when he had fumbled with her body and failed, failed and blamed her, saying she was either frigid or too strong-minded to submit, drunkenly castrating her for his castration and then feeling sorry for himself, sulking and berating her and keeping her terrified that she could not function as a whole person when all along he knew that she could. Lilly was choking with sobs. If only he had helped her sooner, shown her he cared, she would have done anything for him, anything. They could have been all right. Oh God, they might really have been all right. But not now, not like this. Her brain was very clearly in control, reminding her that a person does not really love another person and withhold for so long the physical happiness he had just given her.

Lilly did not remember precisely when the tears and anger evaporated that night and the sleep had finally come, but her final thoughts were of the terrible sadness of having to choose between what is right for the soul and what is pleasurable for the body. Poor, twisted, selfish Robbie. She would ask him to leave in the morning.

"A fu... ...verent, and br...y ...ccount
life a... ...ington hostess ...a Fam...
confid... ...enfant terrible."

# 20

SO MANY men had tumbled in and out of her life in the four years between Robbie and Peter—the four years until now, now when she was forty and so discouraged by it all. Instead of protecting herself, she had done just the opposite. After Robbie it had not taken long for her to begin looking for more trouble. She knew the cycle well: the strange hungriness inside and she would start to cast her eye at every man she met—men at parties, on planes, trains, in the street, looking at them for measure, wondering if one of them were meant for her. It would be only a matter of weeks from the hunger to the pounce—yes, pounce was the word—selecting at random and pursuing the affection and romance she craved. And the sex? No, it was nothing so uncomplicated as just sex, but it was not to be discounted—when the body wants something badly enough, the mind and the soul bend to accommodate.

Few of the men after Robbie had lasted long enough to qualify as bona-fide memories. For a while, there had been a shy, introverted short-story writer whom she had pushed and picked at to live up to her fantasy, then tired of him because he did not; the wealthy stockbroker who said she was "charming" and "so game" until once too often, she declined to accompany him to some remote place like Seattle where he was the guest speaker at one fund-raising banquet or another. A Republican. George had been right about him, too! Lilly could not love a Republican, he'd said. Who could ever love a rich man for very long? The rich, she found, honestly believe that everyone else was born for their convenience and that any behavior that ran counter to that convenience was a willful denial of their rights. At the moment, Lilly could not recall the broker's name, only that he had later found an amenable divorcée from Greenwich. Probably rich and Republican and game.

For brief periods there had been one or two younger men, and she had been a rather good sport about George's jokes that she was becoming another Mrs. Robinson—the analogy ruining *The Graduate* for her if not the romances. Actually, it had bothered Lilly that younger men believed she needed to be constantly reminded that she was, for her age, a very desirable woman, even inspirational. The arrogance of youth; not one of them was capable of comprehending the truth; they bored her with their inexperience—they simply had not lived long enough or hurt enough or wanted enough to be emotionally supportive or interesting.

The reverse, older men with young girls, mystified Lilly. There was only so much time and energy for sex, and what else but sex could mature men possibly have in common with unexceptional, untried, unseasoned children? Perhaps only she made the wrong choice. Perhaps somewhere there were twenty-six-year-old men who were understanding and fascinating beyond their years. Well, if she'd found someone like that, she wouldn't have cared what George or anyone else thought, but Lilly was born too old for rock music and it was no fun to go to loud, pot-filled parties and be the only woman in the room wearing eyeliner. No, her evenings were better spent with a good book than robbing from a cradle the unripe young men who taught her nothing and for whom a little more living would perhaps be more beneficial than her tutelage. A past, she learned, was a very handy thing to have. She recommended it to the young.

Married men were worse. The entire secrecy thing bored Lilly. It was tiresome to be so cautious and the few such liaisons she stumbled into were quickly terminated, for married men wanted little beyond a more pleasant husband-wife arrangement than they had at home—surrogate wives, comfortable, understanding women to sleep with and for whom they bore no responsibility. Involvement with a married man had none of the redeeming features of being the wife: Lilly still had to pay her own bills and make her own decisions, and worse, she never got taken out to dinner. Nor had she any interest in breaking up anyone's home, taking someone else's husband for her own. In fact, Lilly never thought of marriage now except when she was depressed. Not that the idea of commitment was abhorrent, just the state of being married—contracts, the demands of selfless love, those

289

stamping, invisible male feet that women hear so clearly. Sometimes Lilly wondered if one person could ever be enough to live out a lifetime with. No matter how special the man or woman might be, it seemed to be expecting too much of human beings for one single person to be all things forever. Except for Peter. She had believed he would be enough to last her for the rest of her years.

Lilly walked over to the bar and poured another drink. What she really needed was a woman to talk to, a woman who had traveled the same road, had the same conflicting and destructive needs. Somewhere along the way she should have learned to trust other women. Maybe because she was changing and growing, other women were getting better, too, more trustworthy. Well, perhaps she would give it another try. Lilly shook her head tiredly; right now she would have to make do with George, her one and only friend. Wherever he was.

The odor of something burning caught her attention; the corned beef had been in the stove all this time! She followed the acrid smell to the kitchen, and with several towels extracted the charred remains of dinner and put it in the sink; steam rushed up as she ran water into the burned dish.

It was not until she turned off the tap that Lilly heard the music, a banjo. Or was it a guitar? In addition to being a poor cook, she had a tin ear; she stood quite still, straining to recognize the song. There really was no place like Georgetown for the unexpected; some luckless person was being serenaded by a tone-deaf guitarist. Or was it a ukulele?

Peering into the darkness, she could make out a huge shape on her stoop; adjusting her eyes to the black, she saw that it was George, propped sideways on the steps between the opened gate, his back resting on one brick wall, his feet pushing against the other. He appeared quite comfortable and made no move to get up—the exhausted minstrel, too tired to stroll. Or too drunk?

It was near freezing outside and George was picking the chord of first one song, then blowing on his fingers before changing to a new tune, singing loudly and badly. Lilly giggled to hear him.

*"See her coming down the street. Who's that looking so petite?"* George stopped and blew on both hands at once. *"Wait till you see my baby, my baby, do the Charleston, do the Charleston rag. Sweetest girl from South Caroline . . ."*

Lilly opened the kitchen door and showered him with a handful of Teddy's bus tokens, all she had at hand, and she laughed at his surprise when the metal coins clinked around him. She was so damn glad to see him.

"Hey! You out there. You got the state right but there's nobody in here especially petite."

He did not look up; Lilly pulled her sweater close and walked outside to squat down beside him.

"Play 'Melancholy Baby' and I'll throw real money," she teased. Still he did not acknowledge her. George, she realized, was very, very drunk; girl-watching would give the wandering madrigalist a thumping hangover on the morrow.

She tried again. "Give us a few rounds of 'Hail to the Chief' and we can all march inside," she said and stood up, reaching down to put her arms under his to help him up.

"Fuck off," he said.

"I don't recall the words to that one. But if you'll hum a few bars . . ."

"Cut the shit, Wonder Woman. You're interfering with my music. You interfere with everything."

He was drunker than she realized; she had never seen him this way. Hostile, yes, like that night in some bar when he'd called the redneck a "black-baiting cocksucker"; the cocksucker had lost three teeth and George was forced to dictate his stories for almost a week. But his hostility had never been directed at her. He would take some special handling, she thought, annoyed at the impending ordeal, but bending down again, she tried to make her voice soothing and conversational.

"Look, Maestro, you're going to freeze into that position." For a fleeting instant she could hear Clara chastising her for making ugly faces: "You'll freeze that way, Lilly. God will punish you." Clara was always promising the Lord's wrath.

"Come on inside, pal. We cater to derelict musicians. White House grant. Charity for the cultured."

"I'm sick of your charity."

Lilly sat down on the cold brick, drawing her knees up for warmth; this would be more difficult than she'd expected. A sudden gust of wind blew the kitchen door closed and she hoped the latch was off. George started to sing again: *"Gee, but I hate to go home, alone . . . because—when I climb up the stairs . . ."* He was stringing away, his right foot tapping the ragtime; Lilly's teeth began to chatter. She had best take another tack.

"The soup kitchen is dishing out cups of warm bourbon," she offered.

He shot her a vicious look, switching to yet another

melody: *"You'll find your happiness lies, under your eyes, back in your own back yard . . ."*

"Correction. This is the front yard—it's a crazy mixed-up house, remember?—soup kitchen's up front." Still nothing. "George, it's awful late for street carols. Come on in. Before the law arrives."

"The blues were born in one of your crummy Southern jails."

It was a damnation, the kind of blanket denouncement of all Southerners that lay very close to the surface of Northern liberals.

"So play 'Birmingham Jail.'" She had his attention now.

"Always the one-liners. Always the best and funniest and quickest goddamned one-liners, huh, Lil? A fast retort for good ole Georgie." He started to sing again—*"Hey, there, Georgie boy"*—but stopped abruptly and placed the instrument over his bent knees. "I'm too drunk to stand up." It was a meek voice, more youthful than drunken.

"I'll help," she said.

"Yeah, honey, you do that. You help ole Georgie boy." Then he snarled at her. "Help, my ass. For you, help is something to demand, not give. Shit." He returned the ukulele to the playing position.

*"Oh Lillybelle, oh Susie Jane and Sarah Lee . . ."*

This was hopeless and Lilly stood up quickly, hearing again the popping sound her legs made. The door was not locked; the Almighty was not so vengeful as Clara had prophesied. From the hall closet she grabbed two bushy fur coats, a fox and a lynx, and with one under each arm she rejoined George outside.

"You want the everyday stuff or the Sunday best?"

There was no answer.

She threw the fox over herself and draped the lynx around George. He shrugged it off. "Since when do you offer me Sunday best?"

So that was it. Gently Lilly replaced the fuzzy coat over his thin tweed jacket, thinking that this had been a long time coming. Had she been so stupid as to think it would never happen?

"What is it, George?"

She reached to take the tiny nub of a cigarette from his mouth but he batted her hand away with the musical instrument, tossing the red dot into the gutter himself and swaying slightly from the exertion.

"Tell me what's the matter," she urged.

He sang instead. *"Oh Lillybelle, oh Susie Jane and Sarah Lee . . ."*

"Sarah Lee is a cheesecake, dummy," she corrected, but he continued to ignore her, singing louder. *"Oh, I may have gone a-lookin', but this is why I never fell . . . 'CAUSE . . . I got spurs that jingle-jangle-jingle. And this song ain't so verrrrrrrry far from wrong . . ."*

"Please, George, Susie Jane and Sarah Lee and I have a right to know what's the matter."

"Oh, Lilly"—his voice erupted in disgust—"cut the shit, will you? *Please*. For once in your life talk straight. I'm so sick of you coming at me like gags from Bob and Ray, I could vomit." For a moment he looked as if he might.

"Sorry."

"From you, that's a joke, too. Sorry is what you are when things don't go your way." He was strumming again, more off-key than before; it was pretty awful music if even she could hear the sour notes. A few lights were switching on in the surrounding houses. It was well past two.

"Will you kindly talk to me, tell me what in heaven's name I've done for us to be sitting out here like two hostile gorillas, one of whom may freeze to death before the other beats her about the head and shoulders with a banjo?"

"Uke."

"Please, George, tell me what I've done."

He thought it over for a minute and then reached through the fur coat to his own pocket and brought out a crumpled cocktail napkin.

"You know"—he hiccupped slightly—"I couldn't even call the bastards by their right and Christian names."

"Who?"

"Those guys, those ignorant assholes you take up with. I only counted up to five. My other fingers were tightly wrapped around a glass." He held up his open hand as evidence. "Every one of them shits. So perfect they were in the beginning: 'I've found the right one this time, George. You'll see. He's wonderful.' " His ability to mimic her was amazing if not amusing and Lilly shifted uncomfortably, tense, waiting.

"Yeah, baby," he said, "ring a bell? All those guys, flying down here, holing up. Haling you off, using you, lying to you, screwing you—yeah, screwing you. How do you think I felt all those times you were off with 'the real thing'? Did it ever cross your one-track mind that I hated every single minute of knowing what you were up to? That I despised your mealy-mouthed glamorizing of those guys? That I was so goddamned jealous, jealous and terrified that you wouldn't come back? That I hated what you were like when you did?"

Lilly started to protest but he did not wait. "No. All you knew was that good old George would come running to patch you up, mend your mammoth ego, and hold my fucking breath until the next time. There was always a next time."

"You never let me down," she said, speaking quietly.

"Remember when you finally discovered the glories of sex —'congenial cohabitation' was how you so quaintly put it— you not only had trouble making it work, you couldn't even say the word once you did. Fucking, Lilly. *Fucking.* For you, 'fucking' is a word that precedes bores, nuisances and bad luck. Well, you learned about fucking. Only you couldn't get your pristine tongue around the expression even when you were describing in pretty damn full detail the joys of finally getting properly laid."

Lilly cringed, both at his words and the truth they conveyed.

"I'm up to here with Lillian Shawcross," he said. "I've been having a drink to all your fellows tonight. Even to Harry, poor sucker. To all of them, whatever their names were. I drank a lot of toasts. Especially to yours truly! George Sabberstein. Fucked over but never taken to bed. I've had it with you." He waved his fist and for a moment she thought he might hit her with it.

"No more, baby. I'm hanging up the kid gloves. Going home where I belong. So help me God, I will not be around to clean up your mess this time. And you're in another mess, Lilly. You think I haven't guessed?"

Lilly sat very still, wondering dazedly how she had been stupid enough not to realize that George knew about Peter. He always knew.

"Remember all those nights of tears and recriminations," he said, "the rationalizing, the screaming and crying to me that nobody loved you." His voice dropped very low. "Well, I loved you. I loved you almost from the beginning. I love you now."

Dear God, she thought, I know that, doesn't he know I know that? Her body was rigid. For how long had she been dreading this?

"Just one word, a look, anything. I'd have dropped Harriette, my kids, the world. It's sick, Lilly, a six-year fever. Two things in life I wanted. One was to make myself love Harriette. I couldn't manage that—no fault of yours. Then I wanted you. Couldn't get that one together, either. So I've shunned the one in order to be shunned by the other. Of all the cripples you've collected, I'm the prize trophy. But no more, baby. *No more.* Lonesome George is going home. Maybe it's too late to disprove ole Tom Wolfe's theory but I know one thing—home ain't so painful as having no place away from it."

George began to inch his body upward, still not looking at her. Why should he—her only friend, the single person in forty years who had given her kindness and loyalty and he was the one she'd hurt the most.

Lilly wanted to throw herself at him now, to beg and plead, to make promises, anything, but she understood with a startling clarity that it was the one thing she must not do. She must not do that to George. She owed him that and more. *But what?* She didn't love George. Not that way. He was her friend, someone to grow up on, lean on. Had she known all along that she was draining him? Lilly was certain of nothing at the moment except that she could not heap upon George the further indignity of a hollow pronouncement.

George was standing unsteadily, looking up and down the street; she didn't even know if he had come by car, she only knew that she might not be able to get along without him. But in a way that was good for her or for him? The unspoken question made her shudder. Why in God's name don't people know when and whom to love? Could passion be so all-fired important? She could not answer that now, either; now she only wanted time to think. She was so close to something important but she needed more time.

George was starting down the street, her lynx coat dangling from his shoulders, and she had to smile; it was *Morgan* all over, the same unreal situation as the movie. George was actually walking away from her. There had to be something she could say, anything, call him back, beg! Never had she felt such panic and desperation at losing what she had taken so long for granted.

"George." She was calling to him. "George!" Lilly started down the street after him, running, grabbing at his hand when she caught up and forcing him to stop.

"Have I left anything out? Forgotten something?" He was aware that he was still wearing her coat and pulled it off and flung it into her face—the force of it nearly knocked her down.

"Thanks. I needed that!"

"Lilly, Lilly." He shook his head in utter disgust. "Will you

295

never learn? Damn you to hell, Wonder Woman. You don't need anything but an audience and a Greek chorus."

"I'll settle for a Jewish vocalist." It had slipped out and she was instantly sorry, reaching to embrace him, but he shoved her roughly aside, his fury plainly visible even in the dim light.

"You will never learn. Never!" He was shouting, bellowing now to the entire block. *"High-rent neighbors, come in your denizens. Hear ye! Hear ye! Lillian Shawcross will never learn!"*

Lilly stood frozen, both fur coats in her arms. And then he was moving off down the street again, weaving drunkenly and plunking at the ukulele as he went, his footsteps and the music growing fainter and fainter in the dark, until the sound, like George, disappeared and was gone.

The warmth of the kitchen could not make Lilly stop shivering; her teeth were chattering loudly as she sat at one of the places she had set at the table earlier and reached for her glass of whiskey, still where she had put it when she had gone outside. She took a few swallows, then opened her fist to examine the list of men George had scrawled on the crumpled cocktail napkin. As usual, they had been thinking along the same lines. Men. Well, she was through with doing that. She wadded the napkin and tossed it toward the trash basket, missing by a foot, always missing by a foot.

The kitchen clock pointed to three, reminding her that it was tomorrow. Tomorrow, and she was going to be without George. Shouldn't she be crying? Wasn't that her usual out? To weep and recriminate, to confuse tears with innocence? Lilly was strangely unmoved. Or was she so moved that she was numbed? And what was that peculiar thought that had flashed in her stunned brain when George had walked away from her? Only moments before, she had had it, and now the thought was lost. It was important, too. An important thought about George. Could she have been relieved to see him go? Was that it? Impossible: he was her friend, he had always been her friend. She might never have made it this far without him. The lost thought flashed in her mind again, but disappeared before she could examine it. Some dumb thought it was—like maybe it was time for George to go.

Lilly pushed the chair back and stood up, taking her glass over to the sink to pour liquor down the drain and being very careful to avoid looking into the mirror as she left the kitchen; she did not need her reflection to remind her that she was exhausted and tired, maybe even sick. Yeah, sick and ired of herself! Lilly switched off all the lights, something she had never done before—going to bed in a completely dark house. Always she had left one light burning as if she were waiting for someone.

Upstairs, she got into bed and turned her face into the pillow, wanting now to think of Peter, to feel something, even to play the maybe-if game. *Maybe* he will call *if* I am good. Maybe if, maybe if. It did not work; she could not think of Peter the way she had always been able to do when she needed the distraction. Peter had vanished. How could someone as important as Peter just vanish from her head? Was he ever really that important or only the most recent? Lilly had always had someone else to think about, to dream of, to lull herself into thinking things would be better if they were there or they were only different. There had always been George to talk to, George and that someone else to push reality aside by dreaming of. Lilly missed having thoughts of Peter to distract her, to turn her energy away from what was really bothering her, herself. Yes, Peter was the current someone she used to keep from relying on herself, the crutch to hold on to, to promise herself that if she only had him to love, she would have it all come together. Why did she keep throwing men up as smoke screens between herself and herself?

Again there was that fleeting glimpse of something, some vague understanding that darted in her head. She almost had it this time but it got away again. Lilly shifted positions, pushing a pillow under her stomach and squinting her eyes against the mattress, forcing herself to think of Peter, of those nights when she had kept her phone free during the hours he was likely to call, sitting there and waiting with a pad in her lap to make notes of all the funny or interesting things that had happened to her since she had talked to him last, things that might hold him on the phone a minute or two longer. Their entire relationship had been like that—conducted with bated breath. Her bated breath.

How could she be so attractive and desirable to George without making any real effort, and then try so hard with Peter and still drive him off? Because she wanted nothing from George, made no demands, that's why. She had wanted too much from Peter; she had wanted him to complete her. That was one hell of a demand. She wanted Peter to hand her over to herself, make her total and happy, like some surprise package on a silver platter, and instead she had scared him away. Oh Jesus, she had, just scared him to death with her demands that he take her over and do something with her life. She had pressured him with her needs and he had disappeared, vanished. He had seen all along that he could not do for Lilly what she could not do for herself. If Peter wanted anyone at all, he wanted a real grown-up person and she had run him off with her intensity, her clinging, cloying needs, her sick obsession with romantic love. Peter had left her for months and then showed up as if he thought maybe she had learned something about herself during his absence. Well, she never learned; George was right about that.

Every time Peter reappeared, Lilly had been so glad to see him. She'd had no pride. Pride was a luxury for people who didn't want something the way she wanted Peter. Oh, each time she'd played along carefully, acting as if no vacuum had existed between them, been casual and easygoing for a while before she would start to cling and clutch at him again, desperately compelling him to make the world wonderful for her. What a terrible burden she must have been. Well, the coward hadn't been too hard to chase away. He could have helped her, talked to her. Was that why she hadn't told George about Peter? Because George would have told her to quit leaning on the cowardly son of a bitch and act like a grown woman, for God's sake. Maybe George wouldn't have done that at all. Maybe he would have encouraged her to run Peter off, too, lifting his shoulder or raising his brows to convey his disapproval in that way of his. Had she been fearful of George's disapproval, unconsciously sought to protect her relationship with Peter from George's devastating scrutiny? It was entirely possible that George would have ruined Peter for her before she had the chance to ruin things for herself. Oh God, she was so close to something again, something painful, too painful for the middle of the night. She bolted upright and lit a cigarette, seeing the ridiculous irony of being in bed alone, thinking of two men, two very different men—one who wanted to take over her life, the other terrified of having to. Peter can't stick around because he fears closeness. George goes away because he isn't close enough. It was almost a comedy. Her exchange tonight with George hadn't been so very different from her last encounter with Peter.

"Look," she had said to Peter, "care about me or go away. Get out, for God's sake. I need somebody to keep in touch with me, to let me know that it's all right, that he is as willing to protect me and deal with me as I'm willing to do for him.

Not this here-today, gone-tomorrow business. Peter, look at me, my emotions are so torn apart with you that I can't think straight. Christ, I know it's corny but you either have to love me or leave me."

"I do love you, Lilly," he had said.

"Then why do you fade in and out—like some kind of shortwave radio?"

"I don't know."

"You what?"

"I don't know," he had repeated.

"What do you expect me to do?"

"I don't know that, either."

"Do you want me?"

"Yes."

And, of course, she had been so grateful to hear him say that that she had caved in and promised she would be better and not be so pushy, and she was really going to try not to lean on him, not even to burden him with the easy things that people who love each other are meant to share. Except that Peter had disappeared again before she got the chance.

If only once Peter had held fast, had let her get the security she needed from him—get a real fill of it—she'd have been all right. She could have found her feet and stood alone—just loving him gently, and not make such a fuss of it. But he kept her off balance with his coming and going; a person could go crazy being kept off balance like that. It was such a desperate thing to cling to a man because he didn't give any sense of permanence to their relationship, and then, when he went away, to become all the more desperate so that you made matters worse the minute you got a second chance. Peter couldn't be counted upon, Lilly thought, not even if she were perfect. She—or somebody—would always move too close to him for comfort. Yes, Peter had a digit missing. So did George. And she had digits missing all over the goddamned place.

Lilly threw back the covers and went into the bathroom, her head reeling as she stood before the vanity, staring levelly at herself. It was time to make all these loose ends come together—without Peter or George or anybody. Just Lilly. She took a yellow sleeping pill out of its plastic bottle, swallowing it with some water, and waited there, examining herself in the mirror, wondering just when the hell she was going to get around to belonging to herself and stop this business of handing herself over, body and soul, to every emotional panhandler that came along. Soon, she promised her reflection, very goddamned soon. And then she smiled, blowing a kiss to her image.

"Good-night, sweet princess. Whoever you are."

# 21

IT WAS late when Lilly woke up, well after two; the sun was bright outside the bedroom windows. Generally she hated Sundays but she was ready for this one. This day would be different; she would be different. She felt it the moment she opened her eyes. The body was maybe a bit sluggish, but her head was clearer than it had been for months, maybe clearer than in her whole life. Lilly regretted that so much valuable time had been slept away for there was a lot to do, a lot of bad days to be amended on this good one.

She dressed quickly and went down to put the coffee on, bringing in the papers and scarcely glancing at the headlines: NEW TAPES DISCOVERED. Was it only last week that Nixon had told an audience in Orlando that he was not a crook? Lilly turned the paper face down on the kitchen table, telling herself cheerfully that the world would have to muddle along without her for a while longer. She untangled the phone cord and pulled the receiver over to where she sat. The first call was to Harry. His young wife answered.

"Bitsy?" Lilly never failed to stumble over the second Mrs. Shawcross's name; its cuteness and the diminutiveness it implied annoyed her unnecessarily. "It's Lillian Shawcross," she said. "Is Harry there?"

"Yes, he's here."

There was no sound or movement at the other end of the wire.

"Well, this is not a random Sunday bed check, Bitsy. I want to speak with him. Please." Lilly's conversations with the girl were never satisfactory. Still, Lilly thought she was a good sport about Mags and Teddy—a better trouper than most women burdened with another woman's children.

"I'll call him." Bitsy's reply was not so much sullen as confused; Lilly was a threat to her—as old wives generally are to the new ones—and nothing Lilly said or did seemed to make the situation easier.

"Lilly?" Harry sounded anxious, too. A call from her was unusual.

"Sorry to bother you, but I was wondering if you could bring the children home early today."

"I guess so. Anything wrong?"

"No. I just want to see them. Also, could you block out a few minutes when you come? I want to talk to you."

"What about?" He was apprehensive.

"The phone is probably tapped, Harry. I'll tell you later." Lilly meant to make a small joke; all Washington assumed the wires were monitored since Watergate.

"You're probably right," Harry agreed. He was so literal. Well, he could be literal today. All Washington could be literal and paranoid today. In fact, the whole frenzied world could be double-parked for all she cared.

"Sometime around six," she said. "It won't take long."

"Well—"

Lilly could hear Bitsy chirping in somewhere in the background.

"It's important, Harry, or I wouldn't ask."

"O.K." It was all he said before hanging up.

Lilly dialed George's home, something she had never done before; she'd had to check the directory for the number. A woman's weary voice answered and Lilly asked for George.

"Who is calling?"

"It's Lillian Shawcross. George and I work—"

"Yes. I know." The woman cut her short, using the precise tone Lilly deserved. "He's not here."

"Is he at the office?" Lilly asked, wanting—for some reason —to detain this strange woman who was George's wife. Why? To tell her she was sorry? Sorry for monopolizing her husband's attentions but not committing adultery against her?

"If he isn't with you, then he must be at the office. I haven't seen or heard from him since yesterday morning."

Lilly opened her mouth to speak but the wire was buzzing again. Goddammit, she thought, I haven't said good-bye yet. Well, what more did she have to say to George's wife? Or to Harry?

Lilly called the UPI office and got Jake Turner; he and Lilly had never been compatible—in fact, they had been mutually abrasive since they met. Nothing in Jake's tone when he spoke indicated his feelings for Lilly had altered.

"Jake. It's Lilly. I'm looking for George."

"So's half the Western world, chum. He's not here and we need him. The whole Nixon rat-fuck is breaking wide open. If you run him down before I do, tell him New York is creaming for him. Tell him to move his ass down here pronto—that is, if you can spare him for an hour or so."

Lilly hung up on him. Of all the people she knew, Jake Turner was the most deserving of this famous first.

She released the disconnect button and dialed information. "A listing in the District, please, a new one, for a Hildy Johnson. Southeast, I think, Operator, near the Capitol." Lilly noted the number as commanded and pressed the button once more for the dial tone. She hated to call Hildy, the cockney-accented and not unpleasantly plump young woman who managed the desk phones at the office during the regular work week. George was very defensive about Hildy. Lilly guessed that he spent an occasional night with the girl, and not that it mattered to Lilly one way or another, but she could never keep a smile off her face whenever the girl's name came up, or could she convince George that it was only the name—Hildy Johnson, the one used for Rosalind Russell in *His Girl Friday*—that Lilly found amusing. Hildy answered on the first ring.

"Hi. It's Lilly Shawcross. I'm looking for George."

Hildy's voice was hesitant, almost diffident. "Mrs. Shawcross . . ."

"Please. I'm Lilly."

"Lilly," the young woman repeated, faltering. "I haven't seen him since Friday." She sounded sincere. "I mean, he really isn't here. I'm sorry."

"Hildy." Lilly sighed into the phone. "Don't be sorry. Don't you ever be sorry."

There was a short pause on the other end.

"Good-bye, Hildy," Lilly said and Hildy said good-bye back and they both hung up at the same time. Now that, thought Lilly, is how decent people terminate a telephone conversation.

It worried Lilly where George might be. There was so much between them that needed to be said and it would not do to let too much time elapse before those things were aired. She would write him a letter; yes, a letter would satisfy Lilly's wonderful new need for action. She poured a second cup of coffee and went upstairs to her desk and rolled a clean sheet of white paper into the typewriter.

Dear George:

There is no point in further insulting your intelligence by elaborating on how deeply sorry I am for last night and for all the nights that led up to it. We know each other too well for you not to understand that. I've tried to track you down this afternoon but you always were a hard man to keep up with. Somehow it just might be better this way, writing a letter. There are so many things I want to say, things I wish to God I'd known sooner to say sooner.

First off, I want you to know that I would never deliberately do anything to hurt you and I know you would never intentionally harm me in any way. Which is what we have somehow managed to do to each other anyhow. You see, I've done what I promised on Friday—I've gone back—been everywhere and done everything again—in my head. It's a visit with myself I've put off too long, a bit of soul-searching that should have taken place years ago. Just, George, as you should have told me years ago all the things you told me last night. It isn't fair of either of us. By not speaking up sooner, you have allowed me to get away with falling back on you and depending on you when I should have been depending on myself, running my own life.

I've taken up so much of your time and given you so little in return. And you've done so much for me, so much of my thinking and my feeling, so many decisions, so much buttressing and shoring. God knows, I shudder to think how I would have wound up without you. You have saved my hide so often and I love you for it. It's been easier for me this way but, George, you have filled so many holes in my life that I'm like a big hunk of Swiss cheese without you.

I thought a lot about those holes this weekend—a lot about you and my mother and my children, Harry, and all those men in my life—and, of course, about myself. Too damn much about myself. Look, I'm not sure that there is a particular time of decision for any of us. I mean, at any given moment we are only the sum of our lives up to now but I think that today—the whole weekend, in fact—is kind of a red-letter date for me, a turning point at which I've decided it's high time to begin to do the things I've never made myself do before, to think the thoughts I've always avoided—maybe even get to finally have some of the peace in life that I've missed. People either train themselves unconsciously to handle growing old or they slop around whining and recriminating while the understanding of themselves slips past and they wake up one fine morning to find they have foolishly dribbled themselves away.

I wish I'd figured this out sooner, but, George, if there is any certain year for me, I guess it's now, at forty, and God knows I don't know all the whys and hows or even any of the wherefores, but I am going to take charge of myself. I am going to stand on my own one way or another. I mean it, I just got out of bed today and I understood it all, like I'd had a visitation in the night. It's in my head firm: Lilly is responsible for Lilly. Christ, it's taken me so long to come around to the only solution possible.

Forty, you know, is neither good nor bad. Not that age doesn't matter; it sure God does. Time forces itself on all of us and forty is just that much closer to death. There's nothing to be done about it except to accept it and then try to forget it. I've heard tell that we older women are supposed to arrive at a calmness and state of graceful acceptance—some kind of uncanny exchange for the loss of physical youth and energy. Well, none of that has precisely knocked me over yet and with my restless nature it may not arrive before I die. Hope, however, springs eternal when little else moves so agilely. What I think I'm saying, George, is that I'm going to work out my own life if it takes me the next forty years, and if I never find another adult human being to really love, then I'll get by on my own. A person has to be good alone before she can be good with anyone else.

I don't know where I got the stupid idea that age guarantees wisdom. Hell, it doesn't even ensure judgment or insight or perspective, never mind knowledge. But getting old sure does give you a deadline, if you'll pardon a last smart remark. You see, I've been sitting around waiting for all the good things, stomping my foot and saying, O.K., world, I'm forty years old now, so bring on the goodies and, while you're at it, bring on the perfect man. The weird part is that I feel so hopeful. I know now that I can get on with it, which is a lot better than getting by with it.

I couldn't think or feel this way or even try to make it work unless I had had you as my friend all these years. You have brought me so far, and I guess what I really want to do is thank you for it.

Lil

Lilly folded the letter without reading it over. She had written it to herself as much as to George and it would not do to edit anything. Instead, she took a stamp and three ten-dollar bills from her wallet, and stuck the letter and the cash into the pocket of her coat, pulling the collar around her neck, then locked the door behind her and started to walk down the street in the general direction of the post office. It was a good day for having a purpose, cold for March, but the sun was warm on her back. Actually, she felt warm all over.

Two blocks further, she passed the public playground, its tennis courts and swimming pool closed now for the winter, but there were several children tossing a football on the playing field, their jackets piled carelessly in a heap on the bank near some neighborhood dogs that wandered about despite the sign prohibiting their presence.

Lilly leaned against the wire fence and watched the children for a moment. Far down, by the swings, a young mother was helping a little girl onto a sliding board—an innocent scene that jabbed at Lilly. She had done so little of that sort of thing with Mags or Teddy—just as Clara had done so little of it with her. Passing along what one has had passed on to them, she thought, and it made her sad that she had not known her own mother better, that things had not been different. They might have been such friends, she and Clara —another, better, happier Clara—and with all her heart Lilly wished at that moment to take Clara and sit down on that grassy bank and talk and talk and talk. She would thank Clara for giving her the most precious gift of all, the very one Lilly had taken for granted. Clara had told her every day and in every way that she, Lilly, was special, that she could do anything and everything she wished. It did not matter that the confidence was not accompanied by a formula or a blueprint—it was enough, enough to be told that she was able to do wonderful things with her life. That Lilly had not done wonderful things was not Clara's fault but Lilly's fault. Well, she would do those things now, those funny and elusive things that the little girl still inside Lilly would never forgive her for if she did not try. Lilly felt closer to her mother now than ever before in her life. Yes, Clara had given her the only thing she had to offer. Hope. Hope and an unused belief in herself.

Lilly went on down the street, her feet moving quickly to keep pace with the rhythm in her chest; it was such a glorious day, a perfect day. At an outdoor flower stall on Wisconsin

Avenue she impulsively stopped to buy two giant bouquets of daisies and another of baby's breath, hugging the flowers to her. Maggie loved flowers. Lilly would fill the house with them before Maggie came home. Teddy, of course, would take one look at the flowers and ask if they were having company, but Maggie would know; Maggie always knew. Lilly felt a sudden heaviness, a strange sadness out of sync with her high spirits and the beautiful day, a sadness that flicked over her, indefinable, like a fly that lit and soiled wherever it touched. Maggie. Yes, the sadness had to do with Maggie. She'd felt it before, this feeling, felt it whenever Lilly allowed herself to worry about how the girl would turn out, fearful that she be tarnished by Lilly, tainted by Lilly's own selfish indifference as to what the girl thought of her mother's many romances, of those handful of men whom Lilly had permitted to intrude so harshly into Maggie's life.

That had been on Lilly's mind a great deal lately but she had shoved it aside, the way she usually handled unpleasant thoughts. Actually, there had not really been so many men. There was Dwight, but he did not count because Maggie did not really know him. That relationship had been conducted away from home, in New York, and Maggie was so young then; but there was Robbie. Robbie had been delivered into Maggie's world rather brutally. And Charles? He had only threatened Maggie's sense of belonging, her sense of place. And the others—the men whose names escaped even Lilly's cruel memory—they had not touched her children; they had been kept at bay too, kept away in some strange bed. Nor had the children met Peter—just the two men, just Robbie and Charles. Not a really bad record. Two men in her bed in all the years since Lilly had been divorced. Surely Maggie could forgive her that—forgive those mistakes so honestly and desperately made. Only once had Lilly broached the delicate subject to Maggie. After Charles, wasn't it? Yes, Charles. Lilly had feared that Mags might think her promiscuous, might even think Lilly's behavior was something to emulate.

"I'm not much of a mother, Mags," she had said, feeling both sorry for herself and contemptuous of herself at the same time.

"Oh, who says?"

"Well, I don't guess any of your friends have mothers who have, ah, boy friends who, ah, sleep over and all."

"Suzanne's mother has plenty of boy friends," Maggie had

said. "They don't sleep over, though. Suzanne says her mother sleeps over at their houses. Her mother says she doesn't but Suzanne says she does. Her mother says she's with a friend at the hospital all night or maybe her car ran out of gas, but Suzanne says her mother just doesn't always come home at night. Why doesn't Suzanne's mother say the truth, Mom?"

"I don't know, honey. Maybe she is telling the truth."

"No," Maggie had responded solemnly, "Suzanne's mother doesn't tell the truth."

Lilly thought of Maggie's response and felt the sadness ebb. No one fools children. Children know; they're born knowing. Maybe in this funny world of divorce and partner changing, Lilly had stumbled onto the right way to deal with her child, just selfishly lucked into the kind of honesty that Mags could accept even when she had not wanted to accept the situations. No, by God, two men in her bed did not make Lilly a whore, and Maggie maybe understood that better than Lilly.

Clutching the armload of flowers, Lilly continued down the quiet main street of Georgetown, nearly empty because it was Sunday. Toward the end of Wisconsin Avenue, she could see the river flash in the distance but she turned left, a block short of it, and headed in the direction of a market on M Street that was always open. Inside she disengaged a wire cart, putting the flowers on its upper rack. Usually there was no pattern to her grocery shopping; it bored her so, this business of housekeeping, but today, she knew precisely what she was about. Lilly smiled as she pushed along the aisles. Order, she thought, the order of doing the very mundane things she had always loathed, buying groceries, putting her thoughts in place, food in her refrigerator, providing for her children—yes, the routine, the monotonous routine she despised was the very thing to save her. Lilly had never been so happy in a grocery store before, so happy to have two children coming home, children who gave her life pleasure and purpose. Almost lovingly she shook off a bunch of watercress in the vegetable bin, thinking that she had her children and her work and her life —all of it right there before her all along. All she had to do was put everything in order.

At the checkout counter, she had two chickens, a bunch of carrots, three kinds of cheese, the watercress, some fruit and a loaf of day-old French bread. She pushed the chickens over to the checker, smiling up at him, wanting him to see her as she felt today, a nice-looking forty-year-old mother who was behaving a little foolishly at the prospect of going home and cooking a meal for two damn nice and miraculously unsullied children. Lilly reached in her coat pocket for the loose bills and wished she had brought her purse, wondering what the cashier would say if she opened her wallet and showed him a picture of Maggie and Teddy.

She took the bag of food into one arm, the flowers in the other, nodded serenely to the grocer and went back outside into the wonderful afternoon, not retracing her steps but turning instead up Thirty-first Street to walk the short half-block to the post office, where she dropped the letter to George into the outside box, then continued again up the hill and through the back streets of Georgetown. The sun was not so strong now, she noticed, it had to be five o'clock, maybe even a little later, but the fading sunlight came at a beautiful angle and Lilly took a deep breath of the chilly air. Definitely, the feeling inside her was one of optimism. Spring would happen almost any day.

The phone was ringing as she let herself in through the kitchen door, but Lilly took time to set down her parcels and remove her coat. She knew the call was for her. She had known all day that the call would come and who would be calling. From the very moment she had got up, Lilly had known it would be just this kind of day.

"Hello."

"Hello."

"Peter?"

"Yeah. How are you?"

"Never better. You?"

"Same, I guess. What are you doing?"

"Getting ready to butcher a couple of unsuspecting chickens."

"You? Cooking?"

"If you call it that."

A pause. "I thought maybe we could have dinner together."

"Tonight?" she said.

"Sure. Why not? You could come up and I'll take you anywhere you want to go." Seldom did he give her that prerogative.

"Sorry, but thanks," she said. "I'm expecting the children anytime now."

"Oh?"

"Uh-hum."

"I guess I could come down there."

"Business?"

"Not really. I just want to see you."

"Oh?"

"Yeah. I just finished a screen treatment. Calls for a celebration."

"I don't think that's a very good idea."

"Got a better one?"

"I'm working on it."

"I could do it easily. Make the six o'clock shuttle and be at your place, say, seven-thirty or thereabouts."

"No, Peter. I'm not up to it."

"What's to be up to?"

"You. Me. Us. I don't know, I'm just tired of it all."

"Maybe we ought to talk about it."

"We never do that."

"Well, I'm not good at it."

"Neither am I. I'm also not so good at handling what comes next."

"Listen, I miss you. It's been a couple of weeks now."

"Eleven weeks is how I count."

"Yeah. Well, the time gets away from me when I'm working."

Lilly said nothing. He was not accustomed to her silence.

"Look," he said. "Seven-thirty. I'll take a cab from the airport. O.K.?"

"No. Not O.K. Peter, I just can't do it anymore."

"Sure you can. What's to do, anyhow? We'll talk. I promise. Seven-thirty?"

Lilly stared at the bag of groceries and the flowers; they seemed to lose their appeal. She glanced at the clock: five-fifteen exactly. There was the familiar twinge of impatience that Maggie and Teddy were on their way home, home with their noise and their demands on her. Immediately Lilly shut her eyes and shook her head; she hadn't counted on her new courage being challenged so abruptly. Arguing with herself mentally and chewing at her lip, she stared down into the telephone receiver. Why not? Why not this one last time?

"Peter, let me think it over. I'll call you right back." That was how he usually avoided her. Only he did not call back and the only thinking over had been done by her.

"I'll be there at seven-thirty, Lilly. I want to see you. I miss you."

Lilly despised herself for wanting to hear Peter say those

words, despised herself for wanting him to barge into her life again and take away her resolve. Mostly she despised her silence, for weakly saying nothing and letting Peter ring off with no further protest from her.

Woodenly she replaced the phone in its cradle and automatically turned to the groceries, a sick fear creeping up from her stomach, tightening itself around her throat. And something else. Something not altogether unpleasant. Excitement. A throbbing sense of anticipation, the coming to life of her body. Resolutely she took the chickens from their wrappings, telling herself that maybe today she could handle herself with Peter. Yes, this time she would be in charge. Still, the unease continued to spread through her as she tore the plastic from around the carrots and scraped them furiously into the sink. With a rising sense of panic she glanced at the clock. Five-thirty now. She ran to the phone and dialed Peter's number and got only his answering service. He was out, yes, out of town for several days and would there be any message? Lilly hung up, half annoyed that she had waited too long to call, half pleased that the decision was out of her hands. She ought to sit down now and think things out but there was that damned spring in her movements, the old excitement. What the hell was life without that excitement?

Lilly picked up the chickens and rinsed them, salting their cavities and putting them into a deep pot; they sizzled in the melting butter. She caught her lower lip between her teeth and frowned; the plucked white chickens looked so naked and vulnerable. Quickly she put the lid over the pot.

It was nearly six. She would have to hurry to tidy up the living room before Harry came with the children. First, the water had to be emptied from the ice bucket, then refilled. Rather clumsily she removed the fire screen and began to build a fire, stuffing the logs with half the Sunday *Times,* determined not to be guilty this time because she was using so much paper. Guilt was the most corrosive feeling invented; it ought to be outlawed. Along with vanity. Still, Lilly stopped automatically before the hall mirror and checked herself. She had liked her face earlier, the look of resolution had been so clear then, so encouraging. Had it been only so few hours since she had looked into another mirror and thought that perhaps the battle against gravity was not really lost? She looked somehow older now, older and what else? Frightened? This day that she'd been so cocky and certain of was taking a twist she had not expected; maybe she wasn't going to

311

handle it so well after all. Lilly pinched at her cheeks to return her color and ran her hands a little uncertainly through her hair, aware of a thudding beat in her chest, tom-tom thumps that were like a warning signal, starting some inner device that was a countdown. To what? To Harry's arrival? Lilly jumped, startled by the sound of the door chime. Nervously she opened the door and bent to embrace Mags and Teddy, so glad to see them, so damn glad to have them. They would make her sure again. She squeezed them to her and smiled at Harry over the tops of their heads. She would be all right now.

"Your cheeks are so cold, Mags."

"So's the rest of me. We were at the playground with the baby."

"Oh, well, that'll do it today."

Teddy broke free of her, kissed his father good-bye and shot past, running up the stairs; he was never easy around Lilly and Harry together. It was useless to ask about his homework now. She would see to him later and for once the task of organizing Teddy did not loom as monumental. She was glad of it, glad of the tiny links, the day-to-day things like Teddy's homework, his bath, his teeth—funny little chores that would weave together and somehow hold her up. Maggie went up also and Lilly stood at the bottom of the stairs and watched her. Unbidden, she recalled a brief conversation some weeks earlier with the girl. They had been talking about something, she couldn't remember now what it was, but Maggie had very offhandedly said that Lilly made her laugh at least once every day—did she know that? Lilly had not known that. What else had she said? That Lilly made her think a new thought every day too. "You know, Mom," Mags had said, "sometimes I look at you and I think that when I'm older I'll be free, too, just like you." Distracted by her own problems at the time, Lilly had not made much of the casual exchange. Now it settled in and around her, warming her. Free, Mom, free like you. Lilly straightened her shoulders, ready again, ready for Harry and for Peter, ready even for herself. The noise of the television and the scraping of furniture came down to where she stood—all the comforting sounds of business as usual. Lilly listened to the noise for a moment, calculating that she had at least a half-dozen years before the children went away, to school or off on their own. Six whole years. The best years. These are the best years of my life, she thought, and dismissed all preccupation with Peter. She would not let herself be concerned about him or about anyone else; she didn't need him. he had Mags and Teddy and a lot of years left with them. No, she thought, when I'm really and truly old, when the children are gone, I'll worry again about finding someone to love. When people are old, they may as well love each other because we are all going to die. But not now. Not yet. For now she had enough. Remembering Harry, Lilly turned to him and asked if he would like a drink.

"I guess so." He started to remove his coat. "What's on your mind?"

So formal and distant he is, Lilly thought. Was it ever thus? No, surely there had been a time when— She was staring at Harry, frowning at him without realizing it. Again he asked what was on her mind. Dear God, Lilly thought, what indeed is on my mind?

She laughed. "I don't really know," she said, leading him into the living room, speaking to him over her shoulder. "All weekend I've felt like there was something special I want to say to you, but I don't know what it is." She laughed again.

Harry did not change his expression. "I don't have a lot of time," he said. "You said you wanted to talk. Is it the children?" He was very nervous; they'd always been nervous with each other. Only Harry was a little better than she was at hiding it.

"The children? Yes. For starters," Lilly said. "They aren't so bad, you know?"

He nodded, saying nothing.

"You know something else, Harry, two people are never really divorced as long as they have children."

"What is it you want to say, Lilly?"

She busied herself pouring the drinks, not bothering to ask his preference. He always drank sherry, when he drank at all. Funny that she knew so many little things about him, so much familiarity about nonsense. Harry took the sherry from her as if he had expected her to remember.

"Lilly, this is all very nice but I think you should come to the point."

"I told you, I'm not sure what the point is. I just want to talk to you. Plain ole talk. Children. Me. You. How are you, anyhow?"

Harry was having none of it. "I am very well, thank you."

"The children are very well, too, don't you think?" Lilly

was stalling; what had she wanted to see Harry about? What clue to herself was he meant to surrender?

With exaggerated patience Harry took a swallow of his drink. "Sure," he said, "the children are swell. You do O.K. with them."

"*We* do O.K., Harry. You and me."

He was embarrassed.

"I don't think it would hurt," she said, fumbling for the right words, "if we, ah, if we talked more. About the children. You know, sort of keep in closer touch about them."

Now Lilly was embarrassed. She was sounding the fool and she did not care to sound the fool to Harry. What the hell was it she wanted to sound? What had she thought—that because she was going to make herself be a better person, because she liked herself a little more than she used to, Harry was supposed to feel kindly toward her, too? Tell her that he understood why it had taken a long time to find herself and that it was all right, that he knew she had it in her all along?

Harry's face was totally blank. Lilly stared into the empty face. For what earthly reason did she think she owed him an apology or an explanation? Why did she need his blessing to go on with the business of going on with her life? Were they meant to fall upon each other and forgive? Was that what she wanted—that they sit down like two old friends and catch up? Was that really so unthinkable? One look at Harry's closed-off face told her that it was, of course, unthinkable. And impossible. He felt no nostalgia for what they were, what they might have been. Old friends? They had never been friends at all. None of their life together had mattered. Nothing but the children. Lilly listened again for their sounds.

"Sure." Harry was talking. What had he said?

"Sure what?" Lilly asked, trying to concentrate.

"Sure, we can talk about the children. I suppose we can manage that." He was very uncomfortable, ready to leave.

"Can't we talk about other things, too, Harry?"

"Could we ever?"

"We're older now. Probably have more in common than most people."

"What?" His face was angry.

"Well, the children."

"I just said you're doing a fine job with them."

"We, Harry," she repeated. "You and me. Together."

"Just what is all this, Lilly. Just what more do you want from me?" He set his glass down hard on the coffee table.

"I don't know. I honest to God don't know."

"If you think of it, you know where to reach me." He stood to leave.

Lilly felt a sudden terror that he would go, go before saying to her that something about their life had been important, that any of it had mattered. She knew now what she wanted to say to him. She wanted to say she was sorry, to hear him say that he was sorry, too. Forget and forgive. Set the record straight. So much of her life couldn't just count for nothing. Lilly felt the tears in her eyes; she turned to Harry, wanting him to help— Please, Harry, her eyes said, just this one time, be kind, let me know that something I did over those years was all right. Remember something good. Just this one time. Harry. Please.

But Harry would not give her that today, she knew. Maybe he really had no feeling, no good memories to take from. When it came to Lilly, Harry had not changed; some people never change, nothing changes, not Harry, or Peter. Not even Lilly. Heaviness seemed to hold her captive in her chair.

She managed to stand somehow, and then moved to get Harry his coat. She must see him to the door, not let him walk out unattended. The old battle lines! He should not have the pleasure of seeing her anguish this way, but a storm of emotion was rising inside Lilly—fear, the old fears, all of them, whatever they were they were all coming back. How could she have been so stupid as to think things could change between her and Harry? She held his coat up for him but he took it from her and put it on unassisted.

"I'm sorry, Harry," she blurted out, her voice choked.

"For what?"

Lilly wanted to smile, but her lower lip was trembling. "Mostly, I'm sorry about the Argonne Forest."

He looked puzzled, squinting at her for a minute until a slight light of recognition came into his eyes—that long-ago phone call, the first time he'd asked her out, a thousand, hundred years back when they were young and they had joked about Hemingway and *The Sun Also Rises* and she had believed he could solve the impotency of her life, that she, too, could be what he wanted. Lilly stood rigidly, waiting—if only Harry would smile, nod, anything that would say that they were not totally a mistake.

Harry stared back at Lilly, his face blank once again. She would get nothing from him; there was nothing of significance in their years together.

"I'm really sorry, Harry. So very sorry." Lilly's hand went out to touch him, but he drew back and she saw just the flicker of a smile, a harsh smile that turned his mouth down.

"Sure, Lil. Sure you are." He closed the gate behind him when he left.

Lilly went back to the kitchen and sat down, some very thin cord snapping inside, and she began to cry now, really cry, putting her arms on the table and resting her head on them, sobbing. Who did she think she was that she could wake up today and be different? Nothing she had ever done or been had mattered; she had ruined or lost or broken everything in her path and it was too late to do any different. She wanted George to come, she wanted to go to the phone and surrender, to find George and tell him she needed him, that she couldn't do anything alone. And Peter. She wanted Peter to hurry, to come back into her life and to punish her by leaving her again. The pattern was indestructible; everybody must come back and give her what she deserved. The weak deserve to be used, just settle in and take it until it's time to die. Whoever was that stupid, arrogant girl inside her who had woken up with Lilly this afternoon and told her she could control her destiny? She hated that girl, that silly optimistic girl who had led her on all day, led her on all her dumb, stupid life.

Lilly looked up at the clock; it was a quarter of seven. Peter would be here soon and he would find her just as he'd always found her—an incomplete person. His plane was probably landing now; already he was on his way to get her and drag her back into the semipleasant stupor of their relationship, reclaim her for a short while and then walk away, leaving her worse off than he'd found her. And she would let him; she always let somebody or something drag her back. She would never belong to herself. It was too late. She had just to sit here, sit in this goddamned kitchen, a drink in her hand, and wait, wait for some other, outer forces to take her over. There had never been a choice. All day she had been playing a cruel game with herself. Somehow she must have known, known that Peter would come and she would end up pleading with him to do for her what she could not do for herself. She could not even help herself when she tried, when she wanted to so very, very much.

Lilly went over to the bottle of Scotch on the counter and poured some into a glass. An evening with Peter went better if she had the false courage of the Scotch. Halfway to her mouth, her hand stopped abruptly, pushed the glass away from her face. No! No, no, no, a voice shouted in her head, wait just a bloody goddamn minute. Give yourself a chance, Lilly. For God's sake, give Lilly Shawcross a decent shot at it,

vill you? She took the glass and held it even further in front
of her as she walked to the sink and poured the liquor down
he drain. She grabbed up the nearly full bottle of Scotch
ind emptied it into the sink also, then began opening cabinets
ind taking out every bottle of whiskey and pouring them all
out, one at a time. Liquor splashed over her; one of the empty
bottles fell to the floor and broke, but she noticed nothing,
only the voice in her head saying, Take this chance, Lilly.
Just this one last time and I promise, I swear to God, I'll
never ask anything of you again. Tough it out this time. Run.
Get away. Get away from Peter. Please. You're just not
strong enough to do it all at once, don't you see? You've tried
to do too much in one day. It will come, Lilly, trust me, it
will come if you'll let it. Hide now. Hide until you're ready.
But get the hell out of here. The clock. The clock showed
after seven. Lilly kicked the broken bottle inside and lunged
for the clock, yanked it from its snug hook on the wall and
wadded the cord around it, flinging it into the trash, pushing
at it viciously. Then she ran to the stairs, shouting for the
children.

"Maggie! Teddy! Come here. Hurry. Come fast." Lilly's
voice sounded hysterical—wonderfully, hilariously hysterical.

The children came running down the steps now, frightened.

"What's the matter? What's wrong?"

"I need you. Quick." Lilly opened the closet and flung a
coat at each of them.

"Mom. What is it? Where are we going?"

"Out."

"Out where?"

"Out of all this." Lilly was buttoning up her own coat.
"Teddy," she commanded, "go up and get my purse. Hurry.
Fast as you can."

"Mother!" Maggie said. "What are you doing?"

"Making a run for it."

"A run for what? What in the world is wrong with you?"

"Not wrong, baby. Right. Something is right with me."
Lilly laughed and hugged Maggie to her. Teddy, excited and
keyed up, came bounding down the stairs with her purse and
Lilly reached for him, pulling him close to her and Maggie.

"We'll go out and eat and maybe to a movie. Maybe stay
out all night. Stay out as long as we have to."

Teddy was jumping up and down, already out the door;
Maggie ran after him, following to where the car was parked.
Lilly dashed through the house and turned off every single
light. She was panting when she came back into the kitchen;

she had to lean against the wall to catch her breath. Then very calmly and very deliberately she walked over to the stove and stood quite still in front of it for a moment before she reached forward and, one by one, carefully turned off the gas flame beneath each of the burners.

## ABOUT THE AUTHOR

BARBARA HOWAR is a writer and television personality whose first book, *Laughing All the Way*, is a sharp criticism of society in general and herself in particular. Ms. Howar lives in Washington, D.C., with her two children.

# Laughing All the Way
## by Barbara Howar

She was Southern born and bred, was "finished" at a fanc school, "came out" at the proper time, and then came u to conquer Washington, D.C.

This is the story of Barbara Howar, who has shocke amused, outraged, and hobnobbed with every level of powe in the capital.

*LAUGHING ALL THE WAY* is a real insider's loo at Washington—a place where survival necessitates "a fin madness and a sense of humor."

2-3145-3     $1.95